A GUIDE TO
NATURE RESERVES OF
WALES
—————AND THE—————
WEST MIDLANDS

Researched and written by
Linda Bennett

Based on accounts of the reserves researched and written by
Jeremy Hywel-Davies

MACMILLAN
PRESS

This edition published 1989 by The Macmillan Press Ltd a division of Macmillan Publishers Limited Stockton House 1 Melbourne Place London WC2B 4LF and Basingstoke.

Associated companies in Auckland, Delhi, Dublin, Gaborone, Hamburg, Harare, Hong Kong, Johannesburg, Kuala Lumpur, Lagos, Manzini, Melbourne, Mexico City, Nairobi, New York, Singapore and Tokyo.

Revised edition published 1991.

British Library Cataloguing in Publication Data
A Guide to the nature reserves of Wales and West Midlands.
  1. Wales. Nature reserves. 2. England. Midlands.
  West Midlands. Nature reserves
  639.9'09429

  ISBN 0–333–56323–9

Filmset in Palatino by Photo·graphics, Honiton
Originated by Adroit Photo Litho Limited, Birmingham
Printed in Great Britain by Butler & Tanner Ltd, Frome, Somerset

Picture research: Juliet Brightmore

Cover: Near Betws-y-Coed, Gwynedd
Photo © Janet and Colin Bord/Wales Scene

Contents

Contributors

Editorial Advisers

Robert E. Boote CVO *Vice-President of the Royal Society for Nature Conservation, and Council Member of a number of voluntary bodies.*

Dr Franklyn Perring OBE *Former General Secretary of the Royal Society for Nature Conservation, Vice-President of the Botanical Society of the British Isles, writer and broadcaster.*

Research Officers

Jeremy Hywel-Davies *Writer on wildlife and the countryside. Author of the English and Welsh entries in the Guide.*

Linda Bennett *Editor of* Natural World, *the magazine of the Royal Society for Nature Conservation.*

Authors of the Introductions

A.J. Deadman *Senior Officer, Nature Conservancy Council (Yorkshire District).*

Phil Drabble *Writer and broadcaster.*

D.M. Eagar *Council Member of the British Ecological Society and the North Wales Wildlife Trust.*

F. Fincher *Author, naturalist and active member of many local and national wildlife organisations, including the Worcestershire Nature Conservation Trust.*

Dr Mary E. Gillham *Author, and Past Chairman of the Glamorgan Wildlife Trust.*

P.N. Humphreys *President of the Gwent Ornithological Society, Vice-President of the Gwent Wildlife Trust.*

Will Prestwood *Former Conservation Officer of the Shropshire Wildlife Trust, and Joint Editor of* The Ecological Flora of the Shropshire Region.

David Saunders *Director of the Dyfed Wildlife Trust.*

Dr F.M. Slater *Curator of the University of Wales College of Cardiff Field Centre.*

Dr A. Tasker *Director of the Warwickshire Nature Conservation Trust.*

Peter Thompson *Former Tutor at Bristol Polytechnic and member of the Herefordshire Nature Trust.*

Picture Acknowledgements

Aquila Photographics: 15 photo Neill King; 22 photo J.V. and G.R. Harrison; 24–25 photo A.W. Cundall; 34 photo Michael Leach; 46 photo J.V. and G.R. Harrison; 51, 54–55 photos Mike and Val Lane; 111 *below* photo N. Rodney Foster. Ardea: 19 photo R.J.C. Blewitt; 36 photo Dennis Avon; 75 photo P. Morris; 79 photo David and Katie Urry; 111 *above* photo Ian Beames. Cardiff City Council: 91. John Cleare: 31. Bruce Coleman: 18 photo Jennifer Fry; 118 photo O.A.J. Mobbs. Jeremy Hywel-Davies: 67, 78, 127. John Mason: 71. Mid-Glamorgan County Council: 90. NHPA: 47 photo Stephen Dalton; 60 photo E.A. Janes. Nature Conservancy Council: 74, 94, 95, 102–3, 126. Nature Photographers: 30 photo N.A. Callow; 43–44 photo J.V. and G.R. Harrison. C. Pellant: 66. Dr D.A. Ratcliffe: 14, 114, 115. Richard Revels: 82. R.A. Roberts: 63. Royal Society for the Protection of Birds: 83, 119 photo Michael W. Richards. Colin Titcombe: 106. Wales Scene: Cover photo Janet and Colin Bord. Wildscape: 26 photo Jason Smalley.

Foreword

It doesn't seem all that long ago, when people and organisations who showed concern for the environment and the natural world were considered just a trifle 'cranky'. Not any more. There is increasing public awareness of environmental issues and of the dangers that come from upsetting the ecological pyramid, and increasing concern at the loss for all time of species of flora, fauna and indeed sadly, entire habitats. There is enormous support for protecting and conserving as much as possible of our natural heritage.

Much of the credit for this public appreciation of what is happening around us belongs to the scores of organisations that have been established to protect or conserve various elements of our natural heritage. Almost entirely charitable and supported by volunteers, these organisations have done immense work in educating the public, raising funds to preserve species and to purchase and maintain valuable habitats. Some of the evidence of their success can be seen on the pages of the five regional editions that together make up *The Macmillan Guide to Britain's Nature Reserves*.

British Gas is delighted to sponsor these regional editions, for the Company has itself a long-standing commitment to protect the environment. Of course the product it supplies, natural gas, is the least pollutive of the fossil fuels, burning without soot, smoke or smell, and contributing least to the acid-rain problem and the greenhouse effect. Much of the progress made in Britain with clean air in the 1960s and 1970s was because of natural gas.

Similarly the transportation of natural gas need make little impact on the landscape – or indeed the townscape. The first natural gas pipeline was laid from Canvey Island, Essex, to Leeds and was completed in 1963. Since then, some 3,400 miles of underground transmission pipelines have been laid, networked across the country, transversing environmentally sensitive moorlands, forests, mountains and bogs as well as some of the country's richest farmland.

The British Gas pipeliners have restored the routes to their former status and in some cases have improved conditions with the advice of local naturalists. Although the Company has its own teams of specialists, it takes considerable heed and co-operates closely with local expertise on environmental matters.

The Company's onshore terminals and other vital installations are invariably sited in rural areas – sometimes in places that are outstanding in terms of habitat. However this has always been taken into consideration with natural landscaping and screening and the planting of indigenous trees and shrubs. Indeed, there is actually a nature trail round the perimeter of one of the onshore terminals. Another terminal also was built a half-mile from its ideal position in industrial terms, to accommodate wildlife considerations.

Within the boundaries of gas installations across the country there is an enormous variety of wildlife which has been allowed to develop without the hindrance of man. A typical example is in Derbyshire where a test centre for controlled explosions, combustion and venting of gases in confined spaces has also become a veritable treasure of wildlife. Among the flowers are yellow toadflax, rose-bay willowherb, white field rose, lady's bedstraw and wild orchids as well as the better-known oxeye daisies, foxglove, primroses and cowslips. In this environment the abundance and variety of the flora has attracted a good population of butterflies: red admirals, tortoiseshells, peacocks, commas, brimstones, whites and painted ladies, and if the chatter of wildlife is momentarily silenced by the occasional experimental controlled explosion, the chances are that it will be broken afterwards by the raps of one of the three species of woodpeckers there – green, great spotted and lesser spotted. While the few staff based at the site are regaled by the cabarets given by hares, stoats, weasels and rabbits, their favourite residents must undoubtedly be those stars of the nocturnal world – badgers.

The enclosed land around the Company's compressor stations have also become mini-reserves in their own right and nature lovers working on these installations have reported some interesting sightings.

At one compressor station the Company is establishing an experimental wildflower meadow and conservation area, with the involvement of the local branch of the British Trust for Conservation Volunteers. The site is becoming a haven for a wide variety of species to thrive, in a part of the country where intensive farming, the use of chemical fertilisers and pesticides, the grubbing of hedges and woodland, and the drainage of wetlands have resulted in a serious loss of natural habitat.

British Gas is just one of the many industries proving that if we go about things the right way, industry and nature can co-habitate. It takes a little bit of extra effort and it costs more too. But we think it's a small price to pay for saving something that we have enjoyed for future generations.

Introduction

The publishers are grateful to British Gas plc whose support for these regional guides have made their publication possible.

The entries are based upon detailed work and research by Jeremy Hywel-Davies and since revised and rewritten by Linda Bennett. Their work would not have been possible without the unstinting co-operation of the Royal Society for Nature Conservation, the NCC and many other bodies concerned with conservation.

Our basis for inclusion of a site is that members of the public should have access either by common law rights, or by membership of a club or trust which gives access by right of membership or by special permit. (All sites in the latter category are marked *Permit only* in the text.) Exceptions have been made on two criteria: where we believe that an endangered or rare species would be threatened by publication of any information about the site where it is found, or where the owner of a site at present allowing access to a limited section of the public would be unwilling to continue such arrangements if an account were published here. We have taken the best advice available on these delicate issues, but in the last resort have made our own judgement.

Our aim has been to be comprehensive and 500 sites have been added to the 1984 list. We have taken pains to ensure that the information was accurate at the time of compilation in mid 1988. It has not been possible to evaluate and include all the sites owned or managed by the Forestry Commission, the Woodland Trust, the Ministry of Defence and the various water authorities. Readers should apply for information to the appropriate addresses (see p.133).

Every entry has been shown to a representative of the owner or managing body to ensure accuracy and the text has been read by two other advisers in addition to our own staff.

In the section on Wales we have followed the modern counties. Throughout England we have had to take a more pragmatic approach, using a combination of old and modern counties in our section titles, and basing our structure in general on the areas covered by the wildlife trusts, many of which still retain titles relating to the pre-1974 administrative counties. The geographical area of each section is coloured green on the map.

Each section is introduced by a well-known naturalist living in the area and possessing an extensive knowledge of its characteristics. The longer entries in each section have been selected for their perspective on the magnificent diversity of habitats in Britain, and because they are large enough to sustain much public use; many of them offer interpretative facilities. The increasing emphasis on and support for wildlife in cities is reflected in this Guide.

Readers will no doubt wish to support the work of the trusts and other organisations involved in the management of many of the sites included here. The addresses of the relevant bodies are on p.133.

At a time when public interest in our natural heritage has never been stronger, but when paradoxically threats to its future seem to be gathering force, we hope that this Guide will encourage both the sensitive use and enjoyment of Britain's wildlife.

How to Use the Guide

Entries are arranged alphabetically under counties or regions of England and Wales. The precise order is shown in the Contents list.

Each county or regional section contains a map showing sites open to the general public, with details of size, population, physical features, climate and major land use. An introduction highlights the main points of interest and characteristics of each county or region.

Factual information is given at the beginning of each entry, in this form:

1   2   3

SC 946562: 43ha: Great Bookworthy BC

4 Limestone cliffs, grassland, heath and scrub

5 Restricted access to old quarry: apply to warden

6 Booklet and nature trail leaflet from car park

7 *Spring, early summer*

Key

1 Ordnance Survey map reference (every OS map contains clear instructions on how to read it) or, in the case of very large sites, reference to the map. For sites marked *Permit only* apply to the managing body (see addresses on p.133) unless otherwise stated.

2 Area in hectares, or length in kilometres, as appropriate. (One hectare is approx. 2½ acres; one kilometre is approx. five-eighths of a mile.)

3 Manager/owner of site (for key to abbreviations, see p.132).

4 Brief description of site.

5 Details of any restrictions.

6 Availability of leaflets or other information.

7 Best season(s) for visiting site.

Sites with access limited to members of trusts or other bodies, or to holders of special permits, are not shown on the map or given OS references.

Cross references to other sites mentioned in the text are shown in CAPITALS on their first mention in any entry. These may include sites not in this region but which may be found in the other companion books in this series.

A list of addresses of local wildlife trusts, nature conservation organisations and other managing bodies of sites is on p.133.

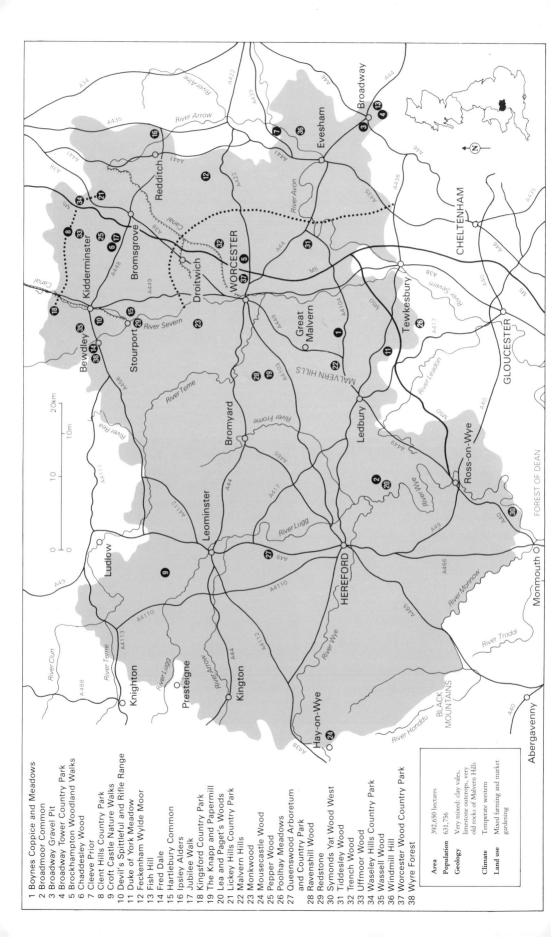

1 Boynes Coppice and Meadows
2 Broadmoor Common
3 Broadway Gravel Pit
4 Broadway Tower Country Park
5 Brockhampton Woodland Walks
6 Chaddesley Wood
7 Cleeve Prior
8 Clent Hills Country Park
9 Croft Castle Nature Walks
10 Devil's Spittleful and Rifle Range
11 Duke of York Meadow
12 Feckenham Wylde Moor
13 Fish Hill
14 Fred Dale
15 Hartlebury Common
16 Ipsley Alders
17 Jubilee Walk
18 Kingsford Country Park
19 The Knapp and Papermill
20 Lea and Paget's Woods
21 Lickey Hills Country Park
22 Malvern Hills
23 Monkwood
24 Mousecastle Wood
25 Pepper Wood
26 Poolhay Meadows
27 Queenswood Arboretum
   and Country Park
28 Ravenshill Wood
29 Redstone
30 Symonds Yat Wood West
31 Tiddesley Wood
32 Trench Wood
33 Uffmoor Wood
34 Waseley Hills Country Park
35 Wassell Wood
36 Windmill Hill
37 Worcester Wood Country Park
38 Wyre Forest

Area	392,650 hectares
Population	631,756
Geology	Very mixed: clay vales, limestone outcrops, very old rocks of Malvern Hills
Climate	Temperate western
Land use	Mixed farming and market gardening

Hereford and Worcester

The MALVERN HILLS with their splendid views form a spectacular divide between the two former counties of Herefordshire and Worcestershire, now known collectively as Hereford and Worcester. Wildlife interests are served by the Worcestershire Nature Conservation Trust, and by the Herefordshire Nature Trust.

With the River Wye, wooded hills, areas of high-quality agricultural land, flood meadows grazed by the characteristic white-faced cattle, many villages linked by narrow lanes, and relatively little industrial development, Herefordshire itself has been described as one of the most uniformly beautiful counties in Britain. It is almost completely surrounded by hills rising to 300m or higher. The Malverns lie to the east, the Black Mountains to the west, and the FOREST OF DEAN (Gloucestershire) to the south, while the north west Herefordshire uplands form a link with the south Shropshire hills to the north. The central area is divided by lower hills into three lowland basins dominated by the city of Hereford in the centre, and the towns of Leominster to the north and Ross-on-Wye to the south.

The underlying rocks of the whole county are Palaeozoic or older, and characteristic of highland Britain. The Malverns, rising to about 425m, are made of Pre-Cambrian schists, gneisses and igneous rocks while, at their south western extremity, around Hollybush Hill, is Herefordshire's only area of Cambrian and Ordovician rocks. The western foothills of the Malverns, the north west Herefordshire uplands between Ludlow and Presteigne and the Woolhope Hills, are all Silurian scarplands formed largely from limestones. These areas are often wooded and do not possess such a rich flora as other limestones in the country, but they are still interesting nevertheless. Reserves found on them include COTHER WOOD near the Malverns, and NUPEND, COMMON HILL AND MONUMENT and LEA AND PAGET'S WOOD situated in the Woolhope Hills.

Most of the rest of the county is underlain by old red sandstone. Marls, producing heavy, rich soils, underlie the Leominster and Hereford lowlands and sands, giving rise to light but fertile soils, as around Ross-on-Wye. Hills such as Dinmore, Aconbury and the uplands around the Golden Valley break the lowlands and contain rubbly limestone bands which add diversity to their plant and animal life. In the south west the Black Mountains provide habitats for ring ouzel and red grouse.

At Symond's Yat the Wye enters the spectacular gorge by which it leaves the county. Rising sharply above it is the Great Doward, the only carboniferous limestone in Herefordshire, and the area with the richest flora. Some of it is now protected in the LEEPING STOCKS, WOODSIDE and WHITE ROCKS reserves, all part of the DOWARD GROUP.

During the ice ages, glaciers left behind morainic deposits, kettle-hole lakes, gravel spreads in the lowlands, diverted rivers and old lake floors. These features are most in evidence in the Lugg and Arrow valleys and the Wye Valley west of Hereford.

Many fine half-timbered buildings bear witness to the former importance of native woodlands, of which many fragments still remain, often on slopes too steep for ploughing or clearance. These woods frequently contain oak as well as ancient coppiced small-leaved lime, large-leaved lime and wild service-tree, while spurge-laurel, herb-Paris and stinking iris are among the ground flora on richer soils. Fallow deer are widespread, many woods boast a badger colony, and dormice may occupy nest boxes intended for pied flycatchers. Woodland paths and rides provide edge habitats for a wealth of butterflies and moths, including silver-washed fritillary and, much more rarely, white admiral. Few of the woods have escaped clearance or coppicing at some time, and coppicing is being reintroduced in some of them. Species-rich 'natural grasslands', with hairstreaks and marbled whites, as well as orchids, cowslips, meadow saffron and adder's-tongue, are now very rare.

The old county of Worcestershire, mainly agricultural, is small and landlocked, but its geographical position brings it within the range of many species of limited distribution. Birds such as nightingale, pied flycatcher, dipper, nuthatch, grey wagtail, ruddy duck, little ringed plover, buzzard and hobby nest, and plants include traveller's-joy, giant bellflower, tutsan, wood crane's-bill, wild liquorice, narrow-leaved everlasting-pea, navelwort, mistletoe, wood spurge, wayfaring-tree, woolly thistle, stone parsley and stinking iris.

The pattern of soils ranges from light sands that suffer from wind blow to very heavy clays which are mainly basic and cover a substantial area in the south east and centre. Acid soils are confined mainly to the Lickey Hills in the north east, an area around Kidderminster, and the Malvern Hills and Castlemorton Common in the south west; but cultivation and enclosure have so altered these soils that heather grows only in a restricted area.

Wetlands have probably suffered most, with the drainage of Longdon Marsh, Feckenham Moors, Moseley Bog, bogs on the Lickey Hills and HARTLEBURY COMMON. The Great Bog of WYRE FOREST still remains but its size hardly justifies the name. Of these areas only Hartlebury Common retains any really acid bog. The best such area lies between Kidderminster and Stourport, at WILDEN MARSH, and attempts are being made to keep as

much as possible. Worcestershire still houses many of the country's marsh warblers.

Probably all the lakes in the county are artificial – either created in the landscape around country houses, or caused by subsidence following brine extraction. The construction of some of these pools has impeded drainage and produced marshy areas to compensate for drainage elsewhere. The Droitwich area has long been known for salt-loving plants associated with its 'salt springs' and normally found near coasts.

Though there is plenty of agricultural grassland, good limestone grassland is now very restricted and unimproved meadows have also greatly diminished in number, but a few good examples remain. EADES MEADOW is considered one of the best examples of its kind in the country.

Worcestershire still retains much woodland, largely through sharing Wyre Forest with Shropshire. Wyre Forest is the only area in which the true service-tree *Sorbus domestica* has ever been found, but it seems fairly certain that the original tree was planted and it never gained a serious hold. These native woods contain small-leaved lime, wild service-tree and yew, with a scattering of large-leaved lime that suggests that some, at least, might be genuinely native. The River Teme is still in good condition, as are other smaller streams that provide haunts for aquatic plants and animals.

F. FINCHER
PETER THOMPSON

Aileshurst Coppice

Permit only; 1.4ha; WNCT reserve
Small mixed woodland
Spring, early summer

The reserve was established to protect some fine colonies of yellow star-of-Bethlehem.

Badgers Hill

Permit only; 2.2ha; WNCT reserve
Scrub woodland
Spring, early summer

Mainly hawthorn but with tree species such as ash, oak and turkey oak, the reserve is on lime-rich clays and includes a small area of grassland with adder's-tongue and greater butterfly-orchid. Nightingale may breed in the scrub.

Betts

Permit only; 2ha; WNCT reserve
Mixed woodland
Summer

Typical sessile oak woodland of the Wyre Forest dominates this steeply sloping reserve above the Lem Brook. Dipper, pied wagtail and redstart breed in the reserve. The steep acid slopes with bilberry and hard fern contrast with the valley floor, where wild daffodil, wood anemone and primroses grow under hazel coppice.

Blind Lane Coppice

Permit only; 1.8ha; WNCT reserve
Old sunken lane and meadow
Spring, early summer

A small plantation woodland which provides a variety of habitats for birds, insects and mammals.

Boynes Coppice and Meadows

SO 830410; 8ha; WNCT reserve
Old-meadow grassland
Permit only off rights of way
Spring, early summer

Ancient ridge-and-furrow meadowland, Boynes Coppice and Meadows is rich in species such as dyer's greenweed, pepper-saxifrage, adder's-tongue and green-winged orchid. Small mixed plantations flank the meadows, some of which have been acquired recently. These are being restored to a herb-rich sward using native wildflower seed.

Bredon Hill

Permit only; 35.7ha; NCC reserve
Unimproved grassland, scrub and old quarries
All year

The grassland, which includes crested hair-grass and quaking grass, also supports squinancywort, stemless thistle and rockrose, as well as the rare purple mild-vetch, chalk milkwort and hound's-tongue. The scrub area, in which mistletoe is found, is an important feeding area for fieldfares and redwings in winter. The old quarries have now become vegetated and autumn lady's-tresses and twayblade grow there.

Briar Hill Coppice

Permit only; 1.6ha; WNCT reserve
Steep woodland
Spring, early summer

Large poplar trees stand with a mixture of other species over a ground cover which includes giant bellflower and small teasel, both rather local species.

Brilley Green Dingle

Permit only; 4.5ha; HNT reserve
Deciduous woodland
Spring, summer

A small valley woodland where bluebells, moscha-tel, sanicle and early purple-orchid grow. There is also a rich birdlife including tree pipits and pied flycatchers. In the stream, where dippers may be seen, there are freshwater crayfish to be found under the stones.

Broadmoor Common

SO 605363; 13.6ha; H and WCC
Grassland scrub
Spring, early summer

The poorly drained grassland has an attractive flora including spiny restharrow, common and heath spotted-orchids. The scrub woodland supports many breeding birds including linnet and yellowhammer. There are good populations of butterflies and fallow deer may be seen. The pond contains all three species of British newts.

Broadway Gravel Pit

SP 087379; 1.2ha; WNCT reserve
Open pools, marsh and willow scrub
Access to hide and marked nature trail only. Hide suitable for wheelchairs
Nature trail leaflet from WNCT headquarters
Spring, summer

Although only a small site, the 111 plant species recorded reflect the diversity of habitats present. The pool supports the locally rare mare's-tail, while the marshy areas around the margins contain five species of rush and five of willow. Other plants recorded include wild carrot, hoary ragwort, wild lettuce, bristly ox-tongue and nar-row-leaved pepperwort. Snipe, moorhen, wood-cock, linnet, yellowhammer, corn bunting and goldfinch have all been seen on the reserve.

Broadway Tower Country Park

SP 114360; 14ha; Mr Hans Will
Cotswold scarp parkland
Guidebook from shop
Spring, early summer

Two trails lead through the mixed broad-leaved

woodland which crowns the summit, giving spectacular views across the lowlands into Wales. The woods contain badger and fox together with a typical range of woodland birds.

Brockhampton Woodland Walks

SO 893543; 1.6km, 2.4km; NT
Mixed woodland and lakeside walks
Leaflet from post office
Spring, early summer

Mixed broad-leaved and coniferous woodland and stands of mature oak encourage birds, including buzzard, raven, pied flycatcher and woodcock, while the small lake adds mallard and little grebe.

Brotheridge Green

Permit only; 2ha; WNCT reserve
Disused railway line
Spring, early summer

A variety of slope and soil type encourages a wide range of plants attracting over 30 species of butterfly. These include marbled white, white-letter hairstreak and both dingy and grizzled skipper. Badger setts are present and there is a good variety of breeding birds.

Chaddesley Woods

SO 914736; 100ha; NCC reserve
Oak woodland and conifer plantations
Permit only off rights of way
Leaflet from NCC
Spring, early summer

Oak with birch, rowan and areas of hazel coppice forms the main tree cover, while small-leaved lime, wild service-tree and Midland hawthorn indicate that it is probably ancient woodland. The ground cover varies with the change in soils and includes bracken, bilberry and bluebell with yellow archangel and herb-Paris. The plantations demonstrate that conservation need not necess-arily be the enemy of commercial forestry. The JUBILEE WALK has been established here.

Clay Vallets Wood

Permit only; 3.4ha; HNT reserve
Deciduous woodland
Nature trail leaflet from HNT
Spring, summer

Over 100 species of plants have been recorded on this reserve. Cow-wheat grows in profusion with wood sage and sweet vernal grass. Among the birds redstart, tree pipit, lesser spotted wood-pecker and buzzard can be seen. Silver-washed fritillary butterflies feed along the rides.

Cleeve Prior

SP 079496; 11.3ha; WNCT reserve
Limestone scrub and grassland
Nature trail booklet from WNCT headquarters
Summer

The Rhaetic limestone grassland supports species such as bee and pyramidal orchids. Under the hawthorn scrub is a dense growth of deadly nightshade in its only site in the county.

Clent Hills Country Park

SO 940804; 148ha; H and WCC
Grassland and woodland
Leaflet from H and WCC
All year

The hill tops in the Country Park are partly gorse covered with areas of acid grassland where mat grass is found. There are bracken and scrub-covered slopes with conifer and broad leaved plantations. The older woods have many spring flowers including bluebells. The diversity of habitats supports many species of birds such as tree pipit, redstart and sparrowhawk and mammals including fox, fallow deer and badgers which have several setts on the hill.

Common Hill and Monument

Permit only; 2ha; HNT reserve
Limestone scrub and grassland
Spring, summer

Typical limestone plants include spring cinquefoil, adder's-tongue, pale St John's-wort and green-winged orchid. The reserve is rich in insects, in particular marbled white butterfly. Many species of moth, including two of burnet moth, are present, as well as glow-worm.

Cother Wood

Permit only; 1.6ha; HNT reserve
Limestone grassland and scrub
Spring, summer

Dyer's greenweed, yellow-wort, bee orchid and greater butterfly-orchid characterise this attractive small area, pitted by old quarry workings.

Court Wood

Permit only; 2.4ha; HNT reserve
Mixed woodland
Spring, early summer

Oak woodland invaded by ash, birch, wych elm, yew and sycamore, the reserve also contains small plantations of beech and conifers. Despite its small size 21 species of breeding birds occur, including both pied and spotted flycatcher.

Croft Castle Nature Walks

SO 463655; various lengths; NT
Parkland walks
Leaflets from site
Spring, early summer

Splendid avenues and mixed woodland hold buzzard, goldcrest and pied flycatcher while, from the peak of the limestone escarpment, views are said to stretch over 14 counties.

Crow Wood Meadow

Permit only; 9.3ha; HNT reserve
Wood pasture and meadow
Spring, summer

The pasture contains a wealth of flowers such as meadow saxifrage, cowslip, common spotted-orchid, lady's-mantle and adder's-tongue. The wood includes huge mature oaks, wild service-tree and small-leaved lime. There is a long established rookery.

Dagnall End Meadow

Permit only; 2.2ha; WNCT reserve
Old-meadow grassland
Summer

The ancient, permanent pasture is one of the last surviving examples of its kind in this part of Worcestershire. The site supports a rich mixture of grasses and herbs such as sweet vernal-grass, crested dog's-tail, meadow foxtail, common spotted-orchid and lady's-mantle. In the wetter areas there are marsh foxtail, southern marsh-orchid, marsh valerian and water-dropwort. A tributary to the River Arrow gives further diversity and yellow iris, bur-reed and water forget-me-not grow along the margins of the stream.

Devil's Spittleful and Rifle Range

SO 815752; 60ha; WNCT reserve
Heathland and birch woodland
Spring, early summer

One of the best examples of heathland in the county, the reserve shows good spreads of heather with gorse and bracken, blocks of birch woodland and a small oakwood. Grassland reveals harebell and wild pansy. A good range of insects includes the waved black moth.

Doward Group

Permit only; 16.5ha; HNT reserves
Limestone woodland, grassland and scrub
Spring, early summer

High above the valley of the River Wye the three reserves protect an area of characteristic wood- and meadowland. The presence of wild service-tree suggests that one of the woodland areas may be ancient, but generally the woods are secondary, returning to colonise cleared areas. The reserves are close enough to circle through all three, though any one would repay a lengthy study, but taken together they display a splendid range of open grassland, scrub and woodland.

WOODSIDE contains high-forest oak and beech over an understorey which includes ash, dogwood, field maple, whitebeam and yew with blackthorn, hawthorn, hazel and holly, together with wild service-tree. It is varied with stands of almost pure beech where ground cover is extremely thin and with more recently coppiced areas showing a well-developed understorey and a good variety of woodland plants.

LEEPING STOCKS has fine beech trees marking the old field boundaries with coppiced oak and hazel and a great range of tangled scrub woodland.

WHITE ROCKS has the same wide range of species as can be found in Leeping Stocks including spindle and wayfaring-tree with sweet chestnut and sycamore.

Throughout all the woods and scrubland areas the ground cover varies according to the shade or the changes in the soil so that acid-loving species such as bracken, birch and common cow-wheat may stand close to sanicle and marjoram, wood spurge and wood melick.

The more open areas of this reserve range from stands of birch, bracken and rosebay willowherb to scrub-fringed gladed grasslands and have their finest show in a small paddock hidden against the woods. Beneath the cover of taller plants the paths are to be found filled with plants such as ploughman's-spikenard and meadow saffron as well as many other species. The Woodside meadow is rich in lime-loving species and also contains a small area of heather, together with cowslip, common rock-rose and wild thyme, yellow-wort, harebell, marjoram, eyebright and greater knapweed, small scabious, quaking-grass and restharrow. Common bird's-foot-trefoil, vetches, violets and grasses provide attractive larval food for butterflies.

Throughout the area a fine variety of plants includes columbine, deadly nightshade and blue fleabane with bee, fly and green-winged orchid and broad-leaved and white helleborine also present in this region.

Butterflies include common and holly blue, pearl-bordered and silver-washed fritillary, marbled white and, occasionally, white admiral. The birds are typical of scrub and woodland and may include nightingale.

Doward Quarry

Permit only; 1.3ha; HNT reserve
Disused quarry
Spring, summer

The quarry has been worked out and stands as bare limestone walls; the special fascination of this reserve will be to watch the gradual recolonisation of the site.

Drake Street Meadow

Permit only; 0.3ha; WNCT reserve
Rich grassland
Spring, early summer

The tiny meadow, crossed by a stream, contains a great variety of plants including unexpected species such as bluebell and woodland violets, with old-meadow flowers such as cowslip and green-winged orchid.

Duke of York Meadow

SO 782354; 2.3ha; WNCT reserve
Old-meadow grassland
Restricted opening; see board at site
Spring, early summer

An area of lowland unimproved grassland, the meadow is beautiful in spring with a show of wild daffodil, uncommon in the county, and with attractive pasture species such as cowslip and green-winged orchid.

Eades Meadow and Fosters Green Meadows

Permit only; 12.2ha; WNCT reserve
Old-meadow grassland
Access only on open days
Summer

In May the reserve is a perfect wild flower garden

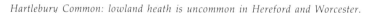

Hartlebury Common: lowland heath is uncommon in Hereford and Worcester.

with large old parklike oak trees standing in a wonderful spread of natural colour. The slightly tilted meadow has damper areas with cuckoo-flower, ragged-Robin and marsh-marigold while the drier grassland is filled with spectacular displays of cowslip and green-winged orchid. Adder's-tongue is also present with hedgerows containing bluebell, bugle, primrose, goldilocks buttercup, wood anemone and violets.

Woodland flowers are present because the area was once part of the Royal Forest of Feckenham, a hunting forest which commoners' rights would probably have maintained as woodland pasture until the farm became established. The hedges are certainly many centuries old. At one time the meadow was subdivided, the oak trees mark the lines of other hedges, and the western parts show evidence of ridge-and-furrow ploughing. No ploughing has occurred in living memory, though, and this is why the grassland is so rich.

Eywood Pool

Permit only; 9.3ha; HNT reserve
Freshwater lake, woodland meadow
All year

This attractive tree-fringed pool has drawn over 100 species of bird including great crested grebe, pochard, shoveler, redstart and pied flycatcher. The reserve lies within the private land of a large estate and the hide overlooks both water and woodland, meadows and arable fields.

Feckenham Wylde Moor

SP 012603; 11.2ha; WNCT reserve
Wetland and open water
All year

An area of undrained peat marsh, the reserve contains wide spreads of rushes and sedgebeds, including sea club-rush, uncommon in inland sites. An artificial lake will attract more wetland birds to add to the numbers of duck and passage waders which already visit and, it is hoped, encourage others to breed. Snipe breed here. A hide is open to the public at all times.

Fish Hill

SP 120368; 4.8ha; H and WCC
Grassland and mixed woodland
All year

The grassy hilltop provides wonderful views of the surrounding countryside. A waymarked trail leads through the mixed woodland of beech, larch and Scots pine overlying former toadstone quarries. The plants include common twayblade, pyramidal, early purple, common spotted orchids and broad-leaved helleborine.

Fred Dale

SO 776763; 22.8ha; WNCT West Midland Bird Club reserve
Woodland and brookside meadows

Access to marked nature trail only
Trail leaflet from WNCT
Spring, early summer

A mixed oak woodland, part of WYRE FOREST.

Grovely Dingle

Permit only; 8.4ha; WNCT–NT reserve
Steep valley woodland
Spring, early summer

The narrow, thickly wooded ravines contain oak, wych elm, wild service-tree, moschatel, wood speedwell and woodruff. It is the only site in the county for the uncommon wood barley.

Hartlebury Common

SO 827715; 81ha; H and WCC
Heath and bog
Leaflets from H and WCC
Spring, early summer

Broom, gorse and heather heathland, scrub woodland, bogs and pools make this one of the most important sandy acid areas in the locality. Marsh cinquefoil and bogbean show in the wetlands while harebell, shepherd's cress and buck's-horn plantain may be found on the heath. Among the birds stonechat and whinchat occur and over 100 moth and butterfly species have been recorded.

Holywell Dingle

Permit only; 3.6ha; HNT reserve
Steep wooded ravine
Spring, early summer

A great variety of tree species stand over bluebell, moschatel and lesser periwinkle. Raven, kestrel, buzzard, pied flycatcher and nuthatch may be seen. Fox and badger may be present.

Hunthouse Wood

Permit only; 24.4ha; WNCT reserve
Mixed valleyside woodland
Spring, early summer

The path twists among mixed tree species standing above an understorey of coppiced hazel, thick with bracken, bramble and rosebay willowherb, while clearings allow a show of bugle, yellow pimpernel, violets and wood-sorrel. Lower down, a bridge crosses a damp flushed area widely spread with dog's mercury and enchanter's-nightshade, overlooked by tall dead elms. The stream has alder, ash and oak above the hazel with broad buckler-fern, tumbles of thickly mossed logs and marsh plants such as giant horsetail and the uncommon alternate-leaved golden-saxifrage and small teasel.

Gigantic wild cherry trees are a feature of the wood, together with large-leaved lime, forming a contrast to slender birch or willow and to the delicate plants of the woodland floor. The variation increases along the winding pathway: wet and dry gullies, steep and shallow banks, tall dead standing trees and fallen giants thick with fungi and filled with burrowing insects. Damper places have square-stemmed St John's-wort and carpets of bugle; richer soils support dogwood, yew and field maple over wood spurge and selfheal; more acid areas show foxglove, honeysuckle and wood sage; the whole is a wonderful complex mix with interest for all.

A variety of animals enjoy the refuge of the reserve. Badgers breed, with an abundance of woodland birds, including several warbler species, reinforced by dipper and grey wagtail at the streamside, and tawny owl, sparrowhawk and buzzard.

Ipsley Alders

SP 076676; 17.8ha; WNCT reserve
Fen marsh
Spring, summer

This fen marsh is supplied with water from a spring emerging under the layer of peat on the marsh. This type of habitat is rare in the area and supports plants such as the marsh stitchwort, marsh woundwort and a number of rushes, especially the blunt-flowered rush. It is attractive to reed bunting and snipe, and many dragonflies inhabit the pools.

Jubilee Walk

SO 914736; 1.5km; NCC
Waymarked trail
Leaflet from dispensers or NCC
Spring, early summer, autumn

The walk passes through CHADDESLEY WOODS. A stream-fed pool adds wetland interest.

Kingsford Country Park

SO 823820; 87ha; H and WCC
Coniferous woodland and heathland
Leaflet from H and WCC
Spring, early summer

The country park adjoins 162ha of National Trust and Staffordshire CC birch heathland at KINVER EDGE (Staffordshire). The wildlife of the heather–bracken heathland and of the birch or coniferous woodland is demonstrated by a way-marked nature trail. The bird life varies from goldcrest to green and great spotted woodpecker while open areas are suitable for adder and common lizard.

The Knapp and Papermill

SO 748522; 24ha; WNCT reserve
Valley woodland, pasture and brook
All visitors should sign record book
Nature trail booklet from site or WNCT
Spring, early summer

The reserve enjoys a wide range of habitat within a relatively small area. The steeper slopes are clothed with woodland which, containing both small-leaved lime and wild service-tree, seems likely to have shaded the valley for many thousands of years. Shallower slopes are grassed, in some places returning to woodland, while the valley bottom is marshy, containing some interesting wetland plants. The Leigh Brook adds the special fascination of running water.

The brook is lined with coppiced alder and ash and pollarded crack willow, standing above small teasel and Indian balsam. Butterbur and common comfrey spread across the banks while water-crowfoot trails in the fast-flowing water. An earlier watercourse has become a marsh with sedges, rushes, marsh-marigold and great horsetail.

The lower land is rich in plants such as early-purple orchid and common spotted-orchid. The drier bank shows cowslip and primrose, growing together with their hybrid form. Longer slopes of grassland further upstream, an area of unimproved meadowland, are rich in common bird's-foot-trefoil, yellow rattle, devil's-bit scabious and musk mallow, contrasting with more acid patches of bracken and broom.

In a small coppice near the brook tangles of traveller's-joy loop over spindle, dogwood and remnants of coppiced wych elm with, where bramble is not too thick, a good variety of plants such as wood melick, woodruff, wood spurge and nettle-leaved bellflower. The woodland proper is varied with standard oak over coppiced hazel and some superb areas of coppiced small-leaved lime where goldenrod blazes in late summer and sprays of polypody decorate the trees. The woods hold good shows of hart's-tongue and soft shield-fern on damp and shaded slopes, and in the shade of the main woodland violet helleborine grows.

The variety of the reserve attracts a range of typical birds while moths include the local silver cloud and waved black, with butterflies such as silver-washed fritillary, holly blue and dingy skipper. Some 20 mammal species have been recorded and include a resident population of badger.

Knowles Coppice

Permit only; 7.7ha; WNCT reserve
Mixed woodland and brookside meadows
Spring, early summer

The woodland is typical of much of WYRE FOREST, consisting in the main of oak with birch, larch and occasional holly. The meadows are rich in cowslip and devil's-bit scabious while the brook attracts dipper, kingfisher and grey wagtail.

Lea and Paget's Woods

SO 597342 and 598344; 9ha; HNT reserve
Mixed limestone wood
Nature trail leaflet from HNT
Spring, early summer

The two separate areas of woodland contain ash, birch and field maple, with a hazel understorey; Paget's Wood also has mature oak and plentiful wild cherry. The ground cover includes wild daffodil and various orchids, while Paget's Wood also supports wild liquorice. Bird life is abundant, with all three native woodpeckers, warblers and other typical woodland species.

The Malvern Hills, composed of some of the most ancient rocks in Britain, rise from the plain.

Leeping Stocks

Permit only; 7.7ha; HNT reserve
Limestone woodland and scrub
Nature trail leaflet from HNT
Spring, early summer

Part of the DOWARD GROUP.

Lickey Hills Country Park

SO 986758; 213ha; City of Birmingham BC
Steep hilly parkland
Spring, early summer

The park gives splendid views from its steep grassed and wooded slopes and contains a children's nature trail.

Lion Wood

Permit only; 3.2ha; WNCT–WARNACT reserve
Acid oak woodland
Summer

Oak dominates this woodland established on acid gravelly ground. The dense shrub layer is of hazel, birch, holly, rowan and alder buckthorn, the latter supporting a large brimstone butterfly population. The ground flora is not rich but has abundant bilberry.

Long Meadow

Permit only; 5.2ha; WNCT reserve
Unimproved hay meadow
Spring

Spring, before the meadow is closed for mowing, shows a fine variety of ancient-pasture species, such as cowslip, green-winged orchid and adder's-tongue.

The Lugg Meadows

Permit only; 16ha; HNT reserve
Flood meadows
Nature trail leaflet from HNT
Spring, summer, winter

In medieval times these fertile flood plain meadows were highly valued; from Candlemas to Lammas the meadows were shut up for hay which would feed the animals through the winter. Many typical meadow flowers occur, including yellow-rattle, pepper-saxifrage, great burnet and fritillaries. The winter floods bring in many wildfowl.

Malvern Hills

SO 768454; 600ha; Malvern Hills Conservators
Narrow ridge of ancient hills
Spring, summer, autumn

Lifting spectacularly from the farmland around, the Malvern Hills are a narrow switchbacked ridge formed from some of the oldest rocks in the country. They are wooded on their lower slopes, blanketed with bracken and scrub, but the ancient hilltops are open to the skies.

Where the rock was quarried to make our roads, plants are beginning to return. The slopes and cliffs and scattered with gorse and broom, with garden escapes such as buddleia, with wood sage and navelwort. Bare rock is thick with stonecrops, such as orpine, while ledges and quarry floors develop a scrub of bramble and wild rose, ash, elder, hawthorn, sycamore and willow. Mosses, lichens and ferns are plentiful, with an abundance of polypody. Small birds breed in the scrub; jackdaw and feral dove nest on the cliffs; kestrels hang in the up-draughts above. The slopes are full of butterflies such as the beautiful small copper or wall brown.

Above the quarries the land lifts steeply upwards, scrub-covered with bracken and bramble, with rosebay willowherb, gorse and broom and an invading woodland of hawthorn, rowan, birch and sycamore. Higher still is open grassland, with harebell and tormentil, heather, sheep's sorrel and bilberry. The complex nature of the rocks gives richer grasslands where lady's bedstraw, common bird's-foot-trefoil and wild thyme grow.

Passing downwards again, the scrub grades into woodland. The mosaic of clumped gorse, hawthorn and heather, standing in a grassland filled with hawkbits, crosswort, broom and wild rose, gives way to oak, ash, birch, hazel and occasional yew, to fine old oak trees over open mossy grasses or richer blocks of coppiced hazel with plants such as violets, wood spurge and wood-sorrel, shrubs such as dogwood and field maple, holly and wild cherry.

Much of the attraction of the site is its variety. For over 15km the hilltops rise and fall and the hillsides change in steepness; the valleys themselves may be grassed or filled with scrub or woodland. Public pressure is high in certain places but quiet areas, rich in wildlife, are plentiful. The woods are rich in typical bird life and, above, the circling of a buzzard may enrich the summer sky.

Marsh Warbler Sites

Permit only; 9ha; WNCT reserves
Nine separate areas of marshland
Summer

Beds of nettle, great willowherb and meadowsweet, often flanked by pollarded willows, hawthorn and blackthorn, provide nest sites for marshland birds such as reed, sedge and marsh warbler and reed bunting. Up to one third of Britain's marsh warbler population breeds on these reserves.

Melrose Farm Meadows

Permit only; 2ha; WNCT reserve
Old-meadow grassland
Spring, autumn
Thick hedges surrounding the meadows add additional variety to the reserve, noted for its grassland species such as cowslip, saw-wort, green-winged orchid and meadow saffron.

Moccas Park

Permit only; 140ha; NCC reserve
Ancient deer park
Spring, early summer

The higher slopes are wooded while the lower areas are occupied by sweeps of grassland under fine old parkland oak and sweet chestnut. Mosses and lichens are particularly notable and the beetles include three species known only from this site.

Monkwood

SO 804607; 61.5ha; WNCT–BBCS reserve
Woodland and rides
Access restricted to paths and rides
Trail guide available from WNCT headquarters
Summer, autumn

This semi-natural woodland almost certainly dates back to the end of the last glacial period. While some of the traditional woodland cover (oak over hazel coppice) still survives, much of the original vegetation was converted by the previous owners to plantations of beech, ash, sycamore, alder, sweet chestnut, Norway maple and spruce. Of those native trees and shrubs still remaining, interesting species include wild service-tree, small-leaved lime, guelder-rose and spurge-laurel.

In total, some 240 plant species have been recorded within Monkwood. Many uncommon or locally abundant species have been discovered such as meadow saffron, lily-of-the-valley, elongated sedge and wood small-reed.

The invertebrate fauna of Monkwood is outstandingly rich, including 538 species of moth, over 30 of butterfly, 100 of beetle, 80 of spider and 36 of hoverfly. The woodland is the most important site for wood white butterfly in Worcestershire, while other interesting species include silver-washed fritillary and white admiral. The terrestrial caddis fly, which is restricted in Britain to a small area of north Worcestershire, is found on the reserve.

A wide diversity of birds inhabits the wood including woodcock, nuthatch, sparrowhawk, tree pipit and grasshopper warbler.

Pied flycatcher, a bird of upland valley woods and tree-lined watersides.

Mousecastle Wood

SO 245427; 21ha; WdT
Mixed woodland
Spring, summer

This beautiful oak woodland overlooks Hay-on-Wye, giving magnificent views of the valley. Within the reserve there is a motte-and-bailey castle which is a scheduled ancient monument.

Mowley Wood Track

Permit only; 1.3ha; HNT reserve
Disused railway line
Spring, early summer

Isolated from roads and houses, the scrub development on the railway banks is well suited to woodland birds.

Newbourne Wood

Permit only; 4.4ha; WNCT reserve
Coniferous and mixed woodland
Spring, early summer

The commercial plantation, now being converted to broad-leaved woodland, has great promise as an educational reserve with a range from dry to damp ground and three small pools.

Nupend Wood

Permit only; 4.8ha; HNT reserve
Superb yew woodland and limestone scrubland area
Spring, summer

Mixed deciduous trees, with wild service-tree, stand above bluebell, stinking iris and stinking hellebore. Elsewhere yew prevents undergrowth. Sparrowhawk and tawny owl are resident, with summer warblers including occasional grasshopper warbler. Butterflies are plentiful and the reserve is well known for its fungi.

Penny Hill Bank

Permit only; 0.8ha; WNCT reserve
Limestone grassland
Spring, summer

Columbine, autumn gentian and ploughman's-spikenard characterise the herb-rich grassland which, sheltered by scrub and belts of woodland, attracts such butterflies as green hairstreak, dingy skipper and wood white.

Pepper Wood

SO 938745; 53.6ha; WdT
Mixed woodland
Spring, early summer

Once managed as coppice with standards, the wood is now overgrown, but the return to regular management should encourage wildlife.

Poolhay Meadows

SO 829308; 2.7ha; WNCT reserve
Old meadow
Permit only off footpath
Spring, early summer

The wetter of the two meadows shows cuckoo-flower, ragged-Robin and a profusion of green-winged orchids. The other is one of the few sites in the county for meadow thistle and great burnet.

Queenswood Arboretum and Country Park

SO 517515; 68ha; H and WCC
Woodland and arboretum
Leaflet available on site
Spring, early summer, autumn

The arboretum contains an important collection of trees on the plateau above a good mixed native woodland dominated by oak. The varied soils of the slopes support devil's-bit scabious, primrose and common spotted-orchid. The bird life is equally varied, including sparrowhawk and woodcock. There is a resident herd of fallow deer.

Randan Wood

Permit only; 4.8ha; WNCT reserve
Mixed woodland
Spring, early summer

The reserve contains a wide variety of trees such as small-leaved lime, wild service-tree, and alder buckthorn, of plants such as ivy broomrape and tutsan, of mammals such as badger and yellow-necked mouse, and many bird species. Over 300 fungi have been the subject of special study.

Ravenshill Wood

SO 739539; 20ha; WNCT Miss M.E. Barling reserve
Mixed coniferous and broad-leaved woodland
Nature trail guides at discovery centre
Open March–October inclusive

The limestone areas support spindle, herb-Paris and broad-leaved helleborine beneath the woodland cover, filled with the birdsong of warblers or the roding flight of woodcock. A pool encourages wetland birds while badger and fox are plentiful. Insects include wood white butterfly.

Redstone

SO 810703; 7ha; Wyre Forest DC reserve
Marsh, wet woodland and damp meadows
Access restricted in accordance with bye-laws
Spring, summer

Hemlock water-dropwort, fine-leaved water-dropwort and slender tufted sedge are amongst the more unusual plants found on this small but valuable Local Nature Reserve. Thirty species of birds were recorded breeding on this reserve in 1984.

Rhydspence

Permit only; 0.2ha; HNT reserve
Tiny woodland
Spring, early summer

Although a small area of woodland, close to the River Wye, it contains a variety of typical plants and birds.

Romers Wood and Motlins Hole

Permit only, 18ha; HNT reserve
Mixed woodland
Spring, early summer

The two woodlands are separated by a large field and contain a mix of trees, chiefly oak and ash, over an understorey which includes hazel, holly and guelder-rose, with spring-fed streams thick with great horsetail. Over 30 breeding bird species have been recorded from the woods.

Spinneyfields

Permit only, 1.6ha; WNCT reserve
Heathland, scrub and pond
Summer

A small pool and stream add diversity to the grassy heathland with banks of heather and gorse, hawthorn scrub and bramble.

Symonds Yat Wood West

SO 557158; 5.6ha; WdT
Deciduous woodland
Visitors are advised to keep to footpaths due to several derelict mineshafts
Spring, summer

This broadleaved wood is part of the geologically important LOWER WYE VALLEY woodlands. It is noted for the wide variety of tree and shrub species found here and for its rich ground flora. It is an important part of the famous view from Symonds Yat Rock.

Tiddesley Wood

SO 930458; 75.2ha; WNCT reserve
Mixed woodland
Avoid access to south end when red flag is flying
Nature trail guide from WNCT
Spring, summer

In the 1950s and '60s, this wood was planted with conifers by the Forestry Commission; since then much has reverted to native broadleaved coppice dominated by oak, ash, field maple, birch and hazel. Over 300 plant species have been recorded, including herb-Paris, violet helleborine, meadow saffron, bird's-nest orchid and wild pea. Nightingale and sparrowhawk are known to breed here, and amongst the 30 species of butterfly found in the wood are white-letter hairstreak and white admiral.

Trench Wood

SO 926586; 43.1ha; WNCT-BBCS reserve
Woodland and rides
Access restricted to paths and rides
Spring, summer

This damp, semi-natural, ancient woodland has almost certainly been present since the end of the last glacial period. The former vegetation, oak standards with a coppiced understorey dominated by hazel, has now been largely replaced by plantations of sycamore, silver birch, alder and beech. The rich ground cover includes plants such as common spotted-orchid, violet helleborine, broad-leaved helleborine, herb-Paris, meadow saffron and fairy flax.

All three species of woodpecker, eight warblers, sparrowhawk, woodcock and up to twelve pairs of nightingale all breed on the reserve. The wood is also rich in invertebrates with 200 species of moth and some 33 of butterfly including pearl-bordered fritillary, white admiral and white-letter hairstreak.

Uffmoor Wood

SO 953811; 86ha; WdT
Mixed woodland
Spring, summer

This ancient woodland has been worked to provide material for making brushes. A long history of traditional management has encouraged a wide range of woodland plants, birds and insects. Two streams cross the reserve exposing interesting geological strata.

Upton Warren

Permit only, 24ha; WNCT reserve
Pools rich in bird life
All year

The pools, formed by subsidence due to underground salt extraction, range from open shallow ponds to lakes surrounded by bulrush swamp, great willowherb, sedges, rushes, yellow iris and water-plantain; some are surrounded by open fields, others by belts of alder and willow. The larger pools are deep enough for diving duck while the margins and the smaller ponds are ideal for dabblers and waders.

Birds form the main attraction of the reserve and some 150 species are recorded in an average year. Uncommon birds may occur at any time and there is a great variety of breeding species, spring and autumn migrants and wintering birds. The saltmarsh areas are some of the most extensive and important in inland Britain. They contain reflexed saltmarsh-grass, spear-leaved orache and sea-spurrey.

Spring may bring visits from black and common tern, travelling from Africa to breed in continental Europe, or from arctic tern, nearing the end of its stupendous 16,000km journey from the Antarctic seas to nest on sea coasts from Britain up into the Arctic. The waders, similarly, pass through on passage and include bar-tailed and black-tailed godwit, curlew and whimbrel, common and wood sandpiper, dunlin, greenshank and ruff. The summer residents include swallow and house martin, warblers, spotted flycatcher and cuckoo. Great crested grebe, mallard, tufted and ruddy duck, Canada goose and mute swan are resident, together with moorhen, coot and kingfisher. The hedges and woodlands hold a range of other birds, such as finches, tits and crow family species, together with green woodpecker, treecreeper and little owl.

As the breeding season ends, passage birds pass through again and the summer visitors move back to their winter quarters, sometimes preyed upon by hunters such as hobby. The winter birds arrive, driven down by the cold, and until the spring returns they shelter and feed here. Wigeon, pintail and goldeneye join the resident duck species while snipe and jack snipe probe the margins of the pools and water rail skulk in the marshes. Redwing and fieldfare gorge themselves on the hedgerow berries, and goldcrest and siskin feed busily among the trees.

Waseley Hills Country Park

SO 979768; 54ha; H and WCC
Rough grassland, scrub and woodland
Leaflets from H and WCC; visitor centre
Spring, early summer

Sedgbourne Coppice, within the park, is managed as a conservation zone. Two ponds and a marsh increase the interest of the wood which provides a magnificent carpet of bluebell in spring. Gorse and broom encourage scrubland birds such as yellowhammer and linnet, while the Coppice area attracts a typical range of birds that favour woodland habitats.

Wassell Wood

SO 795775; 22ha; WdT
Deciduous woodland
Spring, summer

This wood is an important landscape feature, standing as it does on a prominent hill overlooking the Severn Valley. Much of the mature oak woodland was felled before the site became a reserve. A planting programme is now in progress to restore the tree cover.

Wern Wood

Permit only; 0.8ha; HNT reserve
Steep mixed woodland
Spring, early summer

Ash and oak, with wych elm, holly and grey willow, and a block of poplar over an understorey of elder, form the tree cover of the reserve while the woodland floor is distinguished by both giant and spreading bellflower. Summer warblers fill the wood with birdsong.

Wessington Pasture

Permit only; 10.8ha; HNT reserve
Grassland returning to woodland
Spring, early summer

Spindle and oak are among the trees present, and there is a good show of wild daffodil beneath them in spring. All three British woodpeckers are present, with breeding warbler species. In autumn an interesting and colourful range of fungi can be observed.

White Rocks

Part of the DOWARD GROUP

Wilden Marsh

Permit only; 32.6ha; WNCT reserve
River valley marshes
Spring, summer

Marsh arrow-grass, marsh cinquefoil and southern marsh-orchid are only three of the attractive wetland plants. Willow and alder scrub provides shelter for migrant and resident birds while spectacular old pollard willows form a special habitat. The site forms part of the county's most important area of marshland.

Wilden Marsh: scrub is invading the old grazing marshland.

Windmill Hill

SP 072477; 6ha; WNCT reserve
Limestone scrub and grassland
Nature trail guide from WNCT
Spring, summer

The limestone grassland contains greaterknapweed, wild liquorice and both common and spiny restharrow, and supports a good variety of butterflies. Small birds nest in the scrub and there is evidence of badger and fox.

Woodside

Part of the DOWARD GROUP

Worcester Wood Country Park

SO 878543; 50ha; H and WCC
Woodland
Leaflets on site
All year

The Country Park consists of Nunnery and Perry Woods, two attractive broad-leaved woodlands of oak and ash with wild cherry, hornbeam, wych elm, aspen and wild service-tree. In spring wood anemones and bluebells are particularly beautiful and other plants include common cow-wheat, hairy woodrush and violet helleborine. The woods have varied populations of butterflies and birds such as woodpeckers, nightingale and woodcock. A pond contains all three species of British newts.

Wyre Forest

SO 759766; 300ha; NCC reserve
Mixed woodland
Permit only off rides and paths
Leaflet from NCC
Spring, early summer

This is one of the best remaining native woodlands in the country, lying beside the River Severn and centred around a fast-flowing stream, the Dowles Brook. This stream is one of the richest in the area and the whole reserve forms one of the region's most important wildlife environments.

Wyre Forest was the first site where *Enoicyla pusilla*, our only land-living caddis larva, was discovered. It is known now from a very few other localities but Wyre is still an important site for the species.

More than half of the present woodland is converted to alien trees but the remnant forest still shows a great variation: the old coppiced oak on the plateaus, rich mixed woods in the valleys, woodland meadows and glades filled with a richly varied wildlife.

The oak woodland may form stands of oak and birch, above an acid ground cover of bilberry, bracken, heather, wood sage, common cow-wheat and lily-of-the-valley. Lily-of-the-valley is generally found in hilly limestone woods but occasionally it may be found in sandy oakwoods, as in the DANBURY GROUP (Essex).

Oak and birch may stand above an area of growing oak coppice or give way to oak standards above a thin understorey of birch, of occasional holly or yew, over a spread of bracken and bramble.

Even-aged oak, a closed canopy growing towards high forest, may have a variety of plants beneath it, bracken, bilberry, heather and wood sage.

The forest lies on coal measures, a very mixed range of rocks which includes sandstones, conglomerates, marls and bands of *Spirorbis* limestone. The richer rocks may give rise to less acid soils which were recognised in earlier times and have been cleared for grazing: bright small woodland meadows with a rich spread of plants such as betony, common bird's-foot-trefoil, lady's bedstraw, harebell, yellow rattle and wild thyme, with the more unusual green-winged orchid, adder's-tongue and meadow saffron.

Dowles Brook brings another change of scene, with shrubs such as blackthorn, hawthorn, hazel, guelder-rose and rowan, with ash and alder above a show of wild rose, hard fern, broad buckler-fern, wood melick, wood spurge and wood-sorrel. Alder, dogwood, small-leaved lime, wild service-tree and willow grow in the valley, where damp flushes are marked by clumps of pendulous sedge, hemp-agrimony and meadowsweet.

Britain boasts two native oaks, the sessile and the pedunculate, and typical tracts of both kinds occur here in the forest. Mountain melick and wood crane's-bill also occur here around the southernmost limit of their range. Uncommon plants such as columbine and narrow-leaved helleborine glow in the shade of the woods, with bloody crane's-bill and intermediate wintergreen.

The richness and variety of the habitats of the forest and their associated plant life encourage a range of insects of every shape and size, from tiny creatures which live in the leaf litter, to the southern aeshna, one of our largest dragonflies. Alder buckthorn, common nettle, woodland violets, bilberry, oak, cuckooflower and various grasses are food plants for some of the forest's butterflies: for brimstone, comma, high brown and silver-washed fritillary, for green and purple hairstreaks, orange-tip and speckled wood. An extraordinary range and abundance of moths is recorded, with national rarities such as alder kitten. Similarly, a whole range of snails and slugs, worms, flatworms, spiders and harvestmen, centipedes, millipedes, woodlice and other small animals forms part of the pattern of life here.

Dowles Brook holds trout, salmon, chub, eel and lamprey, freshwater shrimp and crayfish, and a host of insects and insect larvae and other invertebrates. Attracted by this wooded stream, dipper, kingfisher and grey wagtail may often be seen, while the aerial hunter, here in the woods, is the beautiful pied flycatcher, which matches the dancing insect flight with wonderful deftness.

The wood warbler is found only where a closed leaf canopy ensures a sparse ground cover, whereas dense bushes are favoured by occasional grasshopper warbler. Where holes are available they may be taken by redstart, nuthatch or tits, while hole makers, great spotted, lesser spotted and green woodpecker all breed. Other birds include woodcock, kestrel, sparrowhawk and tawny owl, with, from time to time, long-eared owl in the conifers adjoining the reserve.

Wyre Forest: high-forest oak in the Fred Dale reserve.

The wild landscape of Long Mynd, Shropshire.

Shropshire

It has been said that the only element required to render Shropshire the perfect county is a coastline although, ironically, such a feature would probably destroy its most precious asset, tranquillity. Although thousands rush lemming-like towards the Welsh cliffs every summer, few spare more than a glance at Shropshire on the way. For those who stop and explore, the county reveals itself as a place of extraordinary variety. In every sense it is a zone of transition between the cold, bleak English lowlands and the solid, reassuring mass of Wales. The dividing line between many of its contrasting features is the River Severn, once an important trade route. This ponderous waterway once flowed northwards to the Dee, but when blocked in the last ice age turned southwards and cut the impressive Ironbridge gorge. Within an almost complete meander of the river, in the centre of the county, lies the ancient county town, Shrewsbury.

The Severn divides the county into two. To the north and east, a low-lying landscape forms the beginning of the Midland plain. This is a very dry region and the predominantly arable farming needs extensive irrigation in order to grow its barley, wheat, potatoes and sugar beet.

To the south and west lie a great variety of hard rocks, including some of the oldest in Britain. Much of this area, wetter and warmer under the influence of the Welsh massif, lies over 130m and rises to 600m. Farming in this hill country is characterised by beef and sheep rearing. The local sheep breed, the Clun, is now internationally recognised.

Shropshire is a Mecca for geologists who come to see the classical exposures of 10 out of 12 recognised geological ages. Pre-Cambrian rocks, 600 million years old, can be seen in the same valley where there is evidence of a glacier 20,000 years ago.

It is assumed that the inhabitants of the many Iron Age ring forts were the first to change the Shropshire landscape. Most large hills were laid bare of trees at this time, and many remain so. The rich alluvial forests of the Severn plain too were cleared at an early date and this continued with Roman occupation. Clearance of the valley woods by Saxon settlers and those who followed them reduced the great Shropshire forests still more. Many vast areas remaining as oak coppice

were cleared early this century and replaced with conifers, the oak bark no longer being needed for tanning.

Despite the industrial significance of Coalbrookdale, and recently Telford New Town, Shropshire has been little scarred by industry. Locally, the extraction of lead from the Stiperstones area, and limestone from Wenlock Edge and the north west, has had an impact on the countryside, but time has converted these original scars into important wildlife areas, notably disued lime quarries.

The complex interaction of different physical features and land use creates a naturalists' paradise, again characterised by contrasts. Many northern and western species mix with their southerly cousins: dormouse, nightingale and mistletoe go little farther north west, and dipper, bird cherry and globeflower little farther south east. Some plants like rock stonecrop have their English strongholds here, and least water-lily has its only English site.

Agricultural development has so fragmented natural habitats in the fertile north and east that only isolated sites remain. Early extensive heathlands have almost vanished and the area is now notable only for the meres and mosses. These large lakes, such as THE MERE, Ellesmere and COLEMERE, and the accompanying peat bogs like WEM MOSS, have developed in depressions left after the retreating ice. The fascinating meres, some under pressure from recreation, support rich freshwater life and harbour many wildfowl.

There are several 'groups' of Shropshire hills, each with its own geological history, and characteristic landscape and wildlife. The earliest Shropshire rocks, the Pre-Cambrian, form a long series of hog-back hills from the Wrekin to the Stretton Hills with vast stretches of acid grassland and some oak woodland. The remote and desolate LONG MYND provides a haunt for red grouse, merlin and hen harrier, while its valleys conceal many interesting plants. Similar plants and birds, with rarer species such as cowberry and crowberry, can be seen on the nearby gaunt and jagged Stiperstones. This ridge is set in wild country, dotted with small farms, lead miners' cottages and abandoned fields, now being rapidly changed by land reclamation schemes.

In the Clee Hills the distinctive peaks of BROWN CLEE and Titterstone Clee are surrounded by upland grassland and moorland, boggy flushes and scree. On the lower slopes are many tiny hay meadows, some traditionally managed and supporting yellow rattle and spotted-orchid. The fertile border country towards Hereford contains orchards and large, ancient woods. The rolling Clun Forest Hills hold several remaining coppiced oakwoods on the steeper valley sides, providing a habitat for pied flycatcher and redstart. The area's rivers, the Unk, Clun and Onny, are important arteries for wildlife in this otherwise well-farmed area.

Away from these windswept and rugged hills, the naturalist can find peace and quiet in the mellow Silurian limestone country of Wenlock Edge and the carboniferous limestone of the north west, near Oswestry. The 35km wooded scarp of Wenlock Edge is a rich storehouse of delights for the botanist, as are the limestone cliffs, screes and tiny meadows of the north west. Both for the ardent naturalist and the passing visitor, Shropshire is well worth a closer look.

WILL PRESTWOOD

Betton Dingle

Permit only; 2.4ha; SWT reserve
Steep valley woodland and scrub
Spring, early summer

Ash and wych elm, with small-leaved lime and wild cherry, provide dense tree cover to contrast with the slope of bracken and bramble beyond the stream. The ground cover includes species such as toothwort and alternate-leaved golden-saxifrage, while the bird interest is typical of scrub and woodland sites.

Brown Clee Nature Trail

SO 607872; 2km; SCC
Mixed woodland trail
Spring, early summer

The trail is mainly through planted conifers, with some native hardwoods and open grassland on the lower slopes of Brown Clee Hill.

Brown Moss

SJ 564394; 32ha; SCC
Woodland, heath and wetland
Leaflet from SCC
Spring, summer

Drainage and cutting has changed the old peat bog to an area of dry acid heath surrounding a series of pools. Rare and locally uncommon wetland plants include orange foxtail, floating water-plantain, floating club-rush and water-violet which, with the bird life, including some 30 breeding species with visitors such as water rail and black tern, give considerable importance to the site.

Bushmoor Coppice

SO 430880; 4ha; SWT reserve
Mixed woodland
Spring, early summer

Tucked into a tiny valley, no more than a fold in the land between two of Shropshire's huge ridges, the reserve is a sheltered lowland wood, set in a pattern of farmland. In the wood itself tall stands of coppiced trees lift above a tilted woodland floor; hazel with wild cherry, with hawthorn and elder here and there, stands in a springtime show of bluebell, on the higher drier ground, with a rich-wood spread of dog's mercury and plants such as yellow pimpernel where the ground is damper and more clayey near the stream.

Beyond the stream, however, the structure is more varied. Alder grows along the valley bottom and passes upwards into more acid woodland where oak, holly and birch stand above glades of bracken, bramble and rosebay willowherb. The streamside area is damp enough for meadowsweet, marsh bedstraw and common valerian; and in places it is dry enough for field maple to stand over drifts of enchanter's-nightshade and woodruff, violets and wood-sorrel, or perhaps a flower-spike of broad-leaved helleborine.

One of the great attractions of the wood is its range of habitat within so small an area. The stream and marsh area attract large numbers of insects which in turn provide food for breeding and visiting birds. Native trees, too, are rich in insects – a long-growing tree such as the oak has some 300 insects associated with it.

Clunton Coppice

SO 342806; 23ha; SWT reserve
Deciduous woodland
Spring, summer

Cow-wheat, bilberry and wavy hair-grass grow in this fine oak coppice on the north-facing slopes of the Clun valley. Wood warblers and pied flycatchers breed here, and buzzards and ravens are often seen over the wood.

Colemere Country Park

SJ 434328; 50ha; SCC
Lake, woodland and grassland
All year

By the end of the last ice age great spreads of sands, gravels and clays had been laid across these lowlands with, here and there, a sizeable hollow which filled with glacial melt-waters and formed a standing pool. These pools gave rise to the well-known meres and mosses.

Colemere shows much of the magic of the open ice-born lakes. Meadows lie to the west and south east of the mere, while woodland stands around the rest, framing the dark, still waters. Some disturbance occurs from fishing and sailing but generally the site is calm and peaceful.

The meadows are fringed with plants such as water forget-me-not, with bulrush, great willowherb and hemlock at the woodland edge. The woods are very varied. To the north is high-forest woodland, curving round the mere and separating it from the Shropshire Union Canal which runs close by. Holly, birch and rowan grow over a tangle of bramble, raspberry and honeysuckle, beneath a mix of tall alder, ash and oak, birch, Scots pine and sycamore at the corner of the mere. Where the wood narrows between the mere and the canal, a strong spread of rhododendron shades out all other undergrowth. Occasional yew trees grow in this northern belt and it is interesting to see that even the smothering rhododendron is smothered by the yew. The southern bank and the slope above are chiefly planted with conifers and sycamore but also contain native species such as rowan, oak and birch.

A good variety of birds may be seen in the park, with woodland and meadow birds as well as water-birds. As with THE MERE, ELLESMERE, a few kilometres away, migration times bring terns and waders, while winter brings waterfowl and flocks of gulls.

Comley Quarry

SO 483964; 0.8ha; SWT reserve
Geological site
All year

The quarry shows an exposure of the type-section of the Cambrian Lower Comley limestones.

Corbet Wood Trail

SJ 525238; 1.6km; SWT
Mixed woodland trail
Spring, early summer

An attractive variety of trees such as wild cherry and rowan are mixed with birch, beech, oak and conifers above a ground cover which may contain bramble and bilberry or plants such as alkanet, bluebell and common spotted-orchid. The bird life is typical of gladed woodland: blackcap and long-tailed tit, for instance. Jackdaw breed in the quarry face which shows a fine exposure from upper mottled sandstone to keuper marl.

Craig Sychtyn

SJ 232256; 2ha; SWT reserve
Disused quarry and ancient woodland
Leaflet available from SWT
All year

The northern edge of this reserve is bordered by a disused quarry which has its own typical lime-loving species, including at least six species of orchid. The quarry is also of geological interest, as fossil specimens of various brachiopods, bivalves and sea lilies may be found. Beneath the cliff the woodland is composed of oak, ash, sycamore, hazel, aspen and wild service-tree, with a shrub layer of dogwood, spindle and spurge laurel. The ground flora is dominated by dog's mercury but includes orchids, hart's-tongue fern, cowslip, false oxlip, slender St John's-wort and three species of violet.

The Dingle

SO 679991; 3ha; WdT
Old garden
Spring, summer

The area was once laid out as a wooded garden, and now it is full of characteristic flowers in spring. A stream offers another important wildlife habitat.

Dolgoch Quarry

Permit only; 2.75ha; SWT reserve
Disused quarry
Summer

A thin limestone grassland has formed on the quarry floor with felwort and blue fleabane in late summer, whilst on the vertical walls viper's bugloss maintains a tenuous hold. Brown spikes of reedmace ring a small pond where great crested newts and frogs can be found, along with a multitude of damselflies and dragonflies. Following the richer grassy slopes up to the precarious narrow walk between the two quarry faces, the more intrepid will find bee and pyramidal orchids and golden rod.

Ercall Wood

SJ 646103; 15.2ha; SCC
Mixed woodland
Spring, early summer

Set on a ridge, the wood contains a good variety of plant species, birds and other animals and has considerable geological interest.

Goughs Coppice

SO 497928; 2.8ha; WdT reserve
Woodland
Spring, summer

A woodland of great landscape value, lying on the northern side Ragleth Hill and with wonderful views of the LONG MYND.

Helmeth Wood

SO 468938; 23.8ha; WdT
Deciduous woodland
Spring, summer

The wood is a superb landscape feature opposite the LONG MYND. At the top of the hill there are many oaks with ash, alder and wild cherry on the lower slopes. The area is rich in wildlife.

Hope Valley Woodland

SJ 350018; 12.8ha; SWT reserve
Mixed woodland
Spring, early summer

The long narrow valley is to be returned to oakwood by removal of planted conifers. Wood-land birds include pied flycatcher and redstart while the stream attracts dipper and kingfisher and also exhibits unique geological exposures.

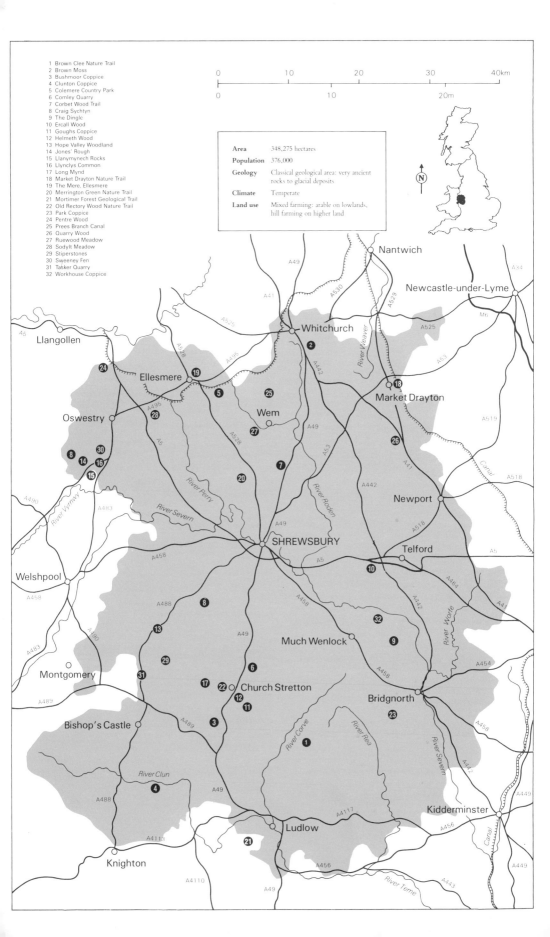

1 Brown Clee Nature Trail
2 Brown Moss
3 Bushmoor Coppice
4 Clunton Coppice
5 Colemere Country Park
6 Comley Quarry
7 Corbet Wood Trail
8 Craig Sychtyn
9 The Dingle
10 Ercall Wood
11 Goughs Coppice
12 Helmeth Wood
13 Hope Valley Woodland
14 Jones' Rough
15 Llanymynech Rocks
16 Llynclys Common
17 Long Mynd
18 Market Drayton Nature Trail
19 The Mere, Ellesmere
20 Merrington Green Nature Trail
21 Mortimer Forest Geological Trail
22 Old Rectory Wood Nature Trail
23 Park Coppice
24 Pentre Wood
25 Prees Branch Canal
26 Quarry Wood
27 Ruewood Meadow
28 Sodylt Meadow
29 Stiperstones
30 Sweeney Fen
31 Tasker Quarry
32 Workhouse Coppice

Area	348,275 hectares
Population	376,000
Geology	Classical geological area: very ancient rocks to glacial deposits
Climate	Temperate
Land use	Mixed farming: arable on lowlands, hill farming on higher land

0   10   20   30   40km

0   10   20m

Nantwich

Newcastle-under-Lyme

Whitchurch

Llangollen

Ellesmere

Market Drayton

Oswestry

Wem

Shrewsbury

Telford

Welshpool

Much Wenlock

Montgomery

Church Stretton

Bridgnorth

Bishop's Castle

Newport

Kidderminster

Ludlow

Knighton

Jagged rocks cap the ridge of Stiperstones.

The old spoil heaps, mounded away from the working floor, have been colonised by grasses and small bright flowers and carry a deep enough soil for woodland to develop. In places they have been planted with conifers or invaded by sycamore scrub but the attractive range of native species such as dogwood, ash and hawthorn implies an eventual mixed wood. The scrub, at present, stands above a show of grassland plants which will disappear as the woodland cover grows, and, eventually, the brighter plants will only survive in the narrow grassland edging the paths.

The thin-turfed quarry floor acts as a storehouse of these grassland plants. In spring and summer, it is beautiful with species such as oxeye daisy and common bird's-foot-trefoil, tangling vetches and clovers, tiny blue milkwort, marjoram and wild thyme, spreads of common rock-rose and vivid star-like yellow-wort, attracting butterflies and songbirds.

The grassland is varied by areas of scree, an open rough shingle of limestone on which little can grow except plants such as herb-Robert, a specialist in rocky places often seen on walls. When soil has accumulated, grassland species will populate the scree and it will be, in turn, a flower garden.

Jones' Rough

SJ 247247; 3.1ha; SWT reserve
Limestone woodland, cliff and scree
Spring, summer

The wood contains many yew trees and some wild cherry. The ground cover includes spurge-laurel and stinking hellebore, while the cliff and scree above the wood is rich in hairy rock-cress, common rock-rose and wild thyme.

Knowle Wood

Permit only; 2.2ha; SWT reserve
Mixed woodland
Spring, early summer

Mainly the result of the natural colonisation of abandoned limestone workings, the wood contains more than 20 tree species including ash, wych elm, oak and grey willow. Mammals found in the reserve include badger and yellow-necked mouse and there is a very varied population of scrub and woodland birds.

Llanymynech Rocks

SJ 266218; 2.4ha; STNC SWT–MWT reserve
Disused limestone quarry
Spring, summer

Llanymynech Hill straddles the border between Wales and England. The carboniferous limestone of the hill has been quarried to leave a towering cliff above a spread of grassland, scree and scrub. Beyond the quarry floor and the scrub-covered spoil heaps, a sloping belt of woodland falls to the edge of the fields below.

Llynclys Common

SJ 273237; 36ha; SWT reserve
Grassland, scrub and woodland
Spring, summer

Scrub and birch woodland is invading a splendid area of limestone grassland – a site which contains

Earl's Hill looms above the land around, seen here from Granhams Moor.

some eight species of orchid and attracts a good range of insects, including brown Argus butterfly.

Long Mynd

SO 425945; 1812ha; NT
Plateau moorland
Leaflets from Shropshire Hills Information Centre
Spring, summer

Bilberry, bracken and heather spread across a great plateau rising out of the level land below. At the highest point, 517m, it is possible to see far over the Cheshire plain, across to Wenlock Edge, the BRECON BEACONS (Powys), or CADER IDRIS (Gwynedd).

The trees that returned after the ice have long been cleared and for centuries sheep have grazed here, preventing any return to woodland cover. The Mynd is now managed as a grouse moor, with a regular mowing programme to encourage the growth of young heather without allowing bracken to spread.

The plateau slopes, particularly on the east, are cut by deep winding valleys where ice and melt-waters have carved away the hill. The present streams rise from springs where bog plants such as *Sphagnum* mosses, bog pimpernel, common butterwort and round-leaved sundew grow with less acidic plants such as marsh lousewort and marsh pennywort. The sheltered grassland slopes are scattered with hawthorn and rowan scrub.

The streams are ideal sites for stonefly larvae, which can only survive in such pure waters, for several of the more particular caddis flies, mayflies and dragonflies, and also for a bird which feeds on these insects. The dipper can walk upstream underwater, head-down, leaning forward, held to the bottom by the water flow. Yellowhammer sing from the hawthorn bushes while wheatear and ring ouzel flit from rock to rock. Buzzard or raven may also be seen.

Although the Long Mynd may seem bare and featureless, to the naturalist it is full of fascination. Tiny acid-loving plants such as tormentil and heath bedstraw shine among the grasses, while navelwort grows on the rocks; northern eggar, moth and caterpillar, may be seen among the heather and small brown trout swim in the lower valley streams.

Market Drayton Nature Trail (Walkmill Marsh)

SJ 684343; 6.4km; SWT
Habitat trail, circulating through lanes near the town
Booklet from SWT
Spring, early summer

The trail includes a range of interest from river and canal to woodland, hedge and farmland.

The Mere, Ellesmere

SJ 403348; 46.4ha; SCC
Large glacial lake
Booklet from Meres Centre at site
Winter

Summer disturbance, pleasure-boating for instance, reduces the potential of the mere but in winter the water is a notable gull roost and draws numbers of wildfowl such as goldeneye, pochard, smew and wigeon. A heronry adds to the year-round interest and tern species are among migrant visitors.

Merrington Green Nature Trail

SJ 465209; 2km; SWT
Scrubland trail
Booklet from SWT and trail for the disabled
Spring, early summer

The trail has been established on the old Merrington Green Common which, now that grazing has ceased, is in the process of changing, through scrub, to secondary woodland. A number of pools add wetland interest.

Mortimer Forest Geological Trail

SO 470730; 4.8km; NCC
Trail examining Silurian sediments
Booklet from NCC
All year

The trail, passing through progressively younger rocks in its passage eastwards, covers some 10 million years. From Easter to September the Ludlow Museum, near the end of the trail, is open to visitors daily.

Old Rectory Wood Nature Trail

SO 448959; 2.4km; SCC
Trail through mixed woodland
Spring, early summer

The trail circles through an attractive woodland of beech, varied with other tree species, beneath the slopes of the LONG MYND.

Park Coppice

SO 673869; 1.9ha; WdT
Woodland
Spring, summer

The small coppice contains a good range of tree and shrub species, and typical woodland birds can be seen.

Pentre Wood

SJ 275370; 6.1ha; WdT
Deciduous woodland
Spring, summer

The reserve lies right on the Welsh border on the banks of the River Ceiriog. Much of the area has been felled in recent years, but a management programme will ensure that it is replanted with the typical broadleaved species of the area which include ash, wild cherry and oak with some beech, field maple and hazel.

Prees Branch Canal

SJ 497332; 0.8km; SWT reserve
Disused canal
Spring, summer

The canal has been invaded by alder, reedswamp and yellow water-lily. Spring brings a waterside show of cowslip and marsh-marigold, while summer plants found in the reserve include frogbit and flowering-rush.

Preston Montford Nature Trail

Permit only; 275m; FSC
Short riverside trail
Booklet and permit from site at SJ 432143, also permit for hide
Spring, early summer

A variety of habitats, particularly the range associated with glacial materials overlying clay, is found on the trail, together with opportunities to study the bird life of the river from the bankside hide.

Quarry Wood

SJ 686273; 2.8ha; SWT reserve
Mixed woodland
Spring, early summer

Winter migrants, such as fieldfare and redwing, roost in the dense rhododendron cover which shades out much of the woodland floor. Some 20 other tree species add colour and variety to the reserve and encourage an interesting range of summer breeding birds.

Ruewood Meadow

SJ 495280; 2.6ha; SWT reserve
Wet unimproved grassland
Leaflet from SWT
Spring, summer

The two fields are separated by a drainage ditch and lie over glacial drift with the River Roden as the northern boundary. This now rare wetland habitat provides feeding areas for snipe, curlew and lapwing, and is home to many amphibians and insects. Over 100 species of plant have been recorded, notably meadow-rue and marsh-orchid in the wetter, more acid field, and yellow iris, meadowsweet and yellow rattle in other areas.

Sodylt Wood

SJ 343409; 8.5ha; WdT
Woodland
Spring, summer

These two areas of attractive ancient woodland alongside the River Dee have recently been clear felled, but have already been replanted with a variety of native trees and shrubs.

Stiperstones

SO 369976; 437ha; NCC reserve
Moorland with geological exposures
All year

The landscape of the reserve is characterised by steep slopes and deep valleys, and is renowned for its stone stripes and polygons. The block scree, which forms the stripes, split away from the summit by frost action to form the tors of more durable rock like the Devil's Chair.

The moorland is dominated by heather and bilberry, and other plants such as cowberry, crowberry and western gorse also occur.

At Resting Hill there is an area of oak coppice woodland which used to provide the charcoal for smelting. There are several wet flushes and bogs where cottongrass, bog asphodel and bog violet can be found.

There is a small area of unimproved grassland among the abandoned smallholdings on the reserve, where a large population of the yellow mountain pansy grows. Redstarts and tree pipits live among the old hedges and walls.

Sweeney Fen

SJ 275251; 1ha; SWT reserve
Fen and meadow
Leaflet from SWT
Spring, summer

Set in a shallow trough between two outcrops of carboniferous limestone, fenland is a rare habitat in Shropshire. The main vegetation is lesser pond-sedge and blunt-flowered rush, with water avens, marsh-marigold and globeflower (the most south-easterly limit of its distribution) plus the locally rare marsh helleborine. The adjacent grazed area has many meadow flowers, and brooklime and horsetail grow on the transitional land.

Tasker Quarry

SO 326957; 0.8ha; SWT reserve
Geological site
All year

The quarry shows an exposure of Ordovician Stapeley volcanic ashes interbedded with shales.

Wem Moss

Permit only; 20.8ha; SWT reserve
Lowland raised bog
Spring, summer

Contrary to the views of many people, most bogs are neither dangerous nor ugly. Undoubtedly some are dangerous – a schwingmoor or floating bog, for instance, may be a flimsy raft of peat above several metres of mud or water – but most bogs are wonderful places of subtle-patterned colour.

Wem Moss is a small raised bog, a post-glacial mere where mosses and wetland plants have built up peat into a low dome, like a giant sponge. The surface is dipped and hummocked, allowing plants to grow in either damp or wet conditions.

The reserve, surrounded by woodland and fields, appears as a plain of heather-purple divided by a strip of wetter ground where alder and birch grow with tussocks of purple moor-grass and

Llanymynech Rocks: quarried limestone has now become an important nature reserve.

sprays of bog myrtle, with marsh-marigold, lesser spearwort and early marsh-orchid, lesser butterfly-orchid, meadow thistle and royal fern. Bog aspho-del, cross-leaved heath and heather show the change to more acid conditions which marks the bog, where a spread of purple moorgrass and heathers is varied by tormentil and by the special plant life of the wet, small hollows.

These hollows are rich in sedges, such as white beak-sedge and common cottongrass, and are cushioned with *Sphagnum* mosses, decorated with round-leaved sundew and cranberry. Both the other British sundews occur, oblong-leaved and great sundew, together with bog-rosemary.

Adders are abundant on the moss; wetland and woodland birds may visit, hunting the plentiful insects; some notable dragonflies occur and the reserve protects a population of large heath butterfly. The large heath is limited to bogs and wet heathland where its food plants, white beak-sedge and cottongrass, survive, and it occurs in three distinct varieties. Wem Moss holds the one known only in Cumbria, Lancashire and north Shropshire.

Workhouse Coppice

SJ 667028; 5.4ha; WdT
Deciduous woodland
Spring, summer

The wood overlooks the Severn Gorge above the historic Ironbridge where the Industrial Revol-ution had its roots. Once this coppice provided the wood that fuelled the new factories. Today the wood has a different function as an amenity area where residents and visitors alike can stroll among the mature oaks and enjoy the rich wildlife.

The kestrel is one of England's most common birds of prey.

The little owl may be spotted on heaths and lowlands hunting at dusk.

Staffordshire

Staffordshire is a county of exceptional variety. The wild moorlands in the north of the county have grouse and mountain hares, harriers and dipper-haunted streams. At the other extreme, in the south of the county, fossils from the limestone caves at WREN'S NEST (described under Warwickshire and West Midlands) indicate that the industrial sprawl of the Black Country is on what was once the bed of a semi-tropical sea.

Between the industrialised sprawl of the Potteries in the north and the heavy industries in the south is open, unspoilt countryside that strangers hardly ever discover. Its very anonymity rescues it from the fate of the Dukeries in Nottinghamshire, or parts of THE PEAK NATIONAL PARK (Derbyshire), both of which are being ruined by too much pressure from the people who love them well, but not wisely enough.

CANNOCK CHASE, to the west of this central area, consists of conifer plantations, oak and birch woods and open moorland. This acts as a major lung for the industrial areas to the north and south and the planners have done all that they can to supply 'honeypot' areas, to concentrate visitors and minimise damage through overpressure. To the north east of the Chase a number of contiguous large estates stretch across to Needwood Forest and Marchington Woodlands, almost to the edge of Burton-on-Trent. Although these estates have recently been fragmented by taxation, the families who owned them for centuries shielded them from development, so that they now form a large area of beautiful, unspoiled, typical English countryside, still relatively undiscovered. As with other land composed of great estates, this area owes much to generations of hunting and shooting men who laid out their lands with strategically sited coverts for pheasant and fox, which supply ideal breeding and feeding habitat for insects, birds and animals not even remotely connected with sport!

On the edge of the Cannock Chase coalfield great crested newts and water-beetles, horse leeches and sticklebacks can be found in the subsidence pools or 'swags' created as land subsided, or sagged in, when coal was plundered way underground. The waste land around the swags and spoil banks has been for many decades rich with wild flowers that attract goldfinches, while skylarks sing in summer as over any windswept stretch of isolated downland. In recent years the value of such sites, especially for educational purposes, has been widely recognised and the Nature Conservancy Council and county conservation trusts have shown interest in preserving urban reserves.

Remnants of Needwood Forest and Cannock Chase still retain the last few ancient oaks that clothed the area before they were despoiled for charcoal for the iron and glass trades. Trees such as wild service-tree and plants and insects specific to ancient woodland still thrive there, and the light, sandy soil at Cannock is the perfect habitat for lizard and adder.

The rich dairying country round Uttoxeter grows more rugged and wooded to the north. The Rivers Dove, Churnet and Hamps provide superb scenery and a rich pattern of wildlife. Leaving the farmland of central Staffordshire behind, the clays and red marls give way to the millstone grit of the uplands. This is stone wall country, windswept in summer and desolate and forbidding in winter. Curlews sing the wildest song on earth and rabbits survive in crevices of rock, some man-made in walls and some in natural fissures, immune from dogs and spades and men with guns.

The Roaches, above Leek, support grouse and blue hare and also the remnants of a group of wallabies that started in the 1920s as a private collection, escaped during the war, and have survived ever since as a feral population. Besides dipper in the streams there are ring ouzel and stonechat in these wild hills, and red and fallow deer in the woods that clothe their slopes down to the farmland below.

The River Dove that divides Staffordshire from

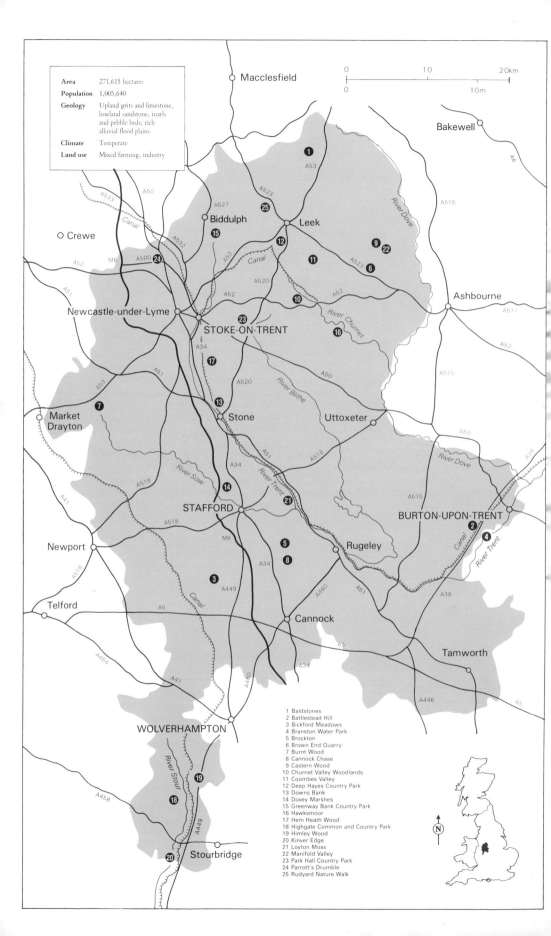

Area	271,615 hectares
Population	1,005,640
Geology	Upland grits and limestone, lowland sandstone, marls and pebble beds; rich alluvial flood plains
Climate	Temperate
Land use	Mixed farming, industry

0   10   20km
0   10m

Macclesfield

Bakewell

Crewe

Biddulph

Leek

Newcastle-under-Lyme

STOKE-ON-TRENT

Ashbourne

Market Drayton

Stone

Uttoxeter

Newport

STAFFORD

BURTON-UPON-TRENT

Rugeley

Telford

Cannock

Tamworth

WOLVERHAMPTON

Stourbridge

1 Baldstones
2 Battlestead Hill
3 Bickford Meadows
4 Branston Water Park
5 Brockton
6 Brown End Quarry
7 Burnt Wood
8 Cannock Chase
9 Castern Wood
10 Churnet Valley Woodlands
11 Coombes Valley
12 Deep Hayes Country Park
13 Downs Bank
14 Doxey Marshes
15 Greenway Bank Country Park
16 Hawksmoor
17 Hem Heath Wood
18 Highgate Common and Country Park
19 Himley Wood
20 Kinver Edge
21 Loyton Moss
22 Manifold Valley
23 Park Hall Country Park
24 Parrott's Drumble
25 Rudyard Nature Walk

N

Derbyshire flows through some of the richest and most beautiful countryside in England, each county claiming that the best of all worlds is on their bank. The stretch flowing through Beresford Dale has been made immortal in Izaak Walton's *Compleat Angler*, and it still holds superb trout. Far more interesting from a naturalist's viewpoint is the fact that the whole valley is rich in wild flowers, and the insects that feed the fish are of no less delight to entomologists. The whole spectrum of bird life in the valley is a constant joy, ranging from curlew on the hills around to kingfisher and dipper along the river banks.

The choice of habitats to study and explore is almost limitless, ranging from the deer-haunted Needwood Forest and Cannock Chase to the wild beauty of the hills or the eerie atmosphere of CHARTLEY MOSS, a floating bog formed by vegetation creating a skin over a deep lake gouged out during the ice ages. In places the surface has formed peat on which large trees have grown. A single person jumping up and down can set the peat quaking until trees 6m high begin to rock and sway in rhythm. If they grow much higher, the weight causes a depression in the peat that makes the trees themselves sink until they die and collapse, to add to the thickness of the skin over the lake below. The next generation of trees will grow a little higher before they in turn sink and add their contribution of support for future generations.

Such curiosities give diversity to an already varied county. Whether your tastes are for woodland with its wide spectrum of birds and flowers, badger, deer and insects, or for the solitude of open hills, the countryside of great estates or wild moorland, you can satisfy them in Staffordshire.

PHIL DRABBLE

Allimore Green Common

Permit only; 2.5ha; SWT reserve
Unimproved pasture
Spring, summer

The deep hedges containing oak, ash, hazel and holly spill into the meadow as a fringe of mixed scrub, bramble, hawthorn and wild rose, or alder, willow and alder buckthorn where the land lies wet. The grassland has not been ploughed or drained for many years and is filled with marshland plants while some areas, at least, show signs of lime enrichment.

The first impression is one of a deep herb meadow, with tall plants such as meadowsweet and hemp-agrimony standing above the grassland. In spring the meadow blazes with marsh-marigold and later the colours of ragged-Robin, greater bird's-foot-trefoil, marsh bedstraw, devil's-bit scabious and common knapweed lay a rich pattern across the spread of meadow grasses and of rushes and sedges which mark the wetter areas. Summer shows the beauty of marsh-orchids and common spotted-orchid, the blue flowers of water mint which are so attractive to butterflies and the fascinating plants of the damp rich spots where marsh pennywort and the white-flowered grass-of-Parnassus grow. The fine hedges and clumps of scrub provide shelter and nest sites for birds as well as attracting insects.

Alvecote Pools

The reserve, mainly in Warwickshire, is described under Warwickshire and West Midlands.

Baldstones

SK 018641; 25.2ha; SWT reserve
Moorland and stream
Spring, early summer

Down the side of the Black Brook valley a small stream cascades to join the brook, cutting its way through the millstone grit to rush down rocky steps or curve through miniature valleys, draining the boggy moor above. The view extends over long sweeps of moorland which are breeding sites for short-eared owl and ring ouzel.

The tilted rocks are bare, fissured and eroded on the east but rising steeply from the west in smooth slopes patched with lichens, heather, bilberry and moorland grasses. Below them the land falls back to the valley – moorland grazing with damper ground where hare's-tail cottongrass and *Sphagnum* mosses grow with purple moorgrass and rushes. These mires drain into the stream and willows lean across the water, where the shelter is sufficient for shrubs to grow, while the banks are topped with heather, bilberry, gorse, rushes and ferns. Clumps of great woodrush grow in the damp deeper soils along the streamside, together with a fine range of fern species.

Ground-nesting birds such as wheatear, whinchat and red grouse frequent the reserve. Grey mountain carpet and perhaps red carpet, both northern species of moth, may occur at Baldstones, together with beautiful yellow underwing.

Battlestead Hill

SK 208211; 2.4ha; WdT
Woodland
Spring, summer

Grazing and Dutch elm disease have badly affected this wood, but fencing and replanting and replacement of dead elms with native species will help to restore the area.

Belvedere Observation Tower

Permit only; FC
Raised viewing hide
Open dawn–2p.m. and 2p.m.–dusk: apply during office hours to Chief Forester, tel. Rugeley 2035
Summer

Set in a sanctuary area of CANNOCK CHASE, the observation tower is open to deerwatchers in two sessions, as above.

Belvide Reservoir

Permit only; 122.4ha; West Midlands Bird Club reserve
Canal feeder reservoir
May be overlooked from public bridleway at SJ 856103
All year

The marshy vegetation of the margins is attractive to breeding birds in early summer and, in autumn, draw-down reveals muds to attract passage waders. The bays and shallows have floating spreads of amphibious bistort with clumps of rushes and stands of reed sweet-grass at the water's edge. Small well-vegetated or gravelled islands add further variety. The surrounding meadows are roosting and feeding grounds for waders and nest-sites for wetland birds, while the shallows are as attractive to dabblers and waders as the deeper waters are to diving birds.

In winter there may be large numbers of mallard, wigeon and teal with tufted duck and pochard, coot and mute swan. Goldeneye and goosander are usually present and, with BLITHFIELD, the reservoir may hold over 50 per cent of the national population of ruddy duck. Pintail and long-tailed duck, scaup, common scoter, shelduck and smew are often seen in bitter weather and, occasionally, true seabirds such as eider and red-breasted merganser may shelter here. Other visitors include geese, swans and rarities such as spoonbill, marsh sandpiper and black-winged stilt. Large numbers of gulls use the reservoir as a night-time roost and there are regular visits by glaucous and Iceland gull.

At times regular numbers of arctic, black and common tern fly through, with occasional visits from a range of other terns. Good numbers of migrant waders occur including spotted redshank and ruff, whimbrel, common, curlew, green and wood sandpiper.

Bickford Meadows

SJ 883141; 1.2ha; SWT reserve
Meadows
Spring, summer

These two small wet fields border a brook which floods in winter. There are extensive beds of wild garlic, some small teazel, marsh-marigold and ragged-Robin. A wide range of common birds may be seen and dragonflies include the southern and brown aeshna.

Black Firs and Cranberry Bog

Permit only; 5.2ha; SWT reserve
Wet woodland, fen and bog
Spring, summer

Swampy woodland covers an area of drained fen while the small floating acid bog is outstanding in that it lies surrounded by rich-fen plants. The bog contains cranberry, cross-leaved heath and common cottongrass, with species such as cowbane, water-violet and royal fern in the surrounding fen.

Blithfield Reservoir

Permit only; 760ha; South Staffs Waterworks Co.
Very large reservoir
May be overlooked from SK 058238 and lanes around
Autumn, winter

Most important for its winter wildfowl, with good numbers of mallard, teal and wigeon, pochard and tufted duck, the reservoir is also visited by passage migrants and provides a winter roost for gulls including occasional glaucous and Iceland gulls. A peregrine is usually seen in the autumn attracted by the large numbers of waterfowl.

Branston Water Park

SK 215205; 2ha; SWT reserve
Gravel pit
All year

Part of an old gravel pit now used as a multi-purpose waterpark. The reserve contains the largest reedbed in Staffordshire and supports a wide range of wildfowl.

Brocton

SJ 967189; 48ha; SCC reserve
Deep-water gravelpit and woodland within Cannock Chase
Spring, summer

Gravel cliffs decorated with birch, broom, heather, rosebay willowherb, grasses and mosses stand above the waters of the pool which are overlooked by a small public hide. Canada geese, mallard, tufted duck and great crested grebe are among the waterfowl. The scrub woodland provides a habitat for smaller birds such as warblers.

Brown End Quarry

SK 090502; 1.4ha; SWT reserve
Geological site with calcareous grassland
Booklet from SWT
All year

The prime interest of this reserve is the exposure of lower carboniferous limestone which is nationally unique, and interpretative signs explain the geology. The surrounding grassland supports cowslips, wild strawberry, meadow crane's-bill and biting stonecrop. Redstarts and garden warblers are summer visitors.

Burnt Wood

SJ 738353; 12ha; SWT reserve
Relict oak woodland
Spring, early summer

Much of the old oak woodland has been felled and turned over to conifers but areas of natural woodland remain, ensuring a continuity of oak which means that animals lost in other woods are able to survive here. For some moth species, Burnt Wood is the only remaining locality in the county.

The oaks stand above an understorey of birch, holly and rowan. The ground cover is mainly of bracken and bilberry with patches of bramble, honeysuckle and fine tussocked grasses. Mosses spread beneath the trees, often with plumes of broad buckler-fern. A characteristic of the wood is the amount of moss-covered fallen timber, while stumps, decorated with sprays of bilberry and moss, add to the dead wood so essential to many insects. Heather shows on the edges of the rides, where rosebay willowherb, raspberry and foxglove grow above tormentil, heath bedstraw, rushes and acid-loving grasses.

The birds include such characteristic woodland species as nuthatch and treecreeper, together with all three native woodpeckers. Tawny owl and sparrowhawk hunt the rides and woodland fringes which, in winter, may be busy with visitors such as redpoll and siskin. Damp places in the rides may show the probe marks of the long slightly flexible beak of the woodcock.

Burnt Wood is important for small pearl-bordered fritillary and for a number of interesting species of spider, but is outstanding for its moths. It is the only known Staffordshire locality for least black arches, a site for the uncommon peacock moth and for three local species, beautiful snout, bilberry pug and silvery arches, which are limited to oak-birch woodlands over heather and bilberry.

Cannock Chase

SJ 971842; 870ha; SCC
Heathland, bog and woodland
Leaflets from SCC or FC
Spring, summer

Late summer is perhaps the most spectacular time on Cannock Chase, when heather seems to blaze purple on the plateau, above spreads of bracken on long curves of the hillside.

After the ice retreated and the climate began to improve the whole plateau was probably covered by forest, but natural woodland is now very limited although much of the Chase is covered with conifers.

The heathland, though, is beautiful, filled with plants such as bell heather and billberry, with upland species such as crowberry and plants of the sandy lowland heaths, such as bird's-foot. Another upland species is cowberry, which not only underlines the link with the northern moors, but where it grows with bilberry forms a hybrid. Sometimes called the Cannock Chase berry, it is known only from two other sites in the county and, elsewhere, only from Derbyshire and Yorkshire.

Below the plateau the valley bottoms have slowly filled to form narrow level flood plains through which the streams meander and which sometimes give way to valley mires where drainage is impeded. In the more fertile valleys, bogbean and marsh cinquefoil, southern marsh-orchid, near the upper limit of its range, and marsh hawk's-beard, a northern plant close to its southern limit, may be found.

The valley bogs also contain species of both north and south but, except for plants such as grass-of-Parnassus, the accent is rather more southern: the bogs are said to be reminiscent of those in the NEW FOREST (Hampshire). Instead of the rich alluvium of the marshes, the bogs are based upon acid peats filled with *Sphagnum*, cross-leaved heath, purple moor-grass and greater tussock-sedge. Plants rare or uncommon in Staffordshire include bog asphodel, common butterwort and cranberry, marsh pennywort and bog pimpernel, common spotted-orchid, great and round-leaved sundew, marsh valerian and marsh violet, together with narrow buckler-fern, marsh fern, dioecious and few-flowered sedge and wood horsetail.

Areas of broad-leaved woodland still remain on the Chase; pedunculate oak may be found at Sycamore Hill and Seven Springs, while sessile oak occurs in BROCTON COPPICE. These Brocton oaks, mainly around 150 to 200 years of age, support a number of beetle species and angle-striped sallow moth which are thought to be indicators of ancient woodland.

In fact, with the fall in grazing pressure, now that the sheep have gone, the Chase may be on its way to a return to woodland. Birch is spreading, pines are seeding themselves from the plantations, and sycamore has seeded from hedgerow trees. For the moment, the heath has the upper hand, with only a scatter of hawthorn, crab apple, elder, holly, rowan and willow to vary the birch and occasional oak. The woods have the typical springtime flowers of acid situations, and also contain less widespread plants such as common cow-wheat and climbing corydalis. In late summer and autumn a wide variety of fungi may be found, with fly agaric and razor-strop fungus in the birchwood and blusher, funnel chanterelle, common earth-ball, shaggy ink-cap, sickener and several *Boletus* species in the mixed woods.

Butterflies include green hairstreak and dingy skipper, with small pearl-bordered fritillary where its food plants, violets, grow in the small valley bogs. The spreads of purple moor-grass around the bogs support the eponymous moth while streamside alders attract such moths as May highflyer, dingy shell and small yellow wave, and stands of willow may hold eyed hawk-moth. The heathlands are sites for typical heather feeders, such as emperor, oak eggar and beautiful yellow underwing, while areas rich in bilberry are sites for northern spinach, July highflyer and golden-red brindle. The woods hold species such as pale brindled beauty, scalloped hazel, September thorn and scorched-wing, with argent, sable and pebble hook-tip flying among the birch trees.

Heathland, scrub and woodland birds include meadow pipit, linnet and great spotted woodpecker. Wetland birds may occur by the streams or, most often, in the flooded quarry at Brocton, where sand martins breed in a dramatic exposure of the pebble beds of the Chase. The coniferous woodlands may be visited by wintering crossbill and hold, besides coal tit and goldcrest, occasional long-eared owl and sparrowhawk. The broad-leaved woods attract typical hole-nesting birds: treecreeper, nuthatch, redstart and tawny owl, with wood warbler, woodcock and hawfinch where hornbeam occurs and lesser spotted woodpecker where alder and willow grow in the valleys. The heathland and scrub provide a habitat for whinchat, tree pipit and grasshopper warbler, as well as for the most important bird of Cannock, nightjar, which seems to be losing ground throughout the country: two-thirds of the whole Midlands population breed here. The heaths are also important as a staging post for migrants such as ring ouzel, stonechat, wheatear, merlin and hen harrier and provide a regular wintering site for great grey shrike.

No discussion of the Chase is complete without mention of the deer. Small numbers of muntjac, red, roe and sika are present but fallow occur in good numbers and are most likely to be seen.

The FC's deer museum and forest office at SK 017171 provide a source of information about the forest and a starting point for waymarked walks.

Castern Wood

SK 116538; 20.4ha; SWT reserve
Mixed woodland, scrub and grassland
Booklet from SWT
Spring, summer

The reserve is set on the steep slopes of the MANIFOLD VALLEY and ranges from open grassland, through mixed woodland, to scrub-invaded grassland beside the winter-born river. Limestone is exposed at the top of the reserve, where shallow turf carries wild thyme, harebell and many colourful plants and deeper grassland contains such species as musk mallow. The woodland contains a wide variety of trees above plants such as giant bellflower, although some parts are thick with bramble. The reserve as a whole is rich in animal life, particularly butterflies and woodland birds.

Chance Wood

Permit only; 2.8ha; WNCT reserve
Small woodland
Spring, early summer

The dry valley originally contained an ornamental woodland which now consists chiefly of oak and beech over a variety of other species. Snowdrop and bluebell make a fine show in spring. Typical woodland birds include nuthatch and tawny owl.

Chartley Moss

Permit only; 42ha; NCC
Large floating bog
Spring, summer

Woodland has formed on the edges of the bog and the thicker areas of floating peat, but generally the reserve consists of a spread of *Sphagnum* mosses, rich in bog plants such as cranberry, cross-leaved heath and bog-rosemary at the south eastern limit of its British distribution. There are important colonies of insects and many adder.

Churnet Valley Woodlands

SK 000480; 74ha; RSPB reserve
Deciduous woodland, river
Spring, summer

The Churnet Valley has many reminders of north Staffordshire's industrial past. Chase Wood has an imposing set of disused limekilns, built from stone excavated from the large quarry within the wood. There is also a network of overgrown tracks of the old horse-drawn railways, known as plateways. The River Churnet, which adjoins part of the reserve, has been deepened to form part of the Cauldon Canal. Booth Wood, part of this reserve, and Rough Knipe – as well as Chase Wood – provided the wood to power the local industries of coal- and iron-mining and charcoal-burning. Rotational cutting has created an uneven-aged woodland ideal for wildlife. There are areas of mature woodland containing oak, birch and ash trees, old coppice of varying ages, and a good shrub layer of birch, cherry, blackthorn, hazel and guelder-rose. In spring the woods are carpeted with wild flowers: bluebells, wood anemones, moschatel and great sweeps of white strong-smelling ramsons. There are patches of giant bellflower and clumps of broad-leaved helleborine.

The woods are especially important for their large populations and varieties of migrant warbler, including wood warbler, whitethroat, garden warbler, blackcap and willow warbler; chiffchaff and

lesser whitethroat occur in smaller numbers. The old trees are ideal for woodpeckers and all three species occur, together with treecreepers, nuthatches, redstarts and five species of tits. Smaller numbers of tree pipit and woodcock occur and sparrowhawks are the main predator. Despite Dutch elm disease, elm is still widespread on the reserve and supports the scarce white-letter hairstreak butterfly.

Clay Mills

Permit only; 8ha; SWT reserve
Gravel pit
Winter

This old, well-vegetated gravel pit adjoins the River Dove and is particularly good for wintering wildfowl. It is used as a roost by cormorants.

Coombes Valley

SK 005530; 95ha; RSPB reserve
Wooded valley, scrub and grassland
Leaflet from information centre
Spring, early summer

The woodland is chiefly oak with a range of species such as ash, birch, holly, rowan and wych elm over a shrub layer of blackthorn, bird cherry, hazel and guelder-rose. Bramble, gorse and wild rose appear where there is enough light and the stream, which was once large enough to carve out the whole valley, is lined with alder and clumps of fern. The woodland does not cover the whole reserve: meadowland lies above and beside the stream, filled with betony, common bird's-foot-trefoil, primrose, self-heal and tormentil, or wet-land plants such as marsh-marigold. In heathland areas heather, bell heather and cross-leaved heath grow with bilberry and purple moor-grass. Early-purple orchid, common spotted-orchid and greater butterfly-orchid may be found in season.

Two observation hides have been built: one overlooking a streamside pool where dipper, kingfisher and grey wagtail may be seen, the other set in a tall oak to view birds such as goldcrest, nuthatch, redstart and treecreeper or the aerobatics of pied flycatchers. Woodland birds include wood-cock, wood warbler, all three British woodpeckers, tawny and long-eared owl and sparrowhawk. Of a total of some 130 species, more than half breed on the reserve. Redpoll and siskin are a feature in winter while large flocks of fieldfare and redwing may make an occasional show.

Cannock Chase: bracken and heather, valley alders, scrub-covered slopes and forestry above.

Badger and fox are both present and there are many small mammals to feed the resident hunters. Adder, grass snake and common lizard are reptiles present and the pond provides a breeding ground for frog, toad and common and great crested newt.

The insect life of the reserve is particularly rich and interesting. There are more than 1200 species of beetle, 500 moths and some 24 butterflies, including high brown fritillary which has no other known breeding site within a 100km radius.

Deep Hayes Country Park

SJ 962535; 57.6ha; SCC
Pools, marshes, meadows and woodland
Spring, early summer

Adder's-tongue, dwarf elder, dyer's greenweed and greater butterfly-orchid are among the interesting plants found on this reserve. Adder and grass snake are plentiful and the birds include kingfisher.

Downs Bank

SJ 901365; 66.4ha; NT
Heathland, stream and woodland
Spring, early summer

Bracken slopes dominate the Downs but there are still areas are colourful showing bilberry and heather. The stream and marshy areas are colourful, showing pink purslane, ragged-Robin and marsh cinquefoil, marsh lousewort, round-leaved sundew and common spotted-orchid.

Alder swamp in the wetland and drier oak–birch woodland with sycamore encourage a good range of birds to the area including marsh tit and yellow wagtail, blackcap, whitethroat and garden warbler.

Doxey Marshes

SJ 904252; 144ha; SWT reserve
Meadow, marshes, reedbed and open water
Booklet from SWT
All year

The construction of the town mill in Stafford and its associated drain in the 11th and 12th centuries was a major factor in the development of the marshes. Then pumping of brine in the 1950s and '70s caused subsidence and flooding, creating a number of pools. The marshes are now extremely varied in the habitats they provide. The reserve is particularly important for breeding wildfowl and waders, including redshank, snipe, pochard, teal and ruddy duck. In winter whooper and Bewick's swan can be seen. Some of the more attractive plants include cuckooflower, flowering rush and purple loosestrife.

Eccleshall Castle Mere

Permit only; 8ha; SWT reserve
Pool, meadow and woodland
Spring, summer

Typical birds of light woodland are abundant on the reserve. Waterbirds may visit the small mere, which is fringed by wet meadowland containing a wide variety of wetland plants.

George Hayes, Piggots Bottom and Square Covert Woods

Permit only; 20ha; SWT reserve
Deciduous woodland
Spring, summer

This ash, wych elm and sycamore woodland has a particularly fine display of wild daffodils in spring. It is the only site in the country where tuberous comfrey can be found and among the other more unusual plants here are broad-leaved helleborine and greater bellflower. Three species of deer – red, fallow and muntjac – have been recorded. The woods are particularly good for breeding warblers including blackcap, garden and wood warbler. Both woodcock and hobby have been seen.

Greenway Bank Country Park

SJ 888552; 44ha; SCC
Woodland, old parkland and canal-feeder reservoir
Spring, early summer

Wetland areas are rich in plants, while the mixed woodlands and waters attract a good range of bird life including redstart, kingfisher and dipper. The Queen Elizabeth II Silver Jubilee Arboretum is an unusual collection of native or long-established British trees.

Harston Wood

Permit only; 4ha; SWT reserve
Woodland
Spring, summer

A wide variety of birds and plants can be found in the reserve which is part of a more extensive woodland in a rocky valley near the end of the Caldon canal.

Hawksmoor

SK 033440; 122.8ha; NT reserve
Mixed woodland and heath
Spring, early summer

Birch, oak–birch and mixed woodlands stand on often steep slopes above bracken, heather and bilberry. The wood is set on the sides of a great ledge of sandstone and pebbles which looks out over the Churnet Valley.

Hem Heath Wood

SJ 885412; 8ha; SWT reserve
Mixed woodland
Booklet from SWT
Spring, early summer

Some 34 trees and shrub species, including alder, ash, birch, beech, oak, wild cherry, wild privet and guelder-rose, grow in the wood, with an array of smaller plants including moschatel, yellow pimpernel and broad-leaved helleborine. A small pond shows wetland plants such as marsh-marigold and marsh cinquefoil. Woodland birds include nuthatch and treecreeper, wood warbler and sparrowhawk.

Highgate Common and Country Park

SQ 844900; 111.2ha; SCC
Heath and woodland
Spring, early summer

The wide area of open heathland and spreads of birch woodland attract a bird life which ranges from skylark, yellowhammer and linnet to woodland species such as woodpeckers and warblers.

Himley Wood

SO 869916; 23.6ha; WdT
Mixed woodland
Spring, early summer

The wood is a fine stand of mature oak, ash, beech, sweet chestnut, lime and Scots pine.

Hodge Lane

Permit only; 1.4ha; SWT–Tamworth BC reserve
Derelict claypit
Leaflet from TBC
Spring, summer

Rough grassland, heathland, scrub and woodland have colonised the old working which also contains a small *Sphagnum* bog and a number of pools. Bulrush and water-plantain are among the wetland plants and a good range of birds is attracted to the gorse scrub and woodland.

Jackson's Coppice

Permit only; 6.4ha; SWT reserve
Oak woodland and marsh
Spring, early summer

The road separates the wood from the marsh here and each is full of interest. The wood is an acid oakwood with a splendid exposure of sandstone outside the reserve boundary, a sudden wall where oak and beech stand above the rock. The wall of stone is rich in mosses, lichens, and ferns such as polypody, and faces out across the valley. Broom, elder, sweet chestnut and wild cherry occur within or around the wood; the ground cover is varied, with dense bramble in well-lit areas or open acid grasses under the trees. Bluebell, foxglove, rosebay willowherb and wood sage, stands of bracken, broad buckler-fern and male-fern add to the show, together with honeysuckle and red campion.

The marsh is fed by a clear stream at its narrow upper end, a stream lined with great willowherb, banked with rosebay willowherb and decorated with the strange clusters of branched bur-reed. Below this point the marsh spreads, sheltered by a belt of willow and thick with reed sweet-grass, with deep stands of meadowsweet, with climbing marsh bedstraw and greater bird's-foot-trefoil. In early spring the brilliant yellow of marsh-marigold blazes from the reedswamp, along with the marsh fern, bogbean and common valerian.

This varied plant life encourages a good range of animals including over 60 species of birds. Grasshopper warbler is among the smaller birds which breed here, while water rail is also present.

Kinver Edge

SO 838828; 123.2ha; NT–SCC
High heath and woodland
Spring, early summer

Despite the number of visitors, the oak–birch woodland over heather, gorse and wavy hair-grass or standing above sweeps of bracken is still attractive, particularly to scrub and woodland birds such as yellowhammer, nuthatch and a variety of tits.

Leomansley Pools

Permit only; 2ha; SWT reserve
Pools and woodland
Spring, summer

Surrounded by wet woodland, the pools contain a good range of water plants and are fringed with wetland species, while the reserve forms a haven for many different birds.

Lime Tree Farm

Permit only; 1.2ha; SWT reserve
Small wood
Spring, early summer

Hedgerows add to the habitat range of a small area of woodland, sloping down to a pool.

Longsdon Woods

Permit only; 92ha; SWT reserves
Three separate woods
Spring, early summer

Close to the riverside, the woodlands are rich in typical plants and bird life, enhanced by the presence of species such as dipper, kingfisher and heron.

Loynton Moss

SJ 989244; 13.2ha; SWT reserve
Wetland and bog
Booklet from SWT
Spring, early summer

Where CHARTLEY MOSS is a superb example of a floating bog, Loynton Moss derived from a similar depression in glacial clays but has been colonised by an immense reedbed. Until relatively recently the centre of the moss was an area of open water but common reed has now completely covered it.

The reserve is approached by a bridge across the Shropshire Union Canal and is bounded by a bank thrown up when the canal was excavated. The bank is relatively rich in lime and is covered with a variety of tree and shrub species which contrast strikingly with the more acid conditions of the moss.

A foot-path marks an internal boundary within the reserve: towards the site of the mere the

Sweeps of bracken below birch woodland are one of the features of Kinver Edge.

wetland is fenlike, rich in plants now uncommon in the Midlands, plants such as yellow loosestrife, yellow iris and greater spearwort, while the further side, lifted by the *Sphagnum* mosses above the richer water, is much more acid. Birch and rowan replace the stands of alder above a spread of broad buckler-fern growing on the *Sphagnum*. Bog myrtle is now limited to this one site in Staffordshire and the colony of alder buckthorn is probably the finest in the county.

Beyond the birch–rowan woodland, further away from the remaining wetter centre of the mere, oak and birch become the dominant trees, a further step in the eventual drying-out process – the reserve is a fascinating study in change.

Manifold Valley

SK 100543; 7km; NT–SCC
Limestone valley footpath
Spring, summer

Above Wetton Mill, water flows fast over the riverbed but, just below, it disappears into the stones, falling through swallet holes to reappear many kilometres south at the boil-holes of Illam. In winter the main flow carries over the swallets and the river runs throughout its course; by summer much of the bed is dry. Water, too, cut the valley itself and the high cave-mouths on the cliffs mark an ancient level of the river.

Beside the present river, narrow meadows lie on the valley floor and give way to steep banks of limestone grassland, to slopes of woodland or to slabby cliffs which lift up to the crags. In some places small quarries have been cut out of the slopes. The whole area is rich in limestone plants with salad burnet, eyebright, harebell, lady's-mantle and marjoram, small scabious, saw-wort and common rock-rose, quaking-grass, common spotted-orchid, greater butterfly orchid and harts

tongue. Damper places in the valley bottom may show water avens, butterbur, great burnet, sweet cicely and comfrey, meadow crane's-bill, raspberry and common valerian, while the moist grottos below the woodland show woodruff and wood melick, giant bellflower and fleshy orpine. The sloping meadows are filled with herbs where devil's-bit scabious and oxeye daisy grow and green-winged orchid may be found in early summer. Mountain currant falls in curtains from the rocks above.

On the gorse and hawthorn of the higher slopes goldfinch, linnet and whinchat may be seen, while jackdaw haunt the high crags. Lower down, the more woodland-adapted birds occur: tree pipit and spotted flycatcher, garden and willow warbler, whitethroat and blackcap come to breed. The river is the site for two attractive and highly specialised birds, dipper and kingfisher.

Mottey Meadows

Permit only; 36ha; NCC reserve
Old-meadow grassland
Spring, early summer

As well as a range of grassland types, the meadows are chiefly notable as the most northerly native site for fritillary, an exotic-looking and very beautiful drooping flower which blooms in May and is limited to only a few areas outside the valley of the River Thames.

Park Hall Country Park

SJ 929447; 133.2ha; SCC
Heath, woodland, canyons and pools
Leaflet from visitor centre or SCC
Spring, early summer

The pools attract waders and wildfowl: golden and grey plover, mallard and tufted duck. Whinchat, stonechat and grasshopper warbler breed on the heaths; the area may be hunted by sparrowhawk, kestrel, short-eared and little owl.

Parrott's Drumble

SJ 817523; 12ha; SWT reserve
Mixed woodland
Spring, early summer

A good diversity of woodland plants grows in the reserve which protects an area of mixed broad-leaved woodland.

Pasturefields

Permit only; 7.7ha; SWT reserve
Mixed grassland including saltmarsh
Spring, summer

The reserve contains an interesting range of habitats from saltmarsh, through wet, neutral grassland and onto semi-improved grassland. It is an important lowland site for breeding snipe, redshank and lapwing.

Rudyard Nature Walk

SJ 955579; 5km; SCC
Disused railway line and canal-feeder stream

Leaflet from SCC
Spring, early summer

The plant life is varied, with lime-loving species growing on the old railway gravels and more acid-loving plants such as tormentil on the sandy banks where gorse, broom and heather show. The wetter land is rich with marsh-marigold and cuckooflower. Snipe and lapwing may be seen. Many hirundines feed on the summer insects.

School Lane Wood

Permit only; 6.4ha; SWT reserve
Mixed woodland
Spring, summer

A pool, marsh and streams add variety to the mainly broad-leaved woodland which supports a good range of birds and insects among an interesting diversity of plants.

Spring Cottage

Permit only; 2.1ha; SWT reserve
Moorland and grassland
Spring, summer

An interesting range of grasses and wild flowers may be seen in this small moorland and unimproved pasture reserve.

Swineholes Wood

Permit only; 24ha; SWT reserve
Mixed woodland
Spring, summer

Areas of open moorland add to the interest of this acid upland reserve which contains a mix of oak, birch and pine woodland and has good populations of associated birds and insects.

Ward's Quarry

Permit only; 0.3ha; SWT reserve
Disused quarry
Spring, summer

The old limestone quarry has been colonised by a flora which includes five species of orchids among over 60 flowering plants.

Widdowson's Plantation

SP 699942; 8ha; WdT reserve
Deciduous woodland
Spring, summer

Part of the wood is a remnant of ancient woodland predominantly of ash and field maple. Crack willow and wild service-tree are among some of the more unusual species.

Warwickshire and West Midlands

Situated at the very heart of England, Warwickshire and the West Midlands are counties of contrasts. Both have been moulded and shaped by the hands of man, but in very different ways. The most obvious effects are in the urbanisation of Birmingham, the Black Country and Coventry, which together have a population of nearly three million. Possibly less obvious but equally affected by man is the agricultural land of Warwickshire, now intensively farmed to maximise food production. Mixed in amongst this background of industry, housing and agriculture are areas rich in wildlife. Some are recent, having developed on derelict land, but others are more ancient, remnants of the countryside of long ago.

Although the entire region is lowland with few hills reaching 250m, Birmingham and the Black Country lie on a slightly raised plateau drained to the east and north by the River Tame. At the time of the second ice age a great lake covered most of Warwickshire, trapped between this plateau and the higher ground of Edge Hill to the south east by giant glaciers. When the ice eventually melted the lake poured out to the south west, creating the basin of the River Avon. Today the Avon flows more gently, crossing the county from Rugby through Warwick and Stratford and then on to the Severn.

The underlying geology of much of the region is keuper marl or 'Mercia mudstone', giving rise to red clay soils, although these are covered in many places by sands and gravels left after the ice ages. In the south east a scarp slope marks the grey calcareous clays of the lower lias, which have associated limestones and overlying ironstones. Coal measures and older, harder rocks are found in both north Warwickshire and the Black Country, the latter rocks outcropping in sites at HARTSHILL HAYES near Nuneaton and WREN'S NEST, Dudley.

Over 4000 years ago the region was almost entirely blanketed by a deciduous forest of oak, ash, alder and birch, but most of this had already been cleared before the Romans came. During the next thousand years agriculture developed in the fertile valleys of the Avon and Tame, with many small towns becoming established. Between these two rivers lay the Forest of Arden, once a continuous tract of woodland from Stratford to Nuneaton but considerably broken up even before the Domesday survey of 1086. By the seventeenth century most of the Birmingham plateau was farmland or heath. These habitats suffered considerably during the Industrial Revolution when large areas of land became covered by thriving factories. Industries, based initially on iron smelting and a multitude of manufactured goods, attracted more people to the towns and demanded more raw materials, more efficient transport and more intensive food production. Although these activities in turn destroyed more of the natural vegetation, by a strange paradox many of the old industrial sites now provide excellent habitats for a wide range of wildlife.

Today rural Warwickshire presents a picture of gently rolling farmland, a patchwork of arable crops and pasture. The destruction of hedgerows to create large, prairie-like fields has happened in only a few areas, so that most fields are still surrounded by living boundaries. Since the ravages of Dutch elm disease 'leafy Warwickshire' is no longer quite so leafy, but subsequent tree-planting schemes may go some way to restore the county's character over the next few decades. Despite the fact that Warwickshire contains large areas of grassland, most are short-term ryegrass leys. Thanks to fertilisers, herbicides and field drains, these are very productive for the farmer but have little value for wildlife and the naturalist.

Heathland, once so widespread throughout the Black Country and Birmingham, and reflected in so many district names, has now largely disappeared. The most important surviving relict is SUTTON PARK, a unique semi-natural area within the city of Birmingham where woodland, bog, heath and grassland give some indication of the landscape of 300 years ago.

As a whole the region is poorly wooded, although small copses are dotted throughout the landscape. Some of these woods may be remnants of the Forest of Arden, but nearly all are later plantings of broad-leaved trees or conifers. Privately owned Ufton Wood, one of the largest deciduous woodlands still managed by coppice rotation, has an excellent record of ground flora and wildlife. CLOWES WOOD near Birmingham, owned by WARNACT, is a more acid wood containing a small area of remnant heath.

Throughout the region the legacy of industrial dereliction has resulted in a wide range of valuable wildlife habitats, from calcareous grassland in old limestone quarries to marshes in worked-out claypits. More recent sand and gravel extraction

in both the Tame and Avon valleys has created wetland sites such as KINGSBURY WATER PARK near Coleshill and BRANDON MARSH near Coventry. Together with mining subsidence pools and reservoirs, these now form vital links in bird migration routes as well as habitats for more permanent residents.

In a short account of the area, one might be forgiven for omitting the towns and cities entirely. However, recent surveys have shown that towns are not seas of lifeless concrete as is sometimes thought, but contain many oases of wildlife. These may be small fragments of wood, marsh or rough grassland, or larger areas with a diversity of habitats. Whatever their size or relative value, they all have what some may think a disadvantage, but in reality is an advantage – they are surrounded by people and so can bring home the message of conservation and the value of wildlife. Man's activities have shaped agricultural landscapes and urban skylines – with the right guidance they can ensure a future for wildlife, too.

A. TASKER

Alvecote Pools

Permit only; 225ha; WARNACT reserve
Pools and damp grassland
Nature trail open to public; booklet from WARNACT
All year

The nature trail demonstrates both ecologically rich and polluted pools south of the railway line, but the wildfowl interest of the reserve is centred on the pools to the north, where in winter flocks of duck, including pochard, shoveler, teal and wigeon, may be seen. Breeding species include great crested grebe, redshank and snipe – the shallow pools and water meadows are particularly suitable for migrant waders.

Ashlawn Railway Cutting

SP 516732; 5.25ha; WARNACT reserve
Disused railway
Spring, summer

A rare urban example of lime-rich grassland, it contains many attractive orchids and butterflies.

Bedworth Sloughs

SP 350871; 5ha; Nuneaton and Bedworth BC
Small wetland
All year

The shallow pool, formed by mining subsidence, is surrounded by a deep bulrush reedmarsh and by small areas of herb-rich grassland. Over 70 species of birds have been recorded including wildfowl, waders and commoner woodland birds. However the major significance of this small site is that it provides one of the largest and most regular roosts of autumn passage swallows in the Midlands, with up to 25,000 birds recorded in one night.

Bracebridge Nature Trail

SP 102980; 2.4km; City of Birmingham DC
Trail past woodland and lake
Leaflet from CBDC
Spring, summer

Set in SUTTON PARK, the trail runs through mainly Scots pine woodland with heather in well-lit glades. Great crested grebe may be seen on the large pond.

Brandon Marsh

Permit only; 53.6ha; WARNACT reserve
Pools, marsh and scrub
All year

A superb wetland reserve has been developed on an area of worked-out gravelpits which now lie among a rich tangle of marsh-plants and scrub. The pools are varied in size and depth, some steep-banked and lined with reedbeds or tall stands of bulrush, others edged with scrub or grading into rough meadowland, with beaches and spits on which waterbirds can preen. Willow and hawthorn scrub, providing shelter and nesting sites, merges into spreads of rosebay willowherb, meadowsweet and common nettle or drier slopes of bramble, clearings bright with ragwort, prickled with thistles and teasel. Damper parts contain rushes, sedges and marshland plants such as gipsywort, while damp grassland supports marsh-orchids.

The deep rich vegetation attracts a good range of insects, with butterflies such as comma, red admiral and an occasional clouded yellow, and moths with wonderful names such as pink-barred sallow, scalloped hazel, burnished brass and copper underwing. The main attraction of Brandon Marsh, however, must be its birds.

Probably the most common breeding species is

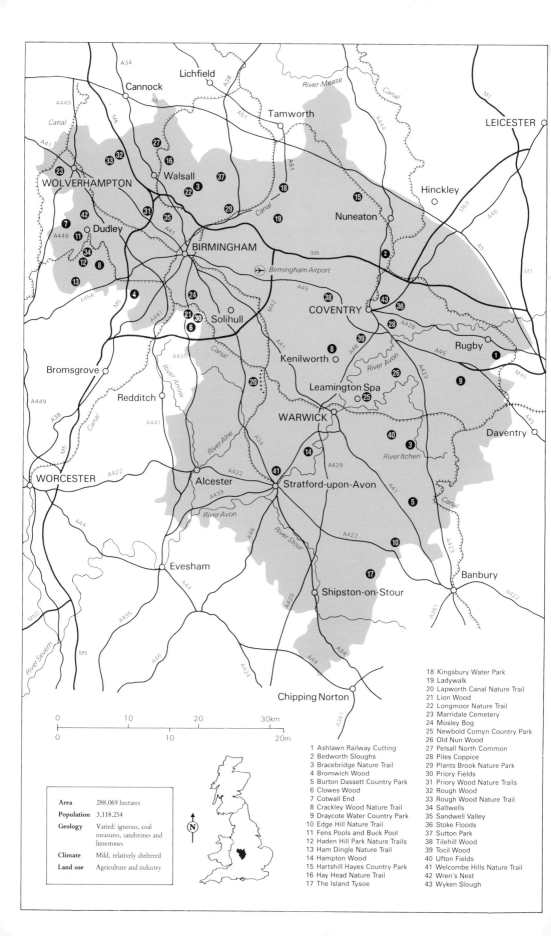

18 Kingsbury Water Park
19 Ladywalk
20 Lapworth Canal Nature Trail
21 Lion Wood
22 Longmoor Nature Trail
23 Marridale Cemetery
24 Mosley Bog
25 Newbold Comyn Country Park
26 Old Nun Wood
27 Pelsall North Common
28 Piles Coppice
29 Plants Brook Nature Park
30 Priory Fields
31 Priory Wood Nature Trails
32 Rough Wood
33 Rough Wood Nature Trail
34 Saltwells
35 Sandwell Valley
36 Stoke Floods
37 Sutton Park
38 Tilehill Wood
39 Tocil Wood
40 Ufton Fields
41 Welcombe Hills Nature Trail
42 Wren's Nest
43 Wyken Slough

1 Ashlawn Railway Cutting
2 Bedworth Sloughs
3 Bracebridge Nature Trail
4 Bromwich Wood
5 Burton Dassett Country Park
6 Clowes Wood
7 Cotwall End
8 Crackley Wood Nature Trail
9 Draycote Water Country Park
10 Edge Hill Nature Trail
11 Fens Pools and Buck Pool
12 Haden Hill Park Nature Trails
13 Ham Dingle Nature Trail
14 Hampton Wood
15 Hartshill Hayes Country Park
16 Hay Head Nature Trail
17 The Island Tysoe

Area	288,069 hectares
Population	3,118,254
Geology	Varied: igneous, coal measures, sandstones and limestones
Climate	Mild, relatively sheltered
Land use	Agriculture and industry

N

0   10   20   30km
0   10   20m

reed bunting; others include reed, sedge and willow warbler, all of them summer visitors, as are yellow wagtail and sand martin, which has a thriving colony here. Snipe and water rail are among the breeding species, together with dabbling duck such as gadwall and divers such as ruddy duck, little and great crested grebe.

The range of wildfowl recorded, particularly in winter, is excellent and includes gadwall, garganey, mallard, pintail, pochard, ruddy duck, shoveler, teal, tufted duck and wigeon. Goldeneye, ring-necked duck, scaup, shelduck and ruddy shelduck occur and the reserve may be visited by Bewick's swan or by wintering white-fronted geese. Migrants such as black-tailed godwit, greenshank, ruff and green sandpiper use the marsh as a feeding ground or roost, while predators such as hobby and merlin may visit, short-eared owl may hunt across the reserve and, occasionally, the great wings of a harrier may sweep the reeds.

Golden eagle and osprey have been sighted overflying Brandon Marsh, while the River Pool, an area of muddy shallows connected to the Avon, can boast a visit by a little egret, only the third recorded in Warwickshire this century. The birds are well studied here due to the work of an active bird-ringing group whose captures and releases include spotted crake, bearded tit, wryneck and barred and great reed warbler.

Bromwich Wood

SO 998813; 4ha; Birmingham City Council
Deciduous woodland
Leaflet from Birmingham City Council
Spring, summer

This attractive broadleaved woodland is a picture in spring with carpets of bluebells, wood anemones and yellow archangel. The damper areas of the wood, where alder grows, also support wood horsetail. There is a good variety of woodland birds.

Burton Dassett Country Park

SP 397519; 38.8ha; WCC
Hilly grassland
Nature trail booklet from Warwickshire Museum or WCC
Spring, early summer

Disused quarries, now richly overgrown, add interest to the large area of unimproved grassland with its views across the farmland plain below.

Clowes Wood

SP 100743; 32.5ha; WARNACT reserve
Mixed woodland
Spring, early summer

Divided by a working railway line, Clowes is composed of two woodlands. Big Clowes is mainly even-aged oak over a thin understorey of birch, holly, rowan and alder buckthorn. The oak trees are not tall, with an almost continuous canopy which shades the low ground cover of bilberry, bramble and grasses. At the bottom of the gentle slope variation is provided by blocks of beech

and sweet chestnut, where bluebells stand thick beneath the trees and the clearings are filled with bracken. Alder appears where the ground is damp and wood-sorrel shows beneath spreads of broad buckler-fern.

Little Clowes is more varied, with mature oak and beech, more tilted and gullied, drained by a stream and containing pools where wetland plants contrast with the woodland around them. The pools are small but attractive, set in clearings and edged with alder, rushes, drooping clumps of cyperus sedge, and plants such as lesser spearwort and branched bur-reed. The woodland floor beneath the beeches is deeply shaded and bare, but where the canopy is mainly oak the understorey resembles that of Big Clowes, with the occasional yellow flowers of common cow-wheat.

The soils throughout the reserve are considerably varied: in Big Clowes a change occurs from bilberry–bramble to a richer mix, and in Little Clowes the western boundary is marked by the presence of ash, dog's mercury, enchanter's-nightshade, woodruff, wood melick and sprays of wild rose. Hazel and hawthorn appear in the understorey and coppicing has been practised, giving a more varied structure to the wood. Both woodlands are noted for mosses and fungi and contain some fine spreads of lily-of-the-valley.

The coppiced areas, clearings and woodland edge provide a suitable habitat for warblers such as chiffchaff, willow and wood warbler, and for blue, great, coal and marsh tit. The bigger trees rich in bark-living insects, provide feeding grounds for great spotted woodpecker or nuthatch.

Just as the birds are those characteristic of mixed woodland, so too are the mammals, which include grey squirrel, wood mouse and bank vole, all competitors for the annual harvest of hazelnuts. A splendid variety of moths includes over 50 scarce species amongst which are ear moth, dark spectacle and the local grey shoulderknot.

Cotwall End

SO 913927; 57ha; Dudley MBC
Woodland, wetland and meadows
Spring, summer

Alvecote Pools attract a good range of birds.

Mixed woodland forms a dingle through which a stream runs, and there is an area of marshland and small *Sphagnum* bog. More interesting plants include broadleaved helleborine and moschatel. The reserve is also an important geological site.

Crackley Wood Nature Trail

SP 287737; 1.2km; Warwick DC
Woodland trail
Leaflet from WARNACT or Warwickshire Museum
Spring, early summer

An acid woodland, mainly oak and birch, Crackley Wood contains a fine show of spring flowers such as wood anemone and bluebell. Woodland birds are plentiful and the site is visited by badger.

Decoy Spinney

Permit only; 1.6ha; WARNACT reserve
Small wood and pools
Spring, summer

A disused duck decoy, now surrounded by developing oak woodland and coniferous plantation. The broadleaved wood has a hazel understorey with dog's mercury and bluebell, whilst the pools are surrounded by common reed and sedges, home for moorhen, coot and reed bunting.

Draycote Water Country Park

SP 467692; 8.7ha; WCC
Hilly grassland
Leaflet from site or WCC
Spring, summer

Overlooking the reservoir, the grassland has the added interest of ridge-and-furrow, the remains of a medieval open-field system.

Earlswood Moathouse

Permit only; 3.6ha; WARNACT reserve
Mature and planted woodland
Spring, early summer

Trees have been planted in abandoned meadowland which, with a strip of mature woodland, will provide a sanctuary for birds.

Eathorpe Marsh

Permit only; 1.4ha; WARNACT reserve
Small marshland
Spring, summer

Wild angelica, water mint and yellow iris add colour to a spread of reed sweet-grass and pond sedge. Pools attract breeding birds such as reed bunting and snipe, which are joined by winter flocks of finches, corn bunting, linnet and redpoll. Insects include white ermine, small square-spot and Hebrew character moths.

Edge Hill Nature Trail

SP 370470; 3.2km; WARNACT
Trail through wide range of habitats with fine views
Leaflet from WARNACT or Warwickshire Museum
Spring, early summer

Grassland, wetland and woodland rich in plants, insects and birds provide considerable wildlife interest to which are added the spectacular views, said to extend to 12 counties, from this northern extension of the Cotswolds.

Elmdon Manor

Permit only; 6ha; WARNACT reserve
Walled garden, wood and ponds
All year

The walled garden in the centre of the reserve is being converted into a wildflower nursery and tree bank. The remainder of the site contains a mixture of habitats, with some mixed woodland, a wet meadow and two shaded ponds.

Fens Pools and Buck Pool

SO 915885; 80ha; Dudley MBC
Wetland, grassland and open water
All year

Yellow oat-grass, knapweed, tansy and the rare adder's-tongue grow in the grassland around Fens Pools. These are also good for butterflies, including the green hairstreak. Frogs, smooth newts and water spiders are found in the pools which attract a good variety of waterbirds.

Haden Hill Park Nature Trails

SO 960856; 1.6–3.2km; Sandwell MBC
Trails through suburban park
Spring, summer

Small wild areas have been established to create pockets of natural vegetation and to encourage a varied range of wildlife.

Ham Dingle Nature Trail

SO 913828; 1.6km; Dudley MBC
Trail through oak woodland
Spring, early summer

The oak woodland contains a good range of mosses and attracts woodland birds such as nuthatch, treecreeper and great spotted woodpecker.

Hampton Wood

SP 254599; 11.1ha; WARNACT reserve
Broadleaved woodland with grass and scrub
Spring, early summer

An excellent wood for its springtime display of flowers, with carpets of primrose and bluebell mixed with red campion and yellow archangel. The hawthorn scrub provides good cover for woodland birds, including goldcrest, wren, spotted flycatcher and whitethroat. Two streams and a deep gully provide moister areas where hard shield-fern hart's-tongue and mosses thrive.

Hanging Wood

Permit only; 7ha; WARNACT reserve
Ancient woodland
Spring, summer

Small-leaved lime and wild service-tree grow in this ancient woodland. The reserve is coppice with oak standards and has an excellent display of bluebells in the spring.

Harbury Spoil Bank

Permit only; 2.4ha; WARNACT reserve
Lime-rich grassland
Spring, summer

The reserve is rich in plants, such as carline thistle, yellow-wort and quaking-grass, and attracts many butterflies. Hawthorn scrub provides winter roosts and feeding for migrants such as fieldfare and redwing.

Hartshill Hayes Country Park

SP 315945; 55ha; WCC
Hill grassland and woodland
Leaflet from site or WCC
Spring, early summer

The wildlife interest of the country park, set high up on a ridge overlooking the Anker Valley, is mainly to be found in Hartshill Hayes. This wood is reputed to be part of the Forest of Arden and was originally coppiced, although replanted now, a few old oaks and limes can still be seen.

Hay Head Nature Trail

SP 041989; 1.2km; Walsall MBC
Old lime workings and canal basin
Spring, early summer

The old lime workings, now colonised by alder and hawthorn shrubs above a ground cover of plants such as ramsons, attract a range of woodland birds. The canal basin may be bright with marsh-marigold in spring and is visited by wetland birds such as kingfisher.

The Island Tysoe

SP 333434; 0.5ha; WARNACT reserve
Woodland and meadow
Spring, summer

A small area of damp woodland and meadow alongside a stream has an attractive display of cowslips in the spring and spindle bright with berries in the autumn.

Kingsbury Water Park

SP 204958; 213.8ha; WCC reserve
Flooded gravelpits
Leaflets from visitor centre or WCC
All year

A part of the much larger compex of flooded pits, grassland and scrub which make up the water park as a whole, the reserve lies at the most northerly, least disturbed end of the park. The water park is, effectively, man-made: gravel extraction has left wide pits, some of them open flooded waters, others filled with fly ash from the power station to form deep reedbeds or spreads of willow swamp. These stands of bulrush and willow form an integral part of the wildlife interest of the site though most of them lie outside the reserve.

Warblers are a feature of the park, with blackcap, chiffchaff, whitethroat and lesser whitethroat, garden, grasshopper, reed, sedge and willow warbler breeding here. Kingfisher, kestrel and tawny owl all breed within the park, but the greatest interest probably lies in the shallow lagoons of the reserve.

In migration times arctic, black and common tern pause to rest and feed on the reserve; waders such as curlew, greenshank, spotted redshank and common sandpiper search the mud and, occasionally, a marsh harrier hunts low across the flood plain. Merlin and hobby, too, will visit in season, the latter following the autumn flocks of swallow and martin as they move south.

In winter the water and the meadows are roosts and feeding grounds for many species. As many as 5000 lapwing may be seen, with thousands of gulls flying in at evening time to roost on the darkening pools. Gadwall, goldeneye, pintail, pochard and wigeon increase the numbers of duck already here, while greylag and white-fronted geese or Bewick's swan add to the variety of waterfowl. Cormorant, water rail and waders such as dunlin and golden plover also winter here, while short-eared owl regularly hunt the meadows. Many duck breed here, with little and great crested grebe, little ringed plover, lapwing and snipe, and common tern on the gravel islands.

Knowle

Permit only; 0.3ha; Knowle Soc. reserve
Educational reserve
Spring, early summer

The tiny reserve includes a spinney, grassland and wetland consisting of a pond and a stream.

Ladywalk

SP 215920; 50ha; CEGB–West Midlands Bird Club reserve
Islands, lagoons and scrub
Permit only from West Midland Bird Club
Leaflet from CEGB or West Midland Bird Club
All year

The reserve, at Hams Hall Power Station, lies in a loop of the River Tame and attracts many wetland birds. There is an environmental studies centre at the site.

Lapworth Canal Nature Trail

SP 186708–188678; 3.2km; NT
Waterside nature trail
Booklet from Warwickshire Museum
Spring, summer

The Stratford-on-Avon Canal falls through 15 locks as it passes down the trail. A fine variety of wetland plants and birds may be seen, together with hedgerow and farmland wildlife.

Lion Wood

SP 084717; 3.4ha; WARNACT WCNT reserve
Acid oak woodland
Spring, summer

This woodland is unusual for the county in being acidic, with bilberry, rowan, alder buckthorn and holly flourishing under a canopy of oak and birch. Despite the wood's small size, blue tit, great tit, wren and robin are all resident, and migratory fieldfare and redwing can reach large numbers.

Longmoor Nature Trail

SP 091955; 3.2km; Birmingham City Council
Heathland and mixed woodland
Leaflet from CBDC
Spring, summer

A SUTTON PARK trail, it circles through the typical heathland where gorse and heath bedstraw show among the heather, and through an area of sweet chestnut where woodland birds add their songs to that of the heathland yellowhammer.

Merridale Cemetery

SO 899979; 2ha; Walsall MBC
Old, well-wooded cemetery
Spring, early summer

The cemetery contains a fine range of mixed tree species both native and exotic, which attracts woodland birds such as nuthatch and spotted flycatcher and forms a wildlife oasis on the western outskirts of Wolverhampton.

Mosley Bog

SP 094821; 11.3ha; Birmingham City Council
Woodland
Spring, summer

A precious fragment of old Worcestershire's countryside, this old wet woodland is associated with Tolkien, who lived nearby as a child and drew inspiration from the area for his books. The site has been well-known for its plants for over 200 years and its specialities include wood horsetail and royal fern.

Nether Whitacre

Permit only; 21.7ha; WARNACT reserve
Willow scrub, marsh and pools
Spring, summer

Bordered by the River Tame, this reserve was previously part of a sand and gravel quarry. It now supports a dense thicket of willow and alder scrub on the drier areas, with marsh grassland and pools in the centre. Although the scrub is generally poor for flowering plants, it provides shelter for the many reedbeds and their associated birds, such as reed warbler, sedge warbler and water rail. The wetland is rich in invertebrate life,

and in summer the emperor dragonfly and banded agrion damselfly flash their irridescent colours over the water. In the open grassier places are centaury and both common spotted and marsh-orchids.

Newbold Comyn Country Park

SP 329659; 128ha; Warwick DC
Riverside habitats
Leaflets from Tourist Information Centre, Jephson Gardens, Leamington Spa
Spring, early summer

Woodland, grassland, marsh and the river combine to form the basis for a varied and interesting nature trail.

Newton Gorse

Permit only; 3.4ha; WARNACT reserve
Mixed woodland
Early summer

Situated in a treeless part of north Warwickshire, this reserve provides a welcome haven for woodland birds such as blue tit, great tit and even woodcock. The predominance of coniferous trees has led to a poor ground flora, but has encouraged both goldcrest and siskin.

Old Nun Wood

SP 382709; 2.1ha; WARNACT reserve
Broadleaved woodland
Spring, early summer

Although small, this reserve is close to the much larger WAPPENBURY WOOD, and so much of the rich animal life moves freely between the two. Predominantly oak and ash, there is a coppice of hazel with field maple, birch and willow also in the scrub layer. Its ancient woodland origins are hinted at by the spring displays of wood sorrel, wood anemone, bluebell and yellow archangel. A recent coloniser is the muntjac deer.

Oxhouse Farm

Permit only; 7.2ha; WARNACT reserve
Lime-rich grassland and disused railway line
Spring, summer

If an insignia for Oxhouse had to be chosen one might suggest traveller's-joy. The rich limestone ridge on which the reserve proper lies is looped and laced with the plant; in autumn the banks are foamed with the creamy white feathery fruits.

The old railway line runs down the spine of the ridge, sheltered with ash, blackthorn, buckthorn, dogwood, elder, hawthorn, oak, privet, wayfaring-tree and willows tangled with bitter-sweet, bramble, traveller's-joy and wild rose. Grassland banks and the ballast of the line are filled with lime-loving wild basil, salad burnet, cowslip, dyer's greenweed, carline thistle and yellow-wort.

The meadow below the line is deeply grassed, humped with colonies of anthills and sheltered by spreading hedges. Pink musk mallow contrasts with vibrant yellow lady's bedstraw and agrimony or the subtler colours of small scabious and greater knapweed, while the spectacular woolly thistle dominates the grassland. A damp corner is thick with meadowsweet which hints at the riches of the river meadows. Although not strictly part of the reserve, these carry a most attractive range from banks of meadow crane's-bill to a vast spread of butterbur and the tall alder, grey poplar and willow trees shading the river.

The insect life is equally diverse and almost 30 species of butterfly have been identified including brimstone and little blue, small copper, dark green fritillary and marbled white, together with both green and white-letter hairstreak. Birds include all three woodpeckers, abundant willow warbler, a fluctuating count of nightingale and occasional redstart. Wide-ranging visitors to the reserve include great grey shrike, hoopoe, peregrine and snow bunting.

Among the unusual plants of the reserve are continental fine-leaved vetch and, among some 45 grasses, spreading meadow-grass at one of its five Warwickshire sites, an unusual variant of tall fescue, and a hybrid between marsh and meadow foxtail not known in the county since 1899.

Pelsall North Common

SK 015043; 55ha; Walsall MBC
Heathland and spoil heap
Summer

The reserve is an interesting mixture of natural heathland and old base-rich spoil heaps from local steelworks. The alkaline areas now support a fascinating flora including common spotted- and southern marsh-orchid, eyebright, blue fleabane, chives and wild asparagus. The heath is dominated by heather with mollinia and cross-leaved heath in wetter areas, where pools support red-eyed damselfly and emperor dragonfly. There is a good population of dingy skipper butterflies.

Piles Coppice

SP 386770; 21ha; WdT reserve
Deciduous woodland
Spring, summer

This ancient semi-natural woodland is thought to be a surviving part of the royal hunting grounds of the Forest of Arden. A rich variety of plants and animals are to be found among the small-leaved lime coppice interspersed with oak standards.

Pinley Abbey Spinneys

Permit only: 2.5ha; WARNACT reserve
Woodland and meadow
Spring, summer

Ponds in the two small spinneys and the rough grassland are all managed to encourage bird life.

Plants Brook Community Nature Park

SP 138922; 13ha; Birmingham City Council UWT
Wetland, lakes, woodland and meadow
Access through kissing gate. Disabled and those with prams should contact warden (021-351 5651) to unlock gate. Very limited parking
Leaflet from visitor centre on site and UWT office
All year

Plants Brook has always been a natural collection place for water. In the past a stream, called the Edbrook, flowed across the site, and in 1748 a forge was constructed harnessing its energy; this became known as Plant's Forge after the man who built it. In the 1860s the need for water once again led to development, and reservoirs with a 33 million gallon capacity were constructed to serve the city of Birmingham; these became redundant at the turn of the century. For some 60 years the site was left to nature, but in 1978 the reservoirs were drained and, after much lobbying, Plants

A superb variety of habitats is contained in the old lime workings of Ufton Fields.

Brook was bought by the City Council as public open space.

With careful management by the UWT the weland habitat now attracts an amazing variety of wildlife. There are beds of bulrush and yellow iris, marsh areas of hard and soft rush and lesser pond-sedge, wet woodland areas with carpets of lesser celandine, ramsons and red campion colouring the ground beneath alders and willows, and wet meadow areas alive with the colours of cuckooflower, southern marsh-orchids and marsh-marigold.

The insect life is abundant: orange tip and meadow brown butterflies are common in summer and later dragonflies come into their own with common sympetrums, common hawkers and brown hawkers gracing the board-walk through the bulrush beds.

Many birds stop off at Plants Brook during migration, and summer visitors include swifts, swallows and house martins as well as willow warblers, blackcaps and lesser whitethroats. Great crested and little grebe, kingfisher, mute swan and sparrowhawk are occasionally seen in the area. Pipestrelle and noctule bats feed over the lakes on summer evenings, and wood mice, water voles, foxes and hedgehogs live in the locality.

Priory Fields

SP 099789; 5.4ha; WARNACT reserve
Grassland
Summer

A damp meadow area on the Birmingham–Solihull boundary fed by a small spring and bounded by the Stratford Canal. The main interest of the site lies in its grassland, where all the common meadow grasses are intermixed with an interesting assortment of colourful flowering plants, including yellow rattle, knapweed, vetches and trefoils. Also of importance is a significant area of heather.

Priory Wood Nature Trails

SP 020913; 1.2 and 2.4km; Sandwell MBC
Wet woodland
Spring, early summer

Oak and hawthorn above spring plants such as wood anemone provide a contrast with wetland areas rich in marsh horsetail and damp-loving species. The woods and scrub attract a good range of songbirds and provide a habitat for great spotted woodpecker.

Rough Wood

SJ 984009; 27ha; Walsall MBC
Woodland and pools
Nature trail guide from Walsall MBC
Spring, summer, autumn

The wood forms part of a large country park and has grown up on the site of a former colliery – the pools have been formed by surface digging for coal. There are some very ancient oak trees with drifts of bluebells in the spring. In autumn a variety of fungi can be found, including the attractive but highly poisonous red and white fly agaric.

Rough Wood Nature Trail

SJ 994010; 2.4km; WMCC
Trail through scrub woodland
Spring, early summer

The spread of scrub woodland includes oak, hazel and acid-loving alder buckthorn, and is particularly rich in birds such as redstart and whitethroat.

Ryton Wood

Permit only; 68ha; WARNACT reserve
Oak woodland
Spring, summer

One of Warwickshire's largest remaining ancient woodlands, Ryton is of oustanding wildlife value in every respect. It is a pedunculate oak wood, with an understorey of hazel and patches of small-leaved lime and both birches. Also in the understorey are spindle, guelder-rose, dogwood and field maple, while the ground flora contains primrose, bluebell, wood sorrel, wood anemone and wood millet. The sunlit rides are home to white admiral, wood white, purple hairstreak, comma, ringlet and brimstone butterflies, while a small pool and damper areas add to the overall diversity. The rich bird population includes six species of tits, six warblers, and tree pipits, while all three woodpeckers, nuthatch and treecreeper are found here.

Saltwells

SO 934874; 70ha; Dudley MBC
Woodland, wetland and disused claypit
Spring, summer

Oak, with aspen, beech and white poplar, stands above a ground cover of bluebell and wood-sorrel and attracts such birds as spotted flycatcher, willow warbler and green woodpecker, while the marshy area is a good site for dragonflies and rich in southern marsh-orchid. The disused claypit is of geological importance.

Sandwell Valley

SP 036931; 10ha; RSPB–Sandwell MBC
Woodland and lakeside trails
Booklet from information centre
Winter, early summer

The trails are laid out in a valley, once parkland, which contains mixed woodland around a number of pools. Trees include oak, alder, ash, field maple, whitebeam and yew above a varied ground cover and hold woodland birds such as spotted flycatcher, willow warbler and kestrel. Wetland birds include passage waders and winter flocks of duck. Tufted duck, coot, little ringed plover and lapwing all breed around the reserve. Curlew, greenshank, and common and green sandpiper occur on migration, while in winter wigeon and pochard feed on the lake. In the marshy areas there are teal, Jack snipe and water rail.

Stockton Railway Cutting

Permit only; 5.5ha; WARNACT reserve
Disused railway line
Spring, summer

Celebrated primarily for its 28 species of butterfly, the reserve supports limestone plants and a range of birds and mammals in mixed scrub and grassland, as well as white-legged damselfly.

Stoke Floods

SP 374791; 7.6ha; WARNACT reserve
Urban wetland area
All year

Summer brings a show of marshland plants to the wet grassland and reedbeds which, in winter, provide an important feeding site for wildfowl.

Sutton Park

SP 103963; 859ha; Birmingham City Council
Lowland heath and woodland
Nature trail leaflets from CBDC
Spring, early summer

Roughly 10km from the heart of Birmingham's bustle, Sutton Park has been preserved as a spread of heath and woodland safe from development. The popular sites are popular indeed, but the park has woodlands where people rarely venture and boggy valleys which people tend to avoid. The land dips and rises, and with wide spreads of heathland stretching to the horizon, one might easily imagine that the city had disappeared.

The woods are mixed with areas of conifers but include large stands of deciduous trees of varying composition. In places the woods are of oak, with birch and rowan over holly, often dense and impenetrable. The holly casts so much shade that virtually nothing grows beneath, but clearings show a mix of acid grasses, bramble, rosebay willowherb, bracken and heath bedstraw, with seedling birch and rowan and occasional oak saplings. Other areas have interplanted larch, with beech and with tall rowan lifting sprays of berries into the high tree canopy. Sweet chestnut and pine trees also occur over a ground cover of bracken and young holly. Parts of the heath have been invaded by birch which stands over grassland, bracken, bilberry and heather with a scrub of gorse and grades into older oak–conifer woodland, again with a holly understorey. Here and there blocks of pure birch stand over spreads of grasses, a slender well-lit woodland contrasting with the holly. A further contrast appears where a small valley mire is filled with an alder swamp standing in cushions of *Polytrichum* mosses, with broad buckler-fern, tussock-sedge and horsetail species.

As with so many acid areas, the wetter parts are often most rich in species and there are several attractive bogs where streams cut through the open heath. The heath itself is mainly of acid grassland with wide banks of gorse and spreads of purple heather, with small copses varying the skyline and with willow and birch marking the lines of the streams. The bogs are marked by a change to purple moor-grass, by cross-leaved heath appearing with the heather, by the soft white plumes of common cottongrass. *Sphagnum* mosses spread in the wettest places surrounded by rushes and sedges. The plants are, perhaps, more marshland than acid bog species and include such attractive species as ragged-Robin, greater bird's-foot-trefoil, devil's-bit scabious, marsh cinquefoil, marsh horsetail and marsh-marigold, with fine stands of marsh-orchids.

Birds of the grassy heath include skylarks and meadow pipits, and occasional pairs of stonechats and whinchats. In the woodland areas willow warblers are common, while marsh and willow tits, tree pipits and redpolls all breed in small numbers. Foxes hunt the woodland and the heath, while insects include dragonflies, with moths such as fox and emperor.

Although one would not recommend a Bank Holiday visit, the sheer size of Sutton Park ensures that despite the public pressures there is always much of natural history interest.

Temple Balsall

Permit only; 4ha; WARNACT reserve
Woodland and wetland
Spring, summer

Reedswamp, wet and dry woodland attract a good range of birds which include blackcap, coal tit and great spotted woodpecker. Butterbur and yellow iris may be found in the wetland, with species such as ramsons and yellow archangel in the woods.

Tilehill Wood

SP 279790; 29.5ha; Coventry City Council
Mixed woodland
Spring, early summer

In spite of heavy urbanisation, the oak–hazel woodland contains an attractive flora including wood anemone, bluebell and wood-sorrel, together with a good range of insects and birds.

Tocil Wood

SP 303753; 4.4ha; WARNACT reserve
Urban oak woodland
Spring, early summer

The wood has been managed as a coppice with oak standards over hazel and provides a show of spring flowers such as bluebell and primrose together with a characteristic range of woodland birds.

Ufton Fields

SP 378614; 31ha; WARNACT reserve
Disused limestone workings
Spring, summer

Ufton Fields includes a tremendous range of habitats in a relatively small area. Open-cast limestone mining has left a ridge-and-dip pattern which has resulted in long narrow pools separated by wooded hills and grassy slopes. Obviously the natural colonisers are mainly lime-loving plants and, although a considerable part of the reserve has been planted with conifers during early 'reclamation', there is a splendid variety of plants.

The pools are fringed with alder and willow with sedges, rushes, bulrush and water-plantain – sheltered areas where warblers sing from the wooded slopes and hawking dragonflies flash as they fly from shade into full sunlight. The slopes – the ridges between the pools – may be covered with conifers or scrubbed with hawthorn, ash, guelder-rose, privet, wild rose and bramble above knee-deep grasses with clovers and vetches, ragwort and knapweeds. Where the ground has been most disturbed primary colonisers such as colt's-foot grow. Where the dips are damp, rather than deeply ponded, narrow marshes develop, thick with bulrush, great willowherb and horsetail species, with plants such as yellow melilot and rosebay willowherb at the drier edges. This marshland may open out on to drier grassland or change again to shallow pools which are surrounded by widespread sedgebeds.

The drier grassland varies according to the depth of the soil. Where a deeper soil has developed, the grasses are coarse, choking out many smaller plants and varied only by stronger species such as ragwort or a scrub of hawthorn, ash and wild rose. Shallow soils, however, give a wealth of lime-loving plants such as wild basil, eyebright, small scabious, yellow-wort and quaking-grass, with very good numbers of common spotted-orchid together with bee and man orchid.

Breeding birds include reed, sedge, willow and grasshopper warbler, with chiffchaff and whitethroat, reed bunting, greenfinch and tree pipit, while on the reedy pools little grebe and tufted duck nest and kingfishers come to feed. Winter may bring goldfinch, lesser redpoll and, occasionally, siskin to feed on the waterside alder. Insect life is varied and interesting, with a colony of marbled white among the butterflies and with a great variety of moths such as five-spot burnet, burnet companion, chalk carpet, Mother Shipton and northern eggar.

Wappenbury Wood

Permit only; 103.2ha; WARNACT reserve
Oak woodland
Spring, early summer

Mainly oak over old coppice, this Forestry Commission woodland also contains ash, birch, holly, hawthorn, buckthorn, aspen and willow. The broad rides are attractive to deer, woodland butterflies – of which 37 species have been recorded – and moths, as well as woodlark, tree pipit and nightingale.

Welcombe Hills Nature Trail

SP 205564; 2km; Stratford DC
Grassland hills and woodland
Leaflet from WARNACT or Warwickshire Museum
Spring, early summer

A mixed spinney, beech woodland, parkland oak trees and conifers provide a good variety of interest and encourage such woodland birds as nuthatch and treecreeper, green and great spotted woodpecker.

Wren's Nest

SO 935923; 29.6ha; NCC reserve
Geological site
No access to fenced workings: many of them are exceedingly dangerous
Booklets from NCC
All year

The colonising vegetation is fascinating for its lime-loving species, but the great importance of Wren's Nest lies in its exposures of Wenlock limestone. These are extremely rich in fossils and the site has long been a Mecca for geologists.

Wyken Slough

SP 363836; 1.2ha; WARNACT reserve
Small urban reedbed
Spring, summer

In late summer the reedbed is an important night-time roost for migrant swallows, while throughout the flying season a good variety of dragonflies and damselflies may be seen.

Wales

Clwyd

Tucked in the north east corner of Wales between rugged Snowdonia and the fertile lowlands of the Cheshire and Shropshire plain, Clwyd offers a remarkable range of wildlife habitat. It is a county of contrasts, a modern amalgam of the former Welsh border counties of Flintshire and Denbighshire with part of old Merioneth, and named after the river which sweeps northwards to the Irish Sea in the Vale of Clwyd.

Apart from the industrial belt along the old coalfield, and recreational and tourist development on the coast, Clwyd is predominantly rural and mostly upland. Traditional sheep rearing on the Berwyn Mountains, Mynydd Hiraethog and elsewhere has perpetuated vast heather and grass moorlands, although afforestation has covered much of Mynydd Hiraethog and the Clwydian range. In the lowlands stock rearing and dairy farming predominate and a close-knit landscape of fields and hedgerows remains.

Land use reflects geological contrasts, with a general east–west succession from newer to older rocks and from lowland to upland. The climate also changes: rainfall ranges from less than 889mm in the lower Dee Valley to 1778mm on the Berwyn Mountains. To the east, the east Denbighshire plain is an extension of the Cheshire plain beyond the Dee which, leaving its spectacular wooded valley between Chirk and Erbistock, meanders north to its estuary and Liverpool Bay. The underlying rocks are Triassic sandstones overlain extensively with clays and, in the Wrexham area, sand and gravels from the last ice age, when a glacier pushed up the DEE ESTUARY from the Irish Sea.

To the west the carboniferous shales and sandstone of the coal measures run north in an arc from the former north Shropshire coalfield to the western shore above the Dee Estuary, and to the west again Ruabon Mountain, rising to 502m, and Hope Mountain are formed on gritstones of the same series. This gives way to a limestone outcrop reaching spectacular proportions in Eglwyseg Mountain in the south above the major fault line of the Vale of Llangollen, thrusting west deep into the uplands. The limestone broadens out to the north on Halkyn Mountain and ends above Prestatyn, separated from the sea by a narrow coastal plain. West again is the eastern flank of the great north–south rift valley of the Vale of Clwyd, the Clwydian range, dominated by MOEL FAMAU at 554m and formed of older Silurian rocks. These also underlie the great dome of Mynydd Hiraethog west of the Vale, separated by a narrow limestone outcrop which runs north to the coast and swings westwards into Gwynedd, terminating in the Great Orme above Llandudno. In the south are the Berwyn Mountains, rising to 827m on Moel Sych on a prominent ridge overlooking a bisected plateau which continues into Powys, and from which the Rivers Ceiriog and Tanat drain into the lowlands of north Shropshire.

In the eastern lowlands of the lower Dee and beyond into the Maelor, agricultural improvement has left little of the former woodland cover. Much of the wildlife interest is related to glacial activity: former small lake basins are now important peatland sites dominated by the extensive Fenns and Whixall Moss.

The industrial belt now only supports two deep coal mines, and much dereliction remains from past extraction of coal, limestone, sand and gravel. There is, however, plenty to interest the naturalist, for many such sites are rich refuges for wildlife.

Beyond Chester the Dee flows past land that was formerly part of the estuary, until it broadens into an estuary of international importance for wintering waders and wildfowl, that has so far survived the pressures of modern development. From the estuary mouth at the POINT OF AYR westwards to the county boundary at Rhos-on-Sea, holiday caravans and chalets between the resorts have left little of the coast undeveloped. However an extensive, if narrow, dune system runs eastwards from Prestatyn to the estuary mouth and supports a rich variety of dune plants and insects.

The limestone outcrops running south from the coast provide many contrasts: the upper slopes are still unploughed and grazed by sheep while, on the coast, they support a number of limestone plants rare in Wales. Elsewhere limestone ash woodland remains and COED CILYGROESLWYD is partly developed on limestone pavement. Lower down the landscape is dominated by small walled fields and, although most are now ploughed, a few flower-rich meadows remain and the roadside verges are awash with spring and summer colour.

Limestone quarrying is a major industry in Clwyd, but some of the smaller disused quarries are rich in flowers and insects.

The most extensive uplands lie to the west of the Vale of Clwyd on Mynydd Hiraethog and the Berwyn Mountains south of the Vale of Llangollen, but extensive areas of heather moor survive on the Clwydian range, Ruabon Mountain and Llantysilio Mountain. Much of Mynydd Hiraethog is now clothed in conifers but the grass and heather moorlands to the west, dotted with reservoirs, and the heather moors on the Berwyn Mountains in southern Clwyd, provide important breeding sites for Welsh upland birds. The high ridges of the Berwyns support some of the most extensive and southerly blanket bog in Britain. Although agricultural improvement and commercial forestry have eliminated most of the original valley oakwoods, a few remnants survive on the lower slopes in the valleys.

From the vast mudflats and saltings of the Dee Estuary to the gentle uplands of Mynydd Hiraethog and the Berwyn Mountains, and from the spectacular limestone outcrops of MYNYDD EGLWYSEG in the beautiful Vale of Llangollen to the sombre peatlands of Fenns Moss, the county of Clwyd reveals all the contrast in landscape and wildlife between highland and lowland Britain.

A. J. DEADMAN

Bigwood

SJ 188675; 8.5ha; WdT
Deciduous woodland
Spring, summer

The attractive mature oak–ash wood stands on a hillside and contains many fine old trees.

Bishopswood Nature Trail

SJ 068813; 2km; Rhuddlan BC
Woodland walk with limestone grassland and quarry
Booklet from RBC,Town Hall, Rhyl and Prestatyn
Information Centre, Nant Hall Road, Prestatyn
Spring, summer

The trail climbs to high grassland where common rock-rose attracts brown Argus butterfly, and the woodlands below hold birds such as blackcap and wood warbler.

Blaen y Wergloedd

SH 914633; 5ha; NWWT reserve
Valley mire
Spring, summer

The mire surface varies in wetness and the vegetation ranges from a wet bogmoss carpet, where sundew, cranberry and bog asphodel grow, to dry banks with sheep's-fescue and devil's-bit scabious. A small base-rich flush supports marsh valerian and marsh arrowgrass. Typical moorland birds such as snipe, woodcock, curlew and golden plover visit the reserve.

Bryn Euryn Nature Trail

SH 834802; 1.2km; Colwyn BC
Hill woodland, scrub and grassland trail
Booklet from CBC
Spring, summer

The woods include yew, spindle, spurge-laurel and wild privet while the rocky grasslands contain such plants as bloody crane's-bill, dropwort and hoary rock-rose.

Coed Bryngwenallt

See COED Y GOPA.

Coed Cilygroeslwyd

SJ 124556; 4ha; NWWT reserve
Limestone woodland
Spring, early summer

Oak and ash form the tree canopy of this woodland, with an understorey of hazel, hawthorn, holly, sycamore and yew. This variety affects the amount of light reaching the ground and has a profound effect on the biology of the wood. Because of the darkness under the yews there is little ground cover but in more open areas there are broad carpets of woodruff while the edges of the clearings are tangled with traveller's-joy. Old field walls within the wood are grown over with ivy, mosses and ferns. Three interesting and unusual plants are stinking hellebore, flowering in February and March, followed by greater butterfly-orchid and bird's-nest orchid in early summer. Of special interest is the presence of giant bellflower, generally typical of northern England, and nettle-leaved bellflower, more usually limited to the south.

The range of habitat provided by the different trees is exploited by many insects and birds. Green and great spotted woodpecker take insect food deep within the bark; coal, blue, great and long-tailed tit may be seen feeding in the high tree canopy, while the pied flycatcher takes its prey on the wing.

Wood mouse, a resident of the wood, moves mainly at night to avoid day-flying hawks, but is hunted by tawny owl instead. Voles and shrews also find cover in the tangled tree roots, banks and old walls of the wood. These small mammals attract other predators – fox, stoat and weasel hunt here and, very occasionally, polecat may be seen.

Coed Tyddyn Halen

SJ 155725; 2.8ha; WdT
Mixed valley woodland
Spring, summer

A secluded woodland in a quiet valley with a wide variety of trees and shrubs and a rich ground flora. A fast flowing stream and marshy area provide added interest.

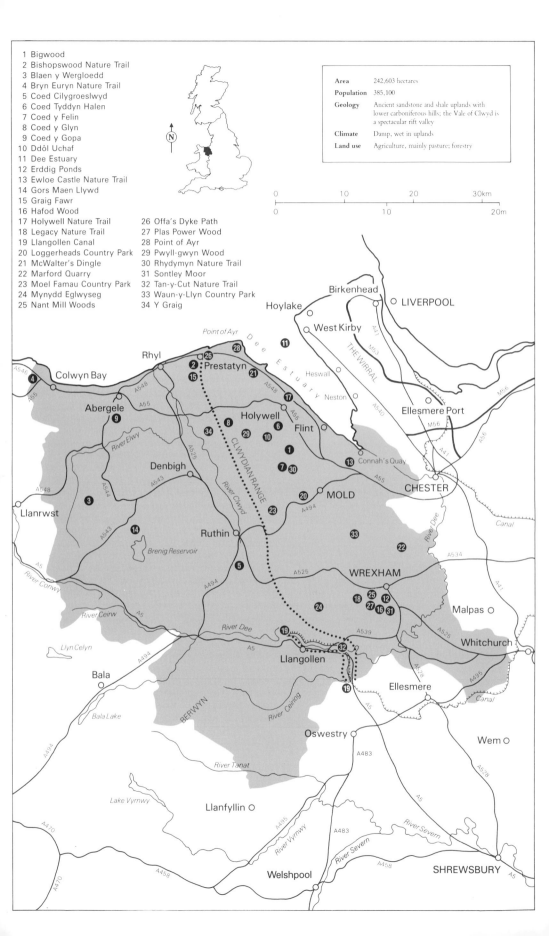

1 Bigwood
2 Bishopswood Nature Trail
3 Blaen y Wergloedd
4 Bryn Euryn Nature Trail
5 Coed Cilygroeslwyd
6 Coed Tyddyn Halen
7 Coed y Felin
8 Coed y Glyn
9 Coed y Gopa
10 Ddôl Uchaf
11 Dee Estuary
12 Erddig Ponds
13 Ewloe Castle Nature Trail
14 Gors Maen Llywd
15 Graig Fawr
16 Hafod Wood
17 Holywell Nature Trail
18 Legacy Nature Trail
19 Llangollen Canal
20 Loggerheads Country Park
21 McWalter's Dingle
22 Marford Quarry
23 Moel Famau Country Park
24 Mynydd Eglwyseg
25 Nant Mill Woods
26 Offa's Dyke Path
27 Plas Power Wood
28 Point of Ayr
29 Pwyll-gwyn Wood
30 Rhydymyn Nature Trail
31 Sontley Moor
32 Tan-y-Cut Nature Trail
33 Waun-y-Llyn Country Park
34 Y Graig

Area	242,603 hectares
Population	385,100
Geology	Ancient sandstone and shale uplands with lower carboniferous hills; the Vale of Clwyd is a spectacular rift valley
Climate	Damp, wet in uplands
Land use	Agriculture, mainly pasture; forestry

Coed y Felin

SJ 190677; 10.8ha; NWWT reserve
Deciduous woodland and grassland
Spring, summer

The reserve consists of a south-facing strip of woodland where bluebell, wood anemone and yellow archangel grow. A disused quarry now supports limestone grassland with basil, marjoram and ploughman's spikenard, while the old railway line is now becoming overgrown with wild cherry, ash, willow and hazel shrub, providing an excellent home for a good variety of woodland birds. The river Alyn has been dammed on the reserve to create two old mill ponds which have now been colonised by alder and great willowherb.

Coed y Glyn

SJ 104732; 1.3ha; WdT
Deciduous woodland
Spring, summer

The wood is on the steep side of a valley with several springs making it very wet in parts. Alder coppice dominates the area, with larger oak and ash over hazel coppice in drier parts. The ground flora is very rich, especially in the damp flushes.

Coed y Gopa

SH 935765; 47.4ha; WdT reserve
Mixed woodland
Spring, summer

A minor road divides this wood from COED BRYNGWENALLT but the two woods are run as one reserve. A mixture of broadleaved and coniferous trees overlooks the town of Abergele; the woods also contain an Iron Age fort, Castell Cawr.

Connah's Quay

Permit only; 90ha; CEGB–DNS reserve
Estuarine saltings and mudflats, large pool, scrub
Field studies centre
Reserve report every two years by DNS
Spring, autumn, winter

Behind the huge towers of the Connah's Quay Power Station the tidal waters of the DEE ESTUARY rise and fall across wide expanses of sand, mud and saltmarsh. About 90ha of foreshore, marsh and reclaimed land have been established as a reserve by the CEGB and are managed by the Deeside Naturalists' Society.

The flats and marsh represent the main features of the estuary and form about half of the site. Here, characteristic plants are common scurvy-grass, lesser sea-spurrey and glasswort. Mallard and shelduck are present at all times, to be joined in autumn and winter by good numbers of pintail, wigeon and teal. Both bar-tailed and black-tailed godwit, together with commoner waders, may be seen on the saltmarsh, but it is most important for the autumn migration of spotted redshank.

The pool, flushed with fresh water from a nearby stream and flooded with salt water only at high spring tides, provides a different range of habitat and, although visited by saltmarsh birds, draws a different range of species. Both great-crested and little grebe may be seen on the pool and heron stalk the shallow waters; common and curlew sandpiper seem to prefer the area. Kingfisher often fish from the willows which grow on the islands and fringe the pool.

In the scrub on the reclaimed land to the east of the reserve, the profusion of clovers, vetches, tares and other flowering plants provides a special attraction for butterflies including comma, around its northern breeding limit, grayling, essentially a coastal butterfly in Britain, and painted lady. This, too, is an ideal site for smaller birds such as blue tit, stonechat and whitethroat.

Grazed fields and a small wood add further interest, and, of course, there is always the chance of some unusual sighting. Oceanic birds such as Manx shearwater or storm petrel may be blown in by autumn gales; hen harrier or merlin are occasional winter visitors; green and wood sand-piper, little and Temminck's stint, arctic skua and Iceland gull have all been recorded here.

Ddôl Uchaf

SJ 142714; 4ha; NWWT reserve
Old marl workings and stream
Spring, summer

Connah's Quay: saltmarsh, mudflats and sandbanks stretch across to the Wirral Peninsula.

Although small, the reserve shows a great variety of habitats. In the woodland the ground cover is not spectacular because of the lack of light, although dog's mercury, ground-ivy and wood avens thrive, but the grassland area has a very rich variety of lime-loving plants. Here the plants have colonised bare marl workings with no competition from the trees and on the dry banks cowslip, kidney vetch, perforate St John's-wort, wild strawberry and ploughman's-spikenard may be found. The damper grassland, from July to September, is graced by grass-of-Parnassus, meadowsweet and hemp-agrimony, while the pools are lanced with bulrush.

As well as the plants, the clearing is filled in spring with birdsong, and in summer with butterflies, bees, dragonflies and damselflies.

The woodland, although less varied than the grassy clearing, still provides a good range of habitat with areas of sycamore, wet and dry willow wood and blackthorn scrub. This provides cover for a wide range of birds and over 40 species have been recorded here.

Some of the old farm buildings have been converted into an interpretative centre.

Dee Estuary

See map; 12,600ha; various bodies
Sand, mudflats and saltmarsh
All year

Walking out on to the sands of Dee, with the wide estuary spreading all around, it is hard to realise that this was once a huge river of sea ice. Since then the sea level has risen, relative to the land, and the estuary, now deeply silted, is formed from the drowned river mouth.

The silts and sands are the key to the wildlife value of the Dee. Upward of 140,000 waders – over 10 per cent of the British population – may be present here in winter, feeding on the rich food supplies of the estuary, together with large flocks of waterfowl and gatherings of finches and other small birds.

Sand and mud form a clogging, difficult environment, while the changing mix of fresh and salt water which occurs in an estuary adds further problems. Although not many species can survive, those that can are present in amazing numbers. Common estuary shellfish, such as Baltic tellin, peppery furrow shell and laver spire shell, provide rich pickings for many birds, together with common cockle – a staple for oystercatcher. *Corophium volutator*, a small crustacean, is present in vast numbers, with ragworm at a density as high as 2500 per square metre and another worm, *Pygospio elegans*, reaching the staggering figure of almost half a million per square metre.

The plants of the bare muds include Townsend's cord-grass and glasswort, while common saltmarsh-grass, sea aster and scurvy-grass species abound where the mudflats are higher and the creeks are fringed with sea-purslane. Sea-milkwort and sea arrowgrass show on higher parts and the fringes of the estuary may be marked by stands of common reed and sea club-rush. These are feeding grounds for winter finches.

The West Hoyle Bank in the estuary mouth is a notable site for grey seal – summer peaks of over 200 have been recorded. It is unusual for a haul-out to be so far away from any large breeding site and it is surprisingly close to a great industrial sprawl. Other sea mammals occur occasionally: bottle-nosed and Risso's dolphin, common porpoise and killer whale may visit while, rarely, large whales have been stranded here.

Other summer animals include breeding duck and waders including shelduck, occasional shoveler and teal, redshank, snipe and a few oystercatchers, and smaller birds: sedge and reed warbler, reed bunting, skylark, meadow pipit and yellow wagtail. Common tern nest on the rafts in the SHOTTON STEELWORKS and little tern may find undisturbed stretches of beach. Stonechat and grasshopper warbler occur in scattered pairs and the summer marshes are hunting grounds for kestrel and sparrowhawk.

Thousands of birds of many species make long migrations to breed in the Arctic and tundra regions and here, on the estuary flats and marshes, they pause to feed on passage or to spend the winter months. Of some 30 wader species normally noted in this country, 26 have been recorded here – in winter the most numerous are knot. These may occur in such numbers as to seem like a living carpet on the flats or, all flying together, like a billowing smoke-cloud whirling at the edge of the tide; over 40,000 dunlin may be present, with thousands of bar-tailed godwit, ringed plover and sanderling – for these five waders, the Dee is one of the six most important estuaries in Britain. Oystercatcher, black-tailed godwit, curlew, grey plover, redshank and purple sandpiper also winter here and, at high tide, the shores and rocky islets may be tightly packed with birds.

The estuary is just as important to wildfowl – 22 out of the 27 British species may occur here. Duck such as pintail and wigeon, from as far away as northern Russia, come to winter on the marshes. The estuary is a prime site for pintail, with flocks of over 5000 – among the largest in Europe; shelduck, too, may exceed 4000. With mallard, teal and other dabblers, these duck are generally gathered in the shallows or on the marshes, but deeper waters also attract diving duck. Smaller numbers of seaduck may be seen, together with great crested grebe, red-throated diver, guillemot and razorbill.

The largest winter roosts of gulls are in the neighbouring Mersey Estuary but the West Hoyle Bank attracts a considerable roost and, with the commoner gulls, species such as glaucous, Iceland, little and Mediterranean gull occur. Winter is the time for gatherings of finches, for foraging groups of greenfinch and chaffinch, for other small birds such as reed bunting, rock and meadow pipit, brambling and twite, for water pipit working the edge of the tide. Hard weather may bring in Lapland and snow bunting, and times of high winter tides force out secretive birds such as spotted crake and water rail. The vast numbers of birds may draw such predators as hen harrier, merlin, peregrine and short-eared owl.

Erddig Ponds

SJ 348473; 0.4ha; NWWT reserve
Two small ponds
All year

In summer wetland plants include greater spear-wort, fine-leaved water-dropwort and bulrush, together with lesser bulrush which is rare in Wales. Willow and hawthorn scrub and oak shelter small birds while the marsh areas attract winter duck, and waders during migration.

Ewloe Castle Nature Trail

SJ 292670; 2.4km; CCC
Trail through open farmland and wooded valley
Booklet from CCC
Spring, early summer

In spring the floor of the valley is filled with primrose and bluebell. The trail also passes a small pond where yellow iris grows and moorhen nests in summer. A good variety of open farmland and woodland birds may be seen.

Gors Maen Llwyd

SH 975580; 267ha; NWWT reserve
Moorland, blanket mire and wetland
All year

Over 110 species of bird have been seen around the reserve. The lake supports large numbers of wildfowl and waders, including whooper swan, goldeneye, goosander and red-breasted merganser, bar-tailed godwit and golden plover. Ospreys occur on migration. On the moorland red and black grouse, hen harriers, merlin and peregrine are all seen. Heather, bilberry and crowberry dominate the drier areas of the moor, while hare's-tail and common cottongrass grow, with bog asphodel around the pools. On cliff edges inaccessible even to sheep shade-tolerant plants such as wood sorrel, lady and beech fern are found.

Graig Fawr

SJ 064802; 24.6ha; NT
Limestone crags, grassland and scrub woodland
Leaflet from NT, Llandudno
Spring, summer

Graig Fawr is a great limestone hill looking out over the Vale of Clwyd, near Prestatyn. The western and northern faces are steep, falling sharply to the valley floor, while the eastern and southern parts slope more gently behind.

The shallow turf is rich with small herbs and lime-loving plants. The presence of hoary rock-rose is of particular interest as it is limited to carboniferous limestone and is found in only a very few sites in Wales and northern England. Here, it grows in thick mats on the steep rocks of the western face.

In the south western part of the site there is a block of woodland scrub which has grown up over some old quarry workings, a typical hills-and-holes system. Here the banks of blackthorn scrub, bramble, gorse and wild rose alternate with clearings and grassy banks, rich with the limestone plants of the plateau above. This grades into semi-mature woodland and there is a similar block of woodland at the foot of the steep faces of the north eastern slope.

The birds of Graig Fawr are chiefly those of woodland, chaffinch and blue tit, for instance, and of scrub, including stonechat, linnet and whitethroat, which may be seen on the gorse clumps. The colourful limestone plants attract many butterflies, including meadow brown, small tortoiseshell and the beautiful common blue.

Hafod Wood

SJ 324477; 8ha; NWWT–NT reserve
Mixed woodland and wetland
Spring, summer

Most of the woodland is open alder wetland, with great horsetail, hemlock water-dropwort, bird cherry, red currant and guelder-rose. The drier woodland, at either end of the reserve, contains wild daffodil and wood spurge beneath a good range of native trees. Breeding birds include spotted flycatcher, lesser spotted woodpecker, tawny owl and kestrel, with mallard and moorhen on the open marsh and pools.

Holywell Nature Trail

SJ 195764; 1.8km; CCC
Trail through wooded valleys and past old industrial ponds
Booklet from CCC
Spring, summer

The valleys have a good variety of trees including oak, ash, rowan and crab apple with characteristic plants such as wood anemone, wood-sorrel and woodruff. Several ponds provide shelter and food for waterbirds, where willow and alder, branched bur-reed, bulrush and yellow iris grow.

Legacy Nature Trail

SJ 295.483; 1km; CFGB
Trail demonstrating the colonisation of man made habitats
Dogs must be kept on leash; no smoking allowed
Leaflet from CEGB
Spring, summer

Mounds thrown up around the substation to preserve the area's rural appearance have been planted with trees and shrubs; the old railway embankment has been colonised by ash. A drainage ditch has been widened to establish a marshy wetland area and open turf provides a further habitat type. The area is populated by hedgerow and woodland birds and hunted by tawny and barn owl.

Llangollen Canal

SJ 198433 284378; 17km; CCC
Canal and towpath
Booklet from CCC
All year

The water of the canal may appear turbid and lifeless but it is filled with all manner of animals and plants, as even a short walk along the towpath will prove.

In spring, marsh-marigold is followed by cuckooflower and water forget-me-not. By mid-summer the banks are full of colour, thick with meadowsweet, hemp-agumony, great and rosebay willowherb, hedge and marsh woundwort and water mint. At the water's edge monkeyflower, a garden escape which has spread along waterways and now grows wild over most of the country, grows in a blaze of yellow. The hedgerow trees, oak, ash and sycamore, tower over hawthorn, hazel, field maple and dogwood.

Heron often visit while coot and moorhen busy themselves at the reedy edges of the canal; mallard dabble. Quick activity among the wagtails and flycatcher signals an insect hatch. Swallow and house martin dip and twist, as do the bats of an evening. Evening, too, is the time for other mammals. Water voles may be seen nibbling at plant material held in their forepaws or heard, especially in spring, chattering and squealing in their territorial squabbles.

Beneath the surface water snails graze the algae and are food for leeches. Dragonfly larvae, and the larvae of the great diving beetle, probably the most voracious of the underwater insects, stalk the canal bed, seizing anything that might be edible. Bream, carp, eel, perch, pike, roach, rudd and tench swim in the slow, dark water.

Although the whole stretch of the canal is an informal nature trail, there is a formal one. JAN-Y-CUT NATURE TRAIL.

Common blue, a beautiful small summer butterfly.

Loggerheads Country Park

SJ 198626; 27ha; CCC
Limestone crags, woodland and river
Nature trail booklet from CCC
Spring, summer

The summer sun strikes the 60m crags with an almost dazzling whiteness relieved only by the darker masses of the trees and the brilliant mosaic of limestone flowers clustering the cliff terraces.

Downstream the land falls in a series of steep banks and semi-dry valleys. Here the tree cover is thick with ash, beech, hazel and sycamore and the resulting lack of light restricts smaller plants to those adapted to this habitat. The limestone ensures a good supply of calcium-rich dampness, so there are dense masses of dog's mercury and enchanter's-nightshade. The parasitic toothwort may also be found.

Above this high-forest area, on the slopes of the limestone hill, the ground becomes drier and a special fascination of such ground becomes apparent. Because water drains very freely through limestone the soil above is often much less rich than that below – the 'goodness' is washed downwards; acid-loving plants can therefore be found growing among the lime-loving plants.

The grassland plateau is filled with lime-loving plants – common rock-rose, bloody crane's-bill and wild thyme. Harebell, small scabious, common milkwort and eyebright grow on the banks and terraces while, lower down, the steep narrow cliff path is edged with the exotic rose-of-Sharon.

Moorhen, dipper, pied and grey wagtail and an occasional kingfisher may be seen at the river. The woodland shelters chittchatt, treecreeper and pied flycatcher. The woodland edge is the home of tits and finches and the grassland holds skylark and meadow pipit.

McWalter's Dingle

SJ 135815; 6. 9ha; WdT
Woodland
Spring, summer

The Dingle is rich in wildlife. Dippers and herons are commonly seen alongside the stream.

Marford Quarry

SJ 357560; 10ha; NWWT reserve
Disused quarry
Spring, summer

These disused quarries now contain open grassland, maintained by rabbit grazing. The site is most important for its butterflies and moths; four nationally rare moths, which include tawny shears and netted pug, have been found. On the warm, south-facing grassland a great variety of butterflies bask in the sun. Especially notable is the grayling, found on less than 20 sites in the county, and a colony of silver-studded blues has been successfully established here.

Moel Famau: a fine spread of heather moorland above the Vale of Clwyd.

Moel Famau Country Park

SJ 171611; 861ha; CCC
High rolling heather moor
Spring, summer, autumn

Moel Famau is a long escarpment, its wide slopes and steep valleys clothed with heather, bilberry and bracken. Gorse and bell heather add bright colour, particularly in sheltered dry stream gullies where rowan and hawthorn grow. A few wet areas show ferns, rushes and plants such as cross-leaved heath and marsh pennywort. A typical grouse moor, the slopes are often hunted by kestrel and buzzard.

Mynydd Eglwyseg

SJ 233485; 490ha; Wynnstay Estates
Limestone crags and acid moorland
No access off rights of way
Spring, summer

The cliffs stand above long, steep scree slopes, in contrast to the purple moorland above and the green farmland below. Sheep graze on the screes, the squat hawthorns heavily pruned by their teeth. In sheltering crannies maidenhair spleenwort and herb-Robert flourish. On the cliffs themselves, less accessible to the sheep, are small scabious and wild thyme, with special plants of the limestone – rigid buckler-fern, limestone fern and uncommon species of whitebeam.

The moorland is managed as a grouse-shoot, with regular burns to ensure a constant new growth of young heather. Small heathland plants such as tormentil also occur, and where the peat thins over the limestone wild thyme reappears.

A right of way from the Eglwyseg scarp and over Ruabon Mountain, shows the contrast between the limestone of Eglwyseg and the acid millstone grit of Ruabon, covered in heather and bilberry. The dark, almost metallic, grit stone does not drain as easily as limestone, so that small areas of *Sphagnum* bog, marked by plants such as round-leaved sundew, become more frequent.

Nant Mill Woods

SJ 285501; 8.7ha; WdT reserve
Deciduous woodland and trail
Spring, summer

The open grassy glades within these oak, beech and ash woods are the richest areas for plants. Here lady's-mantle, meadowsweet, wild angelica, ragged-Robin and common spotted-orchids grow. The Clywedog Valley Heritage Trail follows a path by the river and leads to PLAS POWER WOOD just down the valley.

Offa's Dyke Path

SJ 073822–267206; 85km; CC
Long-distance way
Booklet from HMSO bookshops
Spring, summer

Based upon the defensive dyke built to protect England from the Welsh, Offa's Dyke Path passes through farmland and moorland, upland and lowland, close to GRAIG FAWR and MYNYDD EGLWYSEG and through the great moorland slopes of MOEL FAMAU COUNTRY PARK.

Plas Power Wood

SJ 297495; 31.6ha; WdT reserve
Mixed woodland
Spring, summer

This ancient woodland site in the Clywedog Valley supports a great variety of habitats including streams, rock faces and many woodland types. This diversity provides for many plants and animals. OFFA'S DYKE, the ancient boundary between England and Wales, runs through the wood.

Point of Ayr

SH 125847; 182ha; RSPB
Dunes, sands and saltmarsh
Spring, autumn, winter

This western corner of the DEE ESTUARY is an area of immense sands, shingle banks and mudflats with a small dune system on its western edge.

At high tide Point of Ayr may be a roosting place for thousands of birds. Bar-tailed and black-tailed godwit, dunlin, grey plover, knot, redshank, sanderling and turnstone all wait to return to feed on the mud flats when the tide falls.

As well as a roost for waders, the marsh is a feeding place for wildfowl and attracts good numbers of mallard, pintail, shelduck and shoveler. Inland, the smaller birds shelter and feed – snow bunting, shore lark and water pipit with the commoner winter birds. These small birds, and the plentiful small mammals, attract predators including hen harrier, peregrine and merlin.

Summer brings holidaymakers to the wide sands and the visible wildlife is reduced, but winter storms bring in many interesting vagrants and Leach's petrel, grey phalarope and Sabine's gull have been recorded.

Pwll-gwyn Wood

SJ 127723; 2.3ha; WdT
Deciduous woodland
Spring, summer

Situated on a prominent hill above the River Wheeler, the coppiced woodland of oak, ash and sycamore was last cut during World War II. Older trees are found around the woodland edge and, although Dutch elm disease has had its effect, the gaps created by the loss of elms have now been filled by ash regeneration.

Rhydymyn Nature Trail

SJ 207668; 6.4km; CCC
Trail following River Alyn and returning on higher ground above
Excellent booklet from CCC
Spring, early summer

At times of low rainfall the River Alyn disappears – a swallow-hole takes the river on an underground course when there is insufficient water to drive across the hole. The trail passes woods, small meadows, banks and hedges bright with flowers, especially in spring, and full of commoner birds of woodland, waterside and open country. Twite, siskin and crossbill may be seen in winter.

Shotton Steelworks

Permit only; 22ha; British Steel Corpn reserve
Wetland and pools
Permit from BSC (Personnel Services), Shotton Works, Deeside
All year

A reserve has been established in the marshes, reedbeds and lagoons around the steelworks. Over 200 bird species have been recorded, ranging from terns breeding on nesting rafts to passage waders and winter wildfowl.

Sontley Moor

SJ 337476; 5ha; NWWT NT reserve
Wet grassland, marsh and scrub
Spring, summer

The reserve comprises a complex mosaic of dry to wet grassland. The marsh area is dominated by giant horsetail, *Juncus* species and great willow-herb, while in the wide range of sub-habitats species include bird cherry, wood and water avens, black bindweed and yellow rattle. Birds are not abundant, but willow tit, reed bunting, tawny owl and mallard all breed. Grass snake, frog and toad are common, and polecats have been recorded.

Tan-y-Cut Nature Trail

SH 282411; 0.5km; Wrexham Maelor BC
Woodland trail
Leaflet from WMBC, Guildhall, Wrexham
Spring, early summer

Lying between the Shropshire Union Canal and the River Dee, Tan-y-Cut Wood is a damp mixed woodland with areas of marsh. The plants include great horsetail, pendulous sedge and butterbur.

Waun-y-Llyn Country Park

SJ 284577; 29ha; CCC
Upland moorland
Spring, summer

The heather moorland has a small lake and areas of peat bog. There are good views across the Cheshire plain and the Wirral Peninsula.

Y Graig

SJ 084722; 7ha; NWWT reserve
Grassland and woodland
Spring, summer

This limestone rock outcrop forms a prominant knoll overlooking the vale of Clywd, with wonderful views of Prestatyn in the north, Snowdonia and Berwyn in the south. The woodland of oak, ash, birch and cherry contains areas of beech and Scots pine. On the limestone grassland common rockrose is particularly abundant, and carline and nodding thistle, field madder and thyme are common around the many rock outcrops. In an old quarry sweet-briar, pyramidal orchid and autumn gentian can be found. Purple hairstreak is the most notable among the many butterflies.

Dyfed

The old counties of Carmarthen, Ceredigion and Pembroke together form the present-day county of Dyfed in south west Wales, which has an ancient landscape of great interest to geologists. The oldest rocks in South Wales, of the Pre-Cambrian and Cambrian, occur only in Pembrokeshire where in places they form picturesque outcrops, none more spectacular than Maiden Castle above the Treffgarne gorge. Elsewhere in the county, except for a small pocket of tertiary material, there are no rocks younger than the upper carboniferous period. Subsequently the landscape was shaped by glacial action as a great ice sheet gouged its way from north and central Wales, and by the incessant torrents of meltwater as the ice retreated.

The sea coast, of which Dyfed enjoys a superb variety, has always been a major factor in the development of the county. Most of the main towns are situated on or close to the coast or at the heads of estuaries. According to Nelson one of the finest harbours in the world, Milford Haven, once home port to a thriving fishing industry, now provides a major oil facility with several refineries and terminals together with an oil-fired power station. The only other major industrial zone in Dyfed is around Llanelli and inland along the Amman Valley; otherwise the county is essentially rural.

Iron Age man once lived on SKOMER island and most probably caught and ate seabirds. Nowadays large numbers of seabirds still thrive on the Pembrokeshire islands, of which GRASSHOLM, SKOKHOLM, Skomer and ST MARGARET'S are all nature reserves. Together they form the stronghold for seabirds in south west Britain and the fine colonies are now a major attraction for naturalists. For those unable to make a boat journey as the result of rough weather there are a number of mainland seabird colonies; the one at STACKPOLE HEAD forms part of a National Nature Reserve. Although the estuaries of Dyfed do not support the numbers of wildfowl and waders that occur at some English sites, they are of enough importance for those of the DYFI and CLEDDAU to be designated wildfowl refuges.

The sand dune areas, many of which contain rare plants such as dune gentian and fen orchid, have been much altered as the result of sand quarrying, agricultural reclamation and summer visitors. Four sites of considerable conservation interest do, however, remain – at Ynyslas in the north, and within the boundaries of three Ministry of Defence ranges in the south.

The heathlands of Pembrokeshire, especially those of the north west coastal zone, are especially important. At one time they provided extensive grazing areas, particularly for horses. Such activity would have maintained a more open habitat and allowed smaller plants to thrive, including scarce species such as yellow centaury, wavy St John's-wort and pale butterwort, which still occur. The first of these particularly likes the disturbed ground of animal tracks, a situation where, as the winter floods recede, dainty three-lobed crowfoot can be found.

The upland heather moors have largely vanished as the result of reclamation and afforestation, or are now dominated by purple moor-grass and mat-grass. A few pairs of merlin still nest at suitable sites while the sheep walk areas, which at times provide an abundant supply of carrion, attract that Welsh speciality, red kite. Concerted efforts by naturalists have enabled this superb bird to survive, and in 1986 no fewer than 38 pairs were present here.

There is a scarcity of open freshwater habitats in Dyfed, and extremely few at low altitude. The most important exception is BOSHERSTON PONDS in Pembrokeshire, a major site for aquatic plants and winter wildfowl. Some of the upland lakes are of equal interest, especially those in areas where few changes have taken place in the surrounding catchments.

The two main rivers of Dyfed, the Tywi and the Teifi, both flow through broad valleys. It is to the former that virtually the only wild geese to winter regularly in Wales, a flock of Siberian white-fronted geese, come. The Teifi and its tributaries, and further south west the smaller rivers of Pembrokeshire, form one of the remaining strongholds of otter in England and Wales.

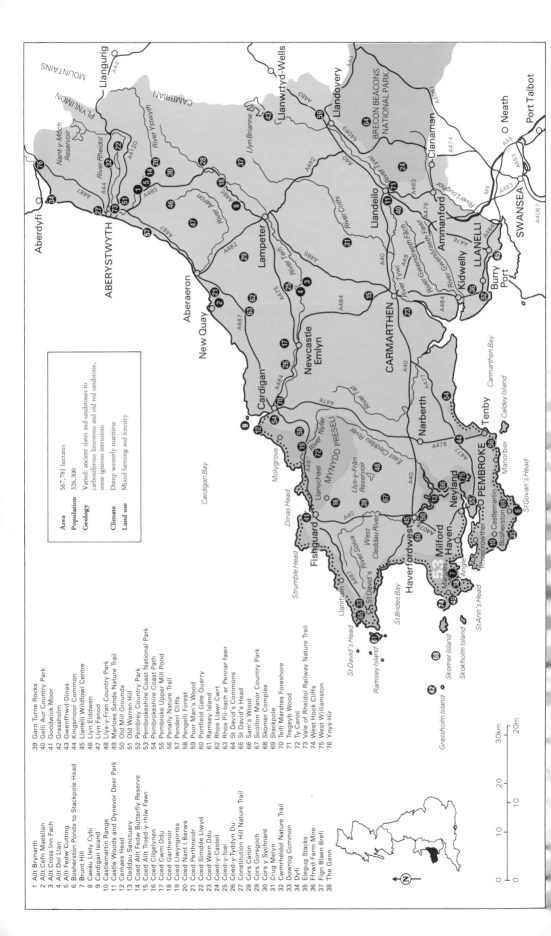

Area	567,781 hectares
Population	326,300
Geology	Varied: ancient slates and sandstones to carboniferous limestone and old red sandstone, some igneous intrusions
Climate	Damp westerly maritime
Land use	Mixed farming and forestry

1 Allt Brynarth
2 Allt Cefn Maesllan
3 Allt Cross Inn Fach
4 Allt Dol Llan
5 Allt Fedw Cutting
6 Bosherston Ponds to Stackpole Head
7 Brunt Hill
8 Caeau Llety Cybi
9 Cardigan Island
10 Castlemartin Range
11 Castle Woods and Dynevor Deer Park
12 Cemaes Head
13 Cleddau Sanctuary
14 Coed Allt Fedw Butterfly Reserve
15 Coed Allt Troed-y-rhiw Fawr
16 Coed Cilgellynen
17 Coed Cwm Ddu
18 Coed Garthenor
19 Coed Llwyngorres
20 Coed Nant t Berws
21 Coed Perthneidr
22 Coed Simdde Llwyd
23 Coed Wern Ddu
24 Coed-y-Castell
25 Coed-y-foel
26 Coed-y-Tyddyn Du
27 Constitution Hill Nature Trail
28 Cors Caron
29 Cors Gorsgoch
30 Cors y Sychnant
31 Crug Melyn
32 Cwmrheidol Nature Trail
33 Dowrog Common
34 Dyfi
35 Elegug Stacks
36 Ffrwd Farm Mire
37 Fign Blaen Brefi
38 The Gann
39 Garn Turne Rocks
40 Gelli Aur Country Park
41 Goodwick Moor
42 Grassholm
43 Gwenffrwd-Dinas
44 Kingsmoor Common
45 Llanelli Wildfowl Centre
46 Llyn Eiddwen
47 Llyn Fanod
48 Llys-y-Fran Country Park
49 Marloes Sands Nature Trail
50 Old Mill Grounds
51 Old Warren Hill
52 Pembrey Country Park
53 Pembrokeshire Coast National Park
54 Pembrokeshire Coast Path
55 Pembroke Upper Mill Pond
56 Penally Nature Trail
57 Penderi Cliffs
58 Pengelli Forest
59 Poor Man's Wood
60 Portfield Gate Quarry
61 Ramsey Island
62 Rhos Llawr Cwrt
63 Rhos Pil-bach ar Pennar-fawr
64 St David's Commons
65 St David's Head
66 Sam's Wood
67 Scolton Manor Country Park
68 Skomer Complex
69 Stackpole
70 Teifi Marshes Foreshore
71 Tregeyb Wood
72 Ty Canol
73 Vale of Rheidol Railway Nature Trail
74 West Hook Cliffs
75 West Williamston
76 Ynys-Hir

Often associated with these rivers are areas of as yet unreclaimed marshland and carr which provide a feeding and resting area for this scarce animal.

Unimproved pastures are rapidly disappearing, and examples have been established in the nature reserves of RHOS GLYN-YR-HELYG, RHOS PIL-BACH and RHOS-Y-FFOREST. However, a number of other sites will have to be acquired if a representative series of pasture habitats with their wide botanical interest is to be maintained. With flowers such as spotted-orchid and marsh-orchid, slender whorled caraway, lousewort and devil's-bit scabious, they contrast strikingly with intensively cultivated farmland nearby.

Much of the semi-natural woodland of Dyfed is now retained only on steep valley slopes where the main species is sessile oak. Several interesting species indicating very ancient sites also occur, including small-leaved lime and wild service-tree. In much of Ceredigion and east Carmarthen the bird of the valley woodlands is pied flycatcher which nested in Pembrokeshire for the first time in 1983. Of the lowland woodland, the most important is the pasture woodlands of DYNEVOR - DEER PARK (see CASTLE WOODS), a treasure-store of lichens, invertebrates, birds and mammals.

DAVID SAUNDERS

Allt Brynarth

SN 669714; 1ha; DWT reserve
Railway cutting
All year

This section of disused railway line is in an almost continuous cutting 1.5km in length. The cutting's sides are well wooded, mainly with oak, but of prime interest are the sheer rock faces. A rich flora of ferns, mosses, liverworts and lichens has developed, especially where water seepage occurs on the most shaded section; these include a number of rare and interesting species.

Allt Cefn Maesllan

SN 425580; 7.7ha; WdT reserve
Deciduous woodland
Spring, summer

This ancient semi-natural woodland in a steep-sided river valley consists of oak and ash coppice. Along the riverside alders grow and the whole reserve has a rich ground flora.

Allt Cross Inn Fach

SN 449396; 4.7ha; DWT reserve
Oak woodland
Spring, summer

The small hillside woodland is dominated by sessile oak, with some downy birch. Crab apple and wych elm grow along the edge of the wood, which also contains old charcoal hearths. Typical woodland birds and mammals occur.

Allt Dol Llan

SN 422402; 14ha; DWT reserve
Coppice woodland
All year

A woodland of high scenic value on the south bank of the Afon Teifi near Llandyssul comprises mainly of mature coppice with sessile oak and downy birch dominant in the canopy.

Allt Fedw Cutting

SN 665730; 1ha; DWT reserve
Disused railway cutting
Spring, summer

This section of cutting and embankment close to the village of Trawscoed was formerly known as Birchgrove Railway Line. The cutting is a shady, sheltered area with numerous mosses, liverworts and ferns, and several species of orchids. The embankment, an open, sunny area, is a particularly rich habitat for butterflies, with some 24 species recorded.

Allt Rhyd-y-Groes

Permit only; 62ha; NCC reserve
Hanging oak woodland
Spring, summer

The wood, on a steep valley side, has some fine mature oaks and includes birch and rowan with ash and alder in the damper areas. Woodland grasses, bilberry and bluebell cover much of the ground, with wood sorrel, meadowsweet and opposite-leaved golden-saxifrage in wetter places. Ferns include oak fern and Wilson's filmy-fern.

Bosherston Ponds to Stackpole Head

SR 966948; 797ha; NT–NCC reserve
Freshwater lakes, dunes, calcareous grassland and sea cliffs
All year

Bosherston Ponds are part of a sea-drowned valley system. The spurs between the ponds are scrub-covered with oak and ash standing among black-thorn, hawthorn and wild privet with a tangle of bramble, ivy and traveller's-joy. Rocky outcrops are thick with ivy-leaved toadflax, maidenhair spleenwort and hart's-tongue. The woodland spread of dog's mercury gives way to bracken and bramble in more open places, while beside the path are betony, slender St John's-wort and marjoram. On the open limestone heath above the woods gorse, bracken and rosebay willowherb grow. The grassland between, where the soil is shallow, is filled with ploughman's-spikenard, kidney vetch, salad burnet, wild thyme, carline thistle, wild privet and wild madder.

At the lake edge are stands of common reed, yellow iris, fleabane, purple-loosestrife and water mint. Nearer the sea typical duneland plants appear – dewberry, lady's bedstraw, common centaury and Portland and sea spurge. The grassland here is rather open and there is obviously much sand blown up from the beach below, but nearer the sea cliffs the plants change again.

The cliffs vary: sometimes a grassed slope with rocky outcrops, sometimes a jumbled series of shelves, sometimes a sheer drop to the sea's edge; caves, stacks and natural arches have been carved out by the waves and there are vertical shafts where blow-holes have collapsed. Here are clumps of rock sea-lavender, thrift, rock sea-spurrey and golden samphire.

Inland, however, the cliff-top plateau is still strongly affected by the dunes behind it and viper's-bugloss and common centaury show among the white flowers of sea campion. The dunes themselves, thrown up over limestone crags, do not have the damp slacks of normal sea-level systems such as KENFIG (Glamorgan), but there is a characteristic cover of mosses and lichens with yellow-wort, common bird's-foot-trefoil and mats of wild thyme.

The cliffs provide nest sites for an important colony of seabirds and the sheltered lakes attract waterfowl in winter.

Brunt Hill

SM 817073; 3.4ha; DWT reserve
Coniferous plantation with some mixed woodland
All year

Numerous oak and birch trees have been planted so as to convert this reserve gradually from coniferous to broad-leaved woodland. There are active badger setts and raptors regularly roost in the quarry. Particularly fine views can be had of the adjoining saltmarsh from the top of the reserve.

Caeau Llety Cybi

SN 603535; 3.4ha; DWT reserve
Four small herb-rich pastures
Spring, summer

These dry fertile fields have fortunately escaped agricultural improvement and provide a sward rich in herbaceous plants. By far the most interesting species is the greater butterfly orchid, rarely seen elsewhere in Ceredigion. The reserve is surrounded by and divided by mixed hedges managed in the traditional manner.

Cardigan Island

SN 160515; 15ha; DWT reserve
Small island
Spring, summer, autumn

A herring gull colony of around 900 breeding pairs dominates this exposed island; other nesting species include great and lesser black-backed gull, fulmar, shag, oystercatcher, raven, jackdaw and rock pipit. Non-breeding kittiwake roost and other visitors include chough. Since 1980 the DWT has been endeavouring to establish a colony of Manx shearwter by transporting fledgelings from SKOMER and by playing sound recordings of their calls at night.

Castlemartin Range

SR 9296; 239ha; MOD
Grazed grassland and limestone cliffs
Access along the coastal path from St Govan's Head to Stack Rocks on non-firing days
Spring, summer

Stack Rocks and a natural arch, Green Bridge, are outstanding. Large numbers of guillemots, kittiwakes and razorbills frequent the cliffs with small numbers of shag, chough and fulmar.

Castle Woods and Dynevor Deer Park

SN 627220; 28ha; DWT–NT reserve
Fine mixed woodland
All year

Castle Woods is one of the finest woodlands in this part of Wales. It overlooks Dynevor Deer Park and a wide area of the valley flood meadows which attract good numbers of wintering wetland birds. The woods lie on a limestone bluff above the River Tywi and, although there are now plantations within the reserve, the ash and wych elm may represent elements of the ancient primary woodland of Wales. Other tree species include some fine oaks, beech, wild cherry and holly with box and privet. The rich ground flora includes spindle and early dog-violet. Parasitic toothwort, known only from two other areas in the old county of Carmarthenshire also grows here.

Dynevor Deer Park is a rare example of fine old parkland, untouched by modern practices and containing a herd of fallow deer and a small group of red deer. The parkland is chiefly open woodland with copses, clumps of trees and some huge old single trees among rough grassland. It also contains ponds and is bordered by an oxbow lake. The trees are mainly oak with beech, sweet chestnut, elm, lime and a number of conifers.

Badger from the six active setts frequent the reserve. Foxes are not uncommon in the area and there are signs of otter on the river. The reserve holds a very good range of woodland birds, including all three British woodpeckers and all the characteristic woodland tit species, together with both nuthatch and treecreeper. Sparrowhawk, buzzard and raven are also present. In winter a wide variety of waterbirds may be seen on the ponds and the flood meadows, with commoner species including mallard, teal, wigeon, moorhen and coot.

The site contains some extremely fine lichen communities. Tree lungwort, a western lichen particularly sensitive to air pollution, is to be found in Castle Woods while the deer park supports a wide range of old parkland lichens now rarely seen in Wales.

Cemaes Head

SN 132500; 16ha; DWT reserve
Coastal cliffs
Permit only away from coastal footpath
All year

A spectacular section of the Pembrokeshire coastline with a range of cliff scenery – steep slopes, cliffs, gullies and small beaches. There is a small population of choughs and peregrines are regularly seen. The seabird population is small and includes cormorant, shag and fulmar, while other species are regularly seen offshore, as are grey seals.

Cleddau Sanctuary

SM 977116; 350ha; DWT reserve
Inland estuary
No access beyond foreshore
Autumn, winter

A large part of the upper estuary has been designated a sanctuary to protect good numbers of migrant and wintering waders and wildfowl; some remain to breed.

Clettwr Valley

Permit only; 21ha; DWT reserve
Lowland valley, oak woodland
Spring, summer

The woodland has been coppiced and contains a rich ground cover. The wide range of habitat throughout ensures great variety. Ferns are plentiful and the 16 species recorded include rustyback, oak and beech fern, and both filmy-ferns.

Coed Allt Fedw Butterfly Reserve

SN 667729; 3ha; FC reserve
Small hilltop area
Leaflet from FC
Spring, summer

Rotational Christmas tree growing encourages butterflies, including silver-washed and small pearl-bordered fritillary, small skipper, small copper, speckled wood and grayling.

Coed Allt Troed-y-rhiw Fawr

SN 413255; 15.8ha; WdT
Deciduous woodland
Spring, summer

The wood stands at the entrance to the wooded gorge of the Afon Gwili and, rising almost vertically from the river to the top of the valley, dominates the view from the south. The reserve is dominated by oak and ash with smaller numbers of birch, cherry and sycamore.

Coed Cilgelynen

SM 985347; 15ha; WdT reserve
Deciduous woodland
Spring, summer

Oak, ash and sycamore coppice are the main components of this woodland on a steep valley side. The wood forms a part of a relatively undisturbed complex of habitats including peat bog, and the whole area is rich in wildlife.

Coed Cwm Ddu

SN 309429; 26ha; DWT reserve
Sessile oakwood
All year

The three blocks of woodland on the steep slopes of the Ceri Valley are mostly coppice regrowth from felling during World War I. There is a well-developed ground flora. The woodland birds include redstart and pied flycatcher, while kingfisher, grey wagtail and dipper occur along the river.

Coed Garthenor

SN 635558; 7.5ha; WdT
Wet woodland, marsh and meadow
Spring, summer

The diverse area of willow carr, marsh and wet meadow is rich in uncommon plants and many animals.

Coed Llwyngorres

SN 092394; 24.8ha; DWT reserve
Woodland and river bank
Permit only off bridleway
Spring, summer

The steep woodland contains oak, holly and rowan at one end and sycamore, oak, ash, hazel and beech at the other. Fox and badger live in the wood where many typical birds may be seen. Willow and alder line the river – a spawning ground for salmon – where heron, kingfisher and dipper may occur.

Coed Maidie B Goddard

Permit only; 9ha; DWT reserve
Woodland and rough grazing
All year

There are several springs in this woodland in the lower Teifi Valley, and a fine display of early-purple orchids can be seen in spring. The reserve has three badger setts.

Coed Nant y Berws

SN 727718; 3.2ha; WdT reserve
Woodland and heathland
Spring, summer

The reserve consists of a small hillside wood of oak, birch and rowan, with open heathy areas dominated by bracken and heather. There is a stream along the northern boundary where a series of small bogs supports an interesting flora.

Coed Penglanowen

Permit only; 6ha; DWT reserve
Mixed woodland with stream
Spring, summer

Alder, grey, goat and crack willow grow by the stream, while the main woodland contains beech, oak, ash, sycamore and wych elm together with some tall conifers. Rhododendron shades out other plants but, where there is sufficient light, the smaller plants are very varied. Birds include all three British woodpeckers with woodcock, pied and spotted flycatcher and sparrowhawk.

The great spread of Cors Caron, filling the Teifi Valley.

Coed Perthneidr

SN 416584; 3.2ha; WdT
Deciduous woodland and scrub
Spring, summer

The small hillside wood is a mixture of oak and ash with some sycamore and a good shrub layer dominated by hazel. At the top of the hill, which provides fine views, are some former fields now becoming overgrown with scrub.

Coed Rheidol

Permit only; 75ha; NCC reserve
Steep oak woodland
Spring, summer

The woodland, cut by river gorges, is generally acidic – birch and rowan among the oaks with a ground cover of bilberry, common cow-wheat, purple moor-grass and wavy hair-grass. Richer areas contain sanicle, globeflower and Welsh poppy. There is a good range of ferns, mosses, liverworts and lichens.

Coed Simdde Llwyd

SN 720786; 39.8ha; DWT reserve
Sessile oakwood
All year

This superb section of the Rheidol Valley woodland on a south-facing slope includes the Rheidol Falls, a hanging valley of great geomorphological interest. The sheltered valley at the east end of the reserve has a great variety of tree species, with cherry, wych elm and small-leaved lime among those found here.

Coed Wern Ddu

SN 372178; 1ha; DWT reserve
Mixed woodland
All year

The wood is predominantly broadleaved, with oak, wych elm and birch and some beech. In spring and early summer there is a striking display of woodland flowers including early-purple orchid and wood anemone.

Coed-y-Castell

SN 667193; 15.7ha; BBNPC
Ash and oak woodland
Leaflet from BBNPC
Spring, summer

Below limestone crags the scree slopes carry thick ash and hazel woodland which gives way to open acid slopes of bracken and oak woodland where the limestone gives way to old red sandstone. This diversity of habitat encourages a wide variety of birds, including wood warbler, pied flycatcher, raven and buzzard.

Coed-y-foel

SN 427425; 20ha; WdT
Deciduous woodland
Spring, summer

The reserve is a fine example of Welsh sessile oak valley woodland, which also contains some ash and birch. Most of the trees are of coppice origin.

Coed-y-Tyddyn Du

SN 272426; 18.8ha; WdT
Mixed woodland
Spring, early summer

Mainly old farmland returning to forest, the ash–birch–oak woodland contains areas of herb-rich old pasture. Over 100 species of fungi and many insects have been recorded.

Comins Capel Betws

Permit only; 7ha; DWT reserve
Marsh, heath and unimproved neutral grassland
Spring, summer

The reserve contains many interesting heath and marsh species, including lesser butterfly orchid, petty whin and whorled carraway. Curlew, snipe and mallard breed.

Constitution Hill Nature Trail

SN 583826; 5km; DWT–Ceredigion DC
Circular trail on coastal hill above Aberystwyth
Leaflet from DWT
Spring, summer

Along the trail coastal grassland gives way to inland woods and hedge bank habitats, each with their own plants and animals. Birds of the open fields, woodland, hedgerow, sea cliff and shoreline may all be seen.

Cors Caron

SN 696632; 800ha; NCC reserve
Raised peat bog and river
Access via permitted route along part of old railway track
Permit and booklet from NCC, Aberystwyth
All year

Cors Caron (formerly known as Cors Tregaron) is one of the classic peat bogs of Britain, demonstrating the development from shallow lake through flood-plain mire (still fed primarily by river-water) to an ombrogenous (rain-fed) mire, the true raised bog. The River Teifi cuts the bog in two, from north east to south west, while the eastern bog is divided again into two. The west bog is the best preserved.

The sloping edge of the bog is tussocked with purple moor-grass whch gives way to a belt of heather, cottongrass and deergrass with occasional small birches. The highest part of the bog is rich with *Sphagnum* mosses. Surface pools are filled with these mosses and with deergrass and white beak-sedge and above these are heather and the wet-loving cross-leaved heath. Other plants include crowberry, bog-rosemary, cranberry and bog asphodel, together with all three sundews. In places the tall fronds of royal fern rise from the covering heathers.

In winter the river floods widely and even in summer the general wetness makes the reserve unsuitable for many mammals, although water voles are plentiful and otter occur. The raised bogs are dry enough for adder, common lizard and slow-worm and may, occasionally, be hunted by polecat.

The wide variety of habitat, river terrace and reed canary-grass bed, raised bog and willow scrub, provides suitable feeding or nest sites for many kinds of bird. Water rail, moorhen, coot, mallard, teal, curlew, redshank and snipe are among the wetland species. Redpoll, willow tit and willow warbler may be found in the trees, with grasshopper warbler, sedge warbler and reed bunting by the river and small numbers of red grouse on the bog itself. In winter there are good numbers of whooper swan together with mallard, teal and wigeon, and hen harrier and merlin may be seen. One of the most exciting sights might be a red kite, wheeling effortlessly above the bog.

Cors Goch

Permit only; 22ha, DWT reserve
Raised mire
Spring, summer

The reserve now includes the whole of the raised mire on the south side of the Carmathen to Haverfordwest railway line. The larger western section has had a number of drainage channels dug at some time in the past. This has resulted in an invasion by birch, and current management includes the blocking of the channels to raise the water table, and the removal of the birch. Interesting species include royal fern, cranberry, bog asphodel and bog myrtle. The marsh fritillary butterfly, bog bush cricket and black sympetrum dragonfly are just three of the invertebrates found.

Cors Gorsgoch

SN 482504; 16ha; DWT reserve
Soligenous valley mire
Spring, summer

The whole of the southern section of the mire which lies to the south of Gorsgoch village is a Trust reserve. The stream forming the headwaters of the Afon Grannell flows north-west through the site, which contains a number of glacial features known as pingoes in which mires have developed, with dominant bog mosses and species like white sedge, round-leaved sundew, cranberry and bog asphodel. The pond close to the eastern boundary attracts wildfowl in winter and is a good dragonfly habitat in summer.

Cors y Sychnant

SN 700688; 1.6ha; DWT reserve
Valley mire
All year

The reserve comprises only a small area at the extreme south-east of a valley mire which drains into the Afon Sychnant. Here the mire is encroached by oak and willow. A striking stand of bog myrtle is present, one of its few sites in Ceredigion. Marsh-orchids, sundew, butterwort, bog asphodel and cranberry can be found in the old peat cuttings and *Sphagnum* moss flushes.

Crug Melyn

SN 502281; 1.5ha; DWT reserve
Heathy grassland
Spring, summer

Sheep-grazed in summer, the upland grassland reserve is dominated by purple moor-grass. Scattered heather and gorse occur with willow and hawthorn. A small stream fringed with rushes runs through the area.

Cwmrheidol Nature Trail

SN 697797; 4km; CEGB
Trail circling the reservoir at Rheidol Power Station
Leaflet from information centre or CEGB
Spring, summer

The trail overlooks the reservoir, a wintering site for Bewick's swan, goosander and tufted duck, and shows much of the plant and animal life of the acid rocky parts of Wales. Salmon and trout pass through the reservoir on their way to breed and a wide range of field, hedgerow, woodland and water birds may be seen.

Dowrog Common

SM 770268; 81ha; NT–DWT reserve
Lowland heath and wetland
Spring, early summer

The common, one of ST DAVID'S COMMONS, is a mosaic of plants, all reflecting the changes in wetness or soil type. Purple-loosestrife, fleabane and sneezewort grow with saw-wort and bog asphodel; small pools are ringed or hidden with wet cushions of *Sphagnum* mosses, and fringed with water mint, yellow iris, ragged-Robin, common cottongrass and bogbean. Nearly 300 plant species have been recorded, including a number of restricted distribution in Britain.

Clumps of grey willow and meadowsweet mark the streams and pools with their stands of bulrush and great willowherb above smaller marsh plants such as square-stalked St John's-wort, marsh lousewort and marsh cinquefoil. Here birds of the open water areas nest – coot, moorhen, water rail, sedge warbler and duck such as mallard. In winter other duck may visit, pintail, pochard, teal, tufted duck and wigeon, and both whooper and Bewick's swan are regularly observed. The birds also include short-eared owl and grasshopper warbler. Hen harrier and merlin are present throughout the winter, while buzzard, kestrel and sparrowhawk are seen regularly.

The wealth of water and flowering plants means that insects are plentiful and varied, with an abundance of dragonflies, including small red damselfly. The butterflies include green hairstreak and the much rarer marsh fritillary using devil's-bit scabious as its food plant.

Dyfi

SN 609942; 1590ha; NCC reserve
Estuary, dune system and raised bog
Permit required, except to Ynyslas Dunes
Leaflets from information centre, Ynyslas
All year

Ynyslas Dunes, rising from a shingle beach, show typical dune development; at low tide sand is blown up to settle around the stems of plants, such as sea rocket and prickly saltwort, which are adapted to grow in the sandy shingle. As sand builds up around these plants marram begins to grow, sending out new shoots as fast as fresh sand covers it – it can tie together a dune as high as 7m. On the sheltered, landward side of the dune, sea spurge can grow and provide shelter in which restharrow, red fescue and duneland mosses begin to consolidate a surface.

When the surface has become more stable, more delicate plants such as Portland spurge, common centaury, biting stonecrop, hare's-foot clover and common bird's-foot-trefoil appear.

Between the ranks of dunes are damp hollows with their own special plants and, because these sands are rich in calcium, they are particularly suitable for many orchids. Among those found at Ynyslas are a subspecies (*coccinea*) of early marsh-orchid, northern marsh-orchid, marsh helleborine and bee and pyramidal orchid.

The reserve is a haven for rabbits, making the dunes a good hunting ground for fox, weasel, stoat and polecat. Small mammals generally are not plentiful, although hedgehogs find plenty of snails, particularly the characteristic duneland banded snail.

Birds, too, are neither plentiful nor widely varied, since the dunes offer little cover; the greatest variety, however, will be seen in the estuary. Summer sightings may include cormorant, shelduck and red-breasted merganser, while waders include bar-tailed godwit, curlew, whimbrel, greenshank and common sandpiper. During spring and autumn migrations the wader population increases dramatically, while the winter population of wildfowl may include about 2000 wigeon, together with mallard, pintail and teal. This is the only regular winter roost, south of the Solway, for Greenland white-fronted geese.

The bog, Cors Fochno, is open only to permit holders. The largest area of unmodified raised mire in the country, it has a magnificent range of wetland plants and insects, many of them of great interest for their range and distribution. It also has probably the lowest-altitude flock of black grouse in the country.

Elegug Stacks

SR 926945; 1ha; MOD–PCNPA
Limestone pillars
Spring, summer

The coastal cliffs here are spectacular, carrying a striking range of plants, and the stacks just offshore provide breeding sites for guillemot and razorbill.

Ffrwd Farm Mire

SN 420026; 19ha; DWT reserve
Fen
Spring, summer

The reserve, which is bounded by a road, disused canal and mineral railway, has a diversity of wetland habitats including species-rich fen, reed-swamp, drier raised dune area, open water in ditches, a new pond and rough pasture. Several scarce species occur, including the marsh pea, frogbit, tubular water-dropwort and floating club-rush.

Fign Blaen Brefi

SN 717547; 45ha; DWT reserve
Blanket mire
Spring, summer

This blanket mire shows a good deal of erosion more usually associated with the peatlands of north-west Scotland. This has been caused by the Afon Brefi eating into the peat-covered watershed, resulting in large areas of peat wastage. The drier sections support heather, cross-leaved heath, bilberry and crowberry, while bog pondweed, bogbean, cottongrass, bog asphodel and star sedge occur in the wetter gullies.

The Gann

SM 808066; 100ha; PCNPA
Coastal shingle, saltmarsh and freshwater pools
Spring, summer, autumn

Near the mouth of the Milford Haven Estuary the coastline bends back on itself, forming the sheltered bay of Dale Roads. The PEMBROKESHIRE COAST PATH crosses the head of the bay, at low water, by an embankment and a tidal ford. From here the Gann, a very wide range of habitat, can be seen.

The foreshore is of shingly sand with rock outcrops. The embankment has led to the development of a saltmarsh behind it and gravel extraction has left a number of pools, some flooded at high tide, some brackish and some freshwater, although these may be washed over at very high spring tides.

The bank is faced with shingle and supports typical shingle plants, such as sea beet and orache, but also some rather unexpected plants, woody nightshade, for instance, indicating that the tides rarely reach here. It is topped with gorse, ragwort, chamomile and mugwort, while common bird's-foot-trefoil and common vetch tangle the undergrowth.

At the eastern end the embankment breaks into a number of tidal islands, thick with sea-purslane, common scurvygrass and greater sea-spurrey. The largest, above normal tide levels, is covered with scrub. Where the shingle and sand-and-shingle become mud glasswort grows. It is at this point that the tidal ford allows crossing of the stream, while upstream of the ford the level ground opens on to the saltmarsh. The saltmarsh, rich in creeks and pools, is full of thrift, sea aster and lax-flowered sea-lavender. Curlew and redshank probe the mud of the marsh, which is also a hunting ground for heron.

The larger gravelpits lie behind the embankment and at the edge of the marsh and there is a good progression of saltwater to freshwater plants with, at the low hill which overlooks the estuary, stands of common reed, hemp-agrimony, fleabane,

silverweed and water mint. A dense mass of thorn and bramble near the west end of the bank gives cover to such birds as stonechat and linnet and the position of the Gann, almost at the mouth of the estuary, means that in spring and autumn a good selection of passage birds should be seen.

Garn Turne Rocks

SM 979273; 3ha; DWT reserve
Archaeological site
All year

The main interest of the site lies in the collapsed cromlech which was once a burial chamber.

Gelli Aur Country Park

SN 596198; 36ha; Dyfed CC
Estate parkland
Spring and summer only, except to organised parties
Leaflets from DCC or warden on site
Spring, summer

The park has a series of natural trails through a variety of habitats. Fallow deer are also present.

Goodwick Moor

SM 946377; 15.4ha; DWT reserve
Reedbed and marsh
Permit only away from boardwalk
All year

A superb mix of wetland – open water, extensive reedbed, marsh and bog – provides habitats for breeding sedge, reed and grasshopper warbler, while snipe and teal are regular winter visitors. Characteristic plants include *Sphagnum* mosses, marsh cinquefoil, bogbean and bog myrtle with bulrush, bur-reeds, reeds and sedges.

Y Goyalt

Permit only; 5.6ha; DWT reserve
Oak woodland
Spring, summer

The reserve, in the upper valley of the Tywi, holds a good range of birds. As in many of the drier Welsh oak woodlands, bracken is thick around the upper edges. There is an active badger sett.

Grassholm

SM 599093; 9ha; RSPB reserve
Rocky offshore island
No visits before 15 June; contact RSPB Wales for advice, access unreliable
Summer

Part of the SKOMER COMPLEX: Britain's second largest gannetry with over 28,000 pairs.

Gwenffrwd–Dinas

SN 787470; 2760ha; RSPB reserve
Upland hill and valley oakwoods and pasture
Dinas open all times; limited access to Gwenffrwd
Leaflet from RSPB or Dinas information centre in summer
Spring, summer

Light filters through the branches of the oaks in Pengelli Forest.

This large tract of typical mid-Wales upland is in two blocks, the Gwenffrwd being the larger and more varied. The smaller is a steeply wooded knoll at the junction of the Towy and Doethie rivers.

There are wide stretches of heather moorland, home of red grouse, snipe and meadow pipit, rich in wet mires with marsh St John's-wort, bog asphodel, bogbean and bog pimpernel. These heather moors provide breeding sites for skylark, whinchat and wheatear and, in spring, may be visited by merlin.

Dropping down from the moors the valley sides begin to show woodland, thin at first and then thickening into the typical woodland, oak and birch, of the wet acid valleys of much of Wales. This is pied flycatcher country, with redstart, wood warbler and woodcock: damp woodland with little ground cover but a tumble of rocks thick with mosses and ferns, with hard, oak and lemon-scented fern, lady-fern, polypody and Wilson's filmy-fern.

Dinas has a nature trail which shows a representative range of the steep valley habitats. The tumbled rocks with the mosses and ferns and oaks climbing the tilted rocks. Where more light penetrates, heather, bilberry, harebell and navelwort grow. Damp, thin grassland shows ivy-leaved bellflower and lousewort; in spring there are bluebells under the trees.

The rivers provide yet another type of habitat, a feeding ground for dipper, heron and kingfisher, a breeding ground for dipper, grey wagtail and common sandpiper. The Towy riverbank is the site for a colony of sand martin, and the rivers themselves hold resident brown trout and are spawning grounds for salmon and sea trout.

Buzzard, kestrel, sparrowhawk, tawny owl and red kite nest on the reserve and peregrine may visit. There are numerous foxes and a number of active badger setts, occasional polecat and a population of both red and grey squirrel.

Kingsmoor Common

SN 123067; 20ha; DWT reserve
Acid grassland and scrub
Summer

The eastern part of the common where the reserve lies is now the only unspoiled area. It is dominated by purple moor-grass with areas of rushes and scrub. In the wetter areas there are common fleabane, water mint, meadowsweet and greater tussock-sedge, while birds found on the common include water rail, snipe, stonechat and short-eared owl.

Llanelli Wildfowl and Wetlands Centre

SS 530983; 89ha; WWT
Saltmarsh and mudflats
Leaflets from visitor centre
All year

The visitor and observation hides overlook the Burry Inlet. Breeding birds include lapwing, red-shank and dabchick, while wildfowl and wader numbers start to build up in the autumn. The area is renowned for oystercatchers but knot, dunlin and bar-tailed godwit also occur in large numbers; wigeon are the most numerous duck, with pintail also often plentiful.

Llanerch Alder Carr

Permit only; 2ha; DWT reserve
Wet alder and grey willow woodland
Spring, summer

Probably the best example in Pembrokeshire of a mature wet alder woodland with an abundance of rotten stumps, fallen trees and open marshy glades. Apart from the glades the tree canopy is dense and the ground cover is thick with bramble, reed canary-grass and greater tussock-sedge.

Llyn Eiddwen

SN 606674; 54.8ha; DWT reserve
Upland lake and grassland
All year

A small water-catchment area of unimproved land has allowed the lake to remain unaltered and encouraged a community of water plants unique in Britain. Here awlwort grows, at its most southerly limit, with quillwort, least bur-reed, shoreweed, water lobelia and lesser and floating water-plantain. The growing basin mire is dominated by bottle sedge and water horsetail. Small numbers of whooper swan winter on the lake.

Llyn Fanod

SN 604645; 4.5ha; DWT reserve
Upland lake
All year

The Trust owns only the northern section of this upland lake, which may aptly be described as a sister to LLYN EIDDWEN to the north. The range of aquatic plants is similar but with the addition of both white and yellow water-lilies.

Llyn Nant-y-Bai

Permit only; 0.9ha; DWT reserve
Pond and scrub-covered bank
Spring, summer

The shallow pond is covered by water horsetail in summer and is edged by soft rush, mosses and purple moor-grass, ideal cover for nesting reed warbler and mallard. The bank is thick with gorse, heather and characteristic heathland plants such as bilberry, heath bedstraw and tormentil. Frog breeds here and it is favoured by heron.

Llys-y-Fran Country Park

SN 040244; 124.5ha; DCC
Reservoir and surrounds
All year

A nature trail demonstrates the interests of the park where moorland birds and waterbirds breed. In winter, wildfowl may shelter on the reservoir.

Marloes Mere

Permit only; 11ha; DWT reserve
Species-rich wetland
All year

Soft rush covers much of the reserve and common cottongrass most of the rest. Reed bunting, curlew, snipe and mallard breed; it is one of the best sites in south Wales for shoveler. Marsh fritillary butterfly has been recorded. A hide is situated at the north-east corner of the reserve.

Marloes Sands Nature Trail

SM 780082; 3.2km; DWT–NT
Trail on coast overlooking Gateholm and Skokholm, returning inland
Leaflet from DWT
Spring, summer

The trail includes streamside interest, an old roadway overlooking MARLOES MERE, and a sunken lane. The cliffs are rich with heather, thrift and wild thyme. Sea and shore birds can be seen, with raven and, occasionally, chough.

Nant Melin

Permit only; 2.9ha; DWT reserve
Mixed woodland and damp grassland
Spring, summer

The slope above the river carries birch, oak, sycamore and rowan, with alder and several willow species in the wetter parts. Wet grasslands on the wood's fringes have plants such as wood horsetail, royal fern and globeflower. Birds characteristic of woodland and river can be seen on this reserve.

Old Mill Grounds

SM 953166; 3.2ha; DWT reserve
Marsh and woodland
Spring, summer

Mixed woodland slopes down steeply to the

Skomer's cliff-top turf may be a carpet of flowers in summer.

western CLEDDAU river, bordering a marsh which lies between it and the water. The marsh has meadowsweet, purple-loosestrife, lesser pond-sedge and wood club-rush. Grasshopper warbler breeds in the marsh, with mute swan on the river islands and birds such as nuthatch, treecreeper, blackcap and goldfinch in the woods.

Old Warren Hill

SN 615787; 8ha; DWT reserve
Mixed woodland
Spring, summer

Varied woodland species form the ground cover under oak, ash, beech and birch and trees such as sycamore and Scots pine. There is an open, bracken-covered hillside, a wooded dingle and a deep valley with a stream. This is a breeding site for many species of birds and contains active badger setts.

Pant Da

Permit only; 4.5ha; DWT reserve
Mixed woodland
Spring, early summer

The woodland, composed of a mix of planted larch and regenerating oak, contains typical birds.

Pembrey Country Park

SN 415007; 210ha; Llanelli BC
Duneland and plantations
Booklet from visitor centre or LBC
All year

The country park is situated on an area of blown sand at the mouth of the Burry Inlet. Four waymarked nature trails demonstrate some of the interest of the pinewoods, scrub, grassland and sands.

Pembrokeshire Coast National Park

See map; 58,275ha; PCNPA
290km of coastline and inlying land
Leaflets from PCNPA
Spring, summer

The park embraces most of the coast from Cardigan to Amroth, swinging inland to include the heather moors of the Mynydd Preseli and the estuary of the DAU CLEDDAU.

The coastal waters are extremely rich, encouraging an important wintering flock of common scoter and providing food for the grey seals which breed on the mainland and offshore islands. These, such as the SKOMER COMPLEX, hold colonies of seabirds while the coastal cliffs and heathlands contain a superb range of colourful plants. The long winding estuaries – deep-cut drowned river valleys – provide shelter and feeding grounds for wildfowl and waders and set in the south west corner of Wales, are important migration routes for birds and insects. The woods have been largely altered by man but form a habitat for typically western as well as more widespread species; the largest area of freshwater lakes, at BOSHERSTON PONDS, has also been modified but is both beautiful and rich in water plants and animals.

DOWROG COMMON, THE GANN and ST DAVID'S HEAD are among a great number of fascinating areas included in the park – the PEMBROKESHIRE COAST PATH runs along its length. Although this is the smallest national park in England and Wales, its range of variety is quite superb: duneland, with uncommon plants such as dune gentian and perennial centaury, give way to cliffs of hard rock above the sea; when the sun is hot on the coast, narrow valleys inland may be cool in the shade of steeply sloping woodlands while the heather moors may be breezy.

Pembrokeshire Coast Path

SN 164468–174073; 270km; PCNPA–CC
Long-distance way
Booklet from CC or HMSO bookshops
Spring, summer

The waymarked footpath follows the coastline through the length of the PEMBROKESHIRE COAST NATIONAL PARK.

Pembroke Upper Mill Pond

SM 993016; 5ha; DWT reserve
Good waterbird pond
Visitors must keep to right of way
Winter

The pond is the only Pembrokeshire site for horned pondweed but its chief interest is probably its waterbirds. Little grebe has nested here and late summer visitors include green sandpiper. Winter is the time for wildfowl – mallard, pochard, tufted duck and teal are among the regular visitors.

Penally Nature Trail

SS 117991; 5.6km; Friends of Penally
Countryside trail
Leaflets from Penally post office, stores or pottery, or PCNPA information centres
Spring, early summer

In an area of farmland set on old red sandstone and limestone, the trail includes hedges, woods, grassland and marsh, together with an old cave system.

Penderi Cliffs

SN 550732; 12.7ha; DWT reserve
Oak woodland and sea cliffs
Permit only away from coastal footpath
Spring, summer

Hanging oakwoods above the sea cliffs have been stunted by exposure to the gales, yet still hold a good variety of woodland plants and birds. Cormorant, shag and herring gull nest on the cliffs and raven and chough may be seen. Grey seal gather in autumn and occasionally breed in inaccessible bays.

Pengelli Forest

SN 132390; 65·8ha; DWT reserve
Oak woodland
Visitors must keep to marked paths
Spring, summer

Even on the hottest day it is cool and quiet under the oak trees of Pengelli. The woodland canopy is fairly high but dense and even, because the forest was clear-felled for charcoal around the time of World War I and so the effect is same-aged coppiced woodland throughout. It represents the largest block of primary oak woodland left in Pembrokeshire and is, in fact, two woods.

The drier wood is chiefly oak with birch and rowan while the wetter wood is more mixed, again with oak but with more birch, with ash and abundant alder. The understorey of the former is rather thin but contains a good range of species including hazel, holly, guelder-rose and gorse, some crab apple, red currant and gooseberry. The ground cover is mainly wavy hair-grass, common cow-wheat, heather and bilberry, the characteristic plants of dry acid Welsh oakwoods. In the damper wood heather is replaced by tufted hair-grass, woodruff, opposite-leaved golden-saxifrage, bramble and marsh violet.

Fox, polecat, badger and rabbit are among the mammals; frogs breed in wetter places and both common lizard and slow-worm may be found. The range of birds is typical of such woodland and includes pied flycatcher, redstart, wood warbler and buzzard.

Poor Man's Wood

SN 784356; 16.7ha; DWT reserve
Sessile oak woodland
All year

An ancient woodland gifted to the nearby town of Llandovery in the sixteenth century with the condition that any wood removed had to be carried away by the person. The area has been coppiced, though some large maiden trees remain. A small number of wild service-trees occur at one spot within the reserve.

Portfield Gate Quarry

SM 923154; 1ha; DWT reserve
Two small pools
Spring, summer

The pools in this tiny reserve are sheltered by willow and blackthorn scrub, and provide an attractive habitat for hedgerow and waterside birds and for dragonflies and damselflies.

Ramsey Island

SM 700235; 200ha
Inshore island
Daily boats from St Justinian's, June–September; otherwise by arrangement, tel. 0437 720648
Summer

The island's complex geology supports an unusual range of plants; its rugged coastline provides sheltered coves and beaches for the most important breeding colony of grey seal in Wales and its cliffs nest sites for the best population of chough.

Rhos Fullbrook

Permit only; 2.5ha; DWT reserve
Herb-rich, unimproved grassland
Spring, summer

The grassland contains a number of slightly base-rich flushes, alluvial marsh and some scrub. Over 100 high plants have been recorded, including devil's-bit scabious, lesser butterfly orchid, heath spotted-orchid, dyer's greenweed, petty whin, round-leaved sundew and butterwort.

Rhos Glyn-yr-Helyg

Permit only; 16ha; DWT reserve
Wet pasture, bog and riverside
Spring, summer

The most important habitat here is an area of unimproved wet heathy pasture, herb-rich and increasingly rare as agricultural practice drains more and more marginal land.

Rhos Llawr Cwrt

SN 411499; 35ha; NCC reserve
Grassland
Access by permit only from chief warden, Dyfed/Powys region, Plas Goggerdan, Aberystwyth, Dyfed SY23 3EE (tel. 0970 828551)
Spring, summer, autumn

An important area of unimproved sedge-rich grassland that includes some excellent examples of pingoes – 10,000-year-old permafrost mounds which melted and partially collapsed at the end of the Ice Age. The area is also rich in plant life which attracts many interesting insects including a colony of marsh fritillary butterflies.

Rhos Pil-bach ar Pennar-fawr

SN 367525; 26.5ha; DWT reserve
Sedge-rich grassland and lowland heath
Spring, summer

The reserve is in two distinct but adjoining sections. Pil-bach, the smaller, is one of the most species-rich extensive areas of neutral and base-rich damp meadows in Ceredigion. Two of the five fields are superb examples of ancient ridge-and-furrow pastures. The grassland is especially rich with common and heath spotted-orchid and northern marsh-orchid. There are three small ponds.

Pennar-fawr is an outstanding area of lowland wet heath dominated by heather and western gorse. Devil's-bit scabious and bog asphodel are particularly plentiful. A single pond has been encroached by *Sphagnum* and willow scrub.

Rhos-y-Fforest

Permit only; 1ha; DWT reserve
Species-rich bog
Spring, summer

The reserve contains an exceptional assembly of

Manx shearwaters nest in burrows under cushions of thrift and sea campion on Skokholm.

bog plants, including a wide range of sedges and wavy St John's-wort, which has a very limited range near western coasts in Britain.

Rosemoor

Permit only; 8ha; DWT reserve
Lake, marsh, rough pasture, scrub and woodland
Spring, summer

Oak and ash, with an understorey of hazel and elder, contrast with dry blackthorn scrub and a wet area of willow scrub. The marsh adds further variation and the range of grassland plants includes adder's-tongue, cowslip, heath spotted-orchid and both northern and southern marsh-orchid. The lake attracts a range of waterbirds.

St David's Commons

SM 770270; 344ha; DWT–NT
Grass heath
All year

A group of 32 commons which form an important range of wet grassland around St David's; DOWROG COMMON is probably the most important. The main habitat is wet grass heath with pale dog-violet, lesser butterfly orchid and twayblade; reptiles and amphibians are plentiful here in particular grass snake, common lizard and frog. Waun Caerfarchell, a reedbed at Waun Sebon, contains areas of tall herb fen, while Sickly Common and Ciliau Moor include coastal cliffs. Grasshopper and sedge warblers, stonechats and linnets breed on the commons, and birds of prey such as merlin, hen harrier and short-eared owl are regular winter visitors.

St David's Head

SM 734272; 208ha; NT
Rocky headland, sea cliffs and coastal moor
Spring, summer, autumn

The tilted rocks and the open heathland topped by the 180m peak with its battlemented tors make St David's Head a popular beauty spot. The views are certainly spectacular but, for the naturalist, are only a part of the area's fascination.

The path rises steeply from the sandy beach of Traeth-Mawr to the edge of the headland. Here kidney vetch competes in brightness with golden-rod. Heather and bell heather, gorse and tormentil clump the edges of the grassland, which runs to the cliff edge and is backed by gorse and heather heathland, broken by boulders and huge slabs of rock before it finally gives way to bracken on the steep slopes up to the tors.

East of St David's Head itself the coastline stretches in a great arc to Strumble Head, a sweep of sheer cliffs and steep gorse and bracken slopes which fall into a sea sharp with rocks or washing tiny unattainable beaches. The cliffs are topped with heathland which rises and falls with the rock beneath. Near the headland the rocks are slanted and form steep, narrow gullies dropping towards the sea. There are mats of rock sea-spurrey, of biting stonecrop and English stonecrop. A near relative, orpine, grows in the shelter of the rocks or in the steep, damp gullies between them. On the heathland above, harebell and saw-wort sway in the strong sea winds which hardly stir the tiny, close-growing heath pearlwort. Uncommon plants of this coastline include *Limonium paradoxum*, a species of sea-lavender, chives, hairy greenweed, and the dwarf coastal form of oxeye daisy.

The hidden beaches and narrow coves beneath the cliffs are hauling-out sites and breeding places for the colonies of grey seal. The cliffs above provide nest sites for buzzard, raven and small numbers of chough and form an ideal site for seabird watching.

St Margaret's Island

Permit only; 7ha; DWT reserve
Island with good bird populations
Landing is by permit only and often dangerous
Spring, summer

In summer there are frequent boat trips around the island to see the bird colonies. The cormorant population is huge and there are good numbers of kittiwake, razorbill, guillemot and great black-backed and herring gull. Manx shearwater are seen regularly and storm petrel occasionally, as well as many other species typical of open sea or rocky shores.

Sam's Wood

SN 004093; 12ha; DWT reserve
Woodland
All year

The ancient sessile oak wood lying on a steep slope overlooks the Daucleddau estuary. Birch and hazel are common but more interesting species are spindle and wild service-tree; the latter is a scarce, but characteristic tree, in the oakwoods around Milford Haven.

Scolton Manor Country Park

SM 991218; 16ha; DCC
Leaflet from DCC or countryside centre
Spring, early summer

The park has a nature trail which circles through the surrounding woodland, including a section in Forestry Commission plantations.

Skokholm

Permit only; 100ha; DWT reserve
Inshore island
Accommodation available; contact DWT
Summer

Part of the SKOMER COMPLEX.

Skomer Complex

See map; 415ha; DWT–NCC–RSPB reserve
Rocky islands
Leaflets from DWT
Spring, summer

Skomer, SKOKHOLM and the smaller Midland Island, or Middleholm, form a group at the base of the curve of St Bride's Bay. Skokholm differs from the others in being made of old red sandstone, repeated in St Anne's Head and the Angle Peninsula, while Skomer and Midland Island are mainly the old volcanic rocks which surface again as the small steep island of GRASSHOLM some 10km further out to sea.

Where vegetation exists on Grassholm it is

Ynys-Hir: a fine dissected saltmarsh spreads from the wooded slopes to the estuary.

mainly a spread of red fescue over the hummocked peat – the earlier deeper peats were tunnelled and eroded by puffins to such an extent that the tunnels collapsed and the puffins were forced to move on. A few may still nest here, together with other species of seabird, but the chief importance of Grassholm is as a gannetry. In 1860 very few gannets nested here; in 1893 numbers had risen to around 250. Now, although still the only western colony in southern Britain, the gannetry has grown to become the third largest in the North Atlantic and around 30,000 pairs may breed on the island.

The much larger island of Skokholm was the site of Britain's first bird observatory. Its coastline is carved into bays and islets ideal for nesting seabirds and, lying just off the mainland, it attracts large numbers of migrants. The cliff tops are lined with a mixture of coastal and common mainland plants, spring squill, Danish scurvygrass and thrift with bluebell, lesser celandine and primrose, while dry inner grasslands are closely cropped by rabbits and damper sites may carry a marsh of purple moor-grass. Unlike Skomer, only 3km away, neither common lizard nor toad is present and an effort to introduce them was a failure. Also a failure was an attempt to infect the rabbits with myxomatosis. Rabbits were introduced, as a food source, by the Normans in the twelfth century and do not carry the fleas which are the normal transmitters of the disease – nor, apparently, were infected fleas attracted to the Skokholm rabbits. Large numbers of seabirds breed here including Manx shearwater, storm petrel, puffin, guillemot and razorbill, together with land birds such as lapwing and raven.

Skomer is the largest of the islands and, like Skokholm, is spectacularly eroded. Erosion is a continuing factor and the narrow ridge of soft sedimentary rock between the main part of the island and the Neck will clearly be broken in the not too distant future.

The island contains a fine range of moorland and cliff habitats, together with those of old farmland, small marshes and pools. Bracken shelters common woodland plants while grasslands are starred with heath pearlwort, rock sea-spurrey and English stonecrop. The heathland contains cross-leaved heath and lesser skullcap in wetter sites and the streamside and damp valley bottoms may be filled with marshland skullcap, yellow iris and meadowsweet. Sea beet, rock samphire and sea spleenwort grow on the rugged cliffs and grade into clifftop turfs, bright with thrift, sea campion and sea squill. Around 200 flowering plants have been recognised on the island, including adder's-tongue, lanceolate spleenwort, wild madder and yellow-eyed grass, the last an American plant possibly introduced by some migrant bird.

Here is the largest kittiwake colony in Wales, with fulmar, lesser and great black-backed and herring gull. Guillemot and razorbill breed on the cliffs while puffin, storm petrel and Manx shearwater nest in burrows beneath the turf. The range of breeding birds is wide and includes waders, curlew, lapwing and oystercatcher, small birds such as wheatear and sedge warbler, and birds of the crags such as chough, raven and peregrine. Among other birds of prey seen on or above the island are buzzard, kestrel and short-eared owl.

Predatory mammals are absent, allowing large numbers of rabbit, common and pigmy shrew, wood mouse and Skomer vole to survive on the island. Skomer vole is a race of bank vole, larger than the mainland variety, lighter in colour and different in skull and teeth. Another speciality of the reserve is the breeding population of grey seal – Skomer is one of the most important sites in south west Britain, second only to RAMSEY ISLAND, some 14km north.

Weather permitting, Skomer may be visited from April until late September, on any day except Monday, Bank Holidays excepted. Details of visits to Skokholm and Grassholm are given under their respective headings.

This quite magnificent and fascinating group of island reserves is complemented by a marine reserve which protects some 1000ha.

Stackpole

SR 977950; 199ha; NT–NCC reserve
Sea cliffs, dunes, calcareous grassland and freshwater lakes
Leaflets from NT, NCC or PCNPA
Spring, summer, winter

See also BOSHERSTON PONDS TO STACKPOLE HEAD.

Teifi Marshes/Foreshore

SN 190453; 40ha; DWT reserve
Freshwater and estuarine marshes
All year

The reserve is part of the Teifi estuary immediately upstream from Cardigan, together with the marshes to the west of the Afon Piliau tributary.

Large numbers of wigeon, teal and mallard and a few shoveler frequent the marshes in winter; while diving ducks such as goldeneye are regularly seen on the river. Water rails breed occasionally and more arrive to winter with the large flocks of lapwing, snipe and curlew. Herons feed on the marshes throughout the year, commuting from the nearest heronry several miles upstream. Reed, sedge and grasshopper warblers nest in the reedbed, where bitterns regularly winter. Purple heron, little egret and marsh harrier are among the rarer winter visitors.

Otters and mink frequent the marshes and there are also sika deer which have escaped from a nearby wildlife park.

Tregeyb Wood

SN 641217; 28ha; WdT
Mixed woodland
Spring, summer

The wood is of great landscape significance within the BRECON BEACONS NATIONAL PARKS (Powys). Now that it has been acquired by the Trust no further large-scale felling will take place. A field within the wood is being allowed to regenerate naturally and a good system of rides throughout the wood provides a variety of attractive walks.

Ty Canol

SN 092369; 69ha; NCC reserve
Woodland
Access via public footpaths
Spring, summer, autumn

The sessile oak and mixed broadleaved wood is of outstanding importance because of its associated lichens. There is also a rich variety of invertebrates, particularly butterflies, moths and snails; as well as breeding populations of dormice and polecats.

Vale of Rheidol Railway Nature Trail

SN 585816; 19.3km; BR
Britain's first railway nature trail
Leaflet, both English and Welsh editions, from WWNT and Aberystwyth bookshops
Spring, summer

The narrow-gauge line runs from Aberystwyth to Devil's Bridge, through the broad flood plain of the lower Rheidol Valley and up the side of the narrowing wooded slopes. The journey takes in a very wide range of man-made and natural habitat.

Wern ddu Wood

Permit only; 1ha; DWT reserve
Mixed woodland and rough pasture
All year

A section of woodland kindly gifted to the Trust. It contains a number of particularly fine oak and beech trees and a typical woodland ground flora. The bryophytes include several rare species.

West Hook Cliffs

SM 762092; 8.1ha; NT–DWT reserve
Coastal cliffs and heathland
Visitors must keep to the coast path right of way
Spring, summer

Above the cliffs rich coastal heathland, thick with bramble, bracken and gorse, contains plants such as autumn squill, heath spotted-orchid and a prostrate variety of broom. Butterflies include small pearl-bordered and dark green fritillary, ringlet and green hairstreak. Buzzard, crow, heathland stonechat and linnet breed here.

West Williamston

SN 028060; 22.4ha; NT–DWT reserve
Mixed coastal and limestone habitats
Permit only away from foreshore
Spring, summer

A limestone outcrop against a saltmarsh deeply cut with tidal creeks provides an interesting reserve. The typical limestone plants include yellow-wort, blue fleabane and bee orchid, while the saltmarsh contains sea couch and marshmallow.

Western Cleddau Mire

Permit only; 16ha; DWT reserve
Flood-plain mire
Spring, summer

Part of the largest remaining flood-plain mire in Wales, through which flows the Western Cleddau. The range of wetland habitats includes superb high tussocks (up to 2m high) of greater tussock sedge. The water dock occurs frequently in the wettest parts of the fen, while there is a stand of the scarce northern bay willow. The Western Cleddau is of exceptional importance for otters and the reserve provides much cover for undisturbed feeding and resting areas.

Ynys-Hir

SN 683963; 255ha; RSPB reserve
Woodland, moorland, estuary and saltmarsh
Leaflet from RSPB or site
All year

Sixty-seven bird species nest at Ynys-Hir, mostly in the oak woodland. Pied flycatcher, very characteristic of Welsh woods, nests here as well as eight species of warbler and the more general woodland birds.

Outside the oak woodland there are conifers, nesting places for goldcrest and coal tit, and the moorland of Foel Fawr, a rocky bracken-covered hill with damp patches holding cross-leaved heath, bog pimpernel and common butterwort. Lesser skullcap and ivy-leaved bellflower also grow here and the drier areas are coloured with heather, bell heather, wild thyme and trailing St John's-wort. Foel Fawr provides nesting sites for wren, for tree and meadow pipit, for stonechat, whinchat, wheatear and yellowhammer, for nightjar and woodcock.

There is a small peat bog, rich with characteristic plants – all three British sundews, bog myrtle, bog-rosemary, bog asphodel, heath spotted-orchid and white beak-sedge. The saltmarsh has typical plants and here are nest sites for grasshopper and sedge warbler, reed bunting, snipe, redshank and lapwing. Here and on the estuary wigeon, mallard, teal, goldeneye, red-breasted merganser, tufted duck and shoveler flock in winter. The Greenland white-fronted geese may move up from their more usual roost in DYFI. Mallard and red-breasted merganser are present all year and breed, as do shelduck, grey wagtail, common sandpiper and, sometimes, kingfisher and dipper. Buzzard, kestrel, sparrowhawk, tawny and barn owl nest here and there is also a small heronry.

The range of habitat supports a wide variety of mammals – small mammals are prey to fox, stoat, weasel and polecat and to aerial predators which, in autumn and winter, may include hen harrier, merlin and peregrine.

Butterflies and moths are also encouraged by the diversity, and 31 species of butterfly have been identified, including pearl-bordered, dark green and marsh fritillary. The more uncommon moths include scarlet tiger, narrow-bordered bee hawkmoth, fox and northern eggar.

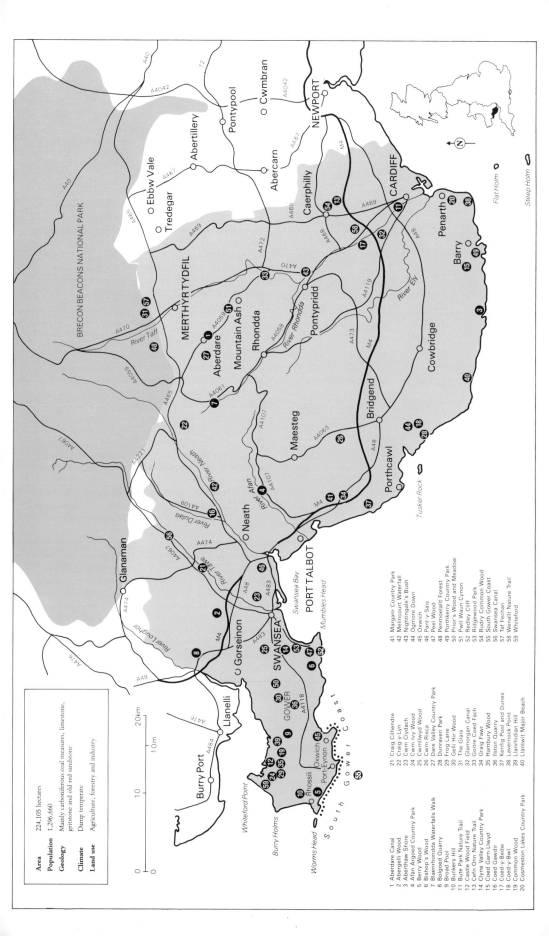

Area	224,105 hectares	
Population	1,296,660	
Geology	Mainly carboniferous coal measures, limestone, gritstone and old red sandstone	
Climate	Damp temperate	
Land use	Agriculture, forestry and industry	

1 Aberdare Canal
2 Abergelli Wood
3 Aberthaw Shore
4 Afan Argoed Country Park
5 Berry Wood
6 Bishop's Wood
7 Blaenrhondda Waterfalls Walk
8 Bolgoed Quarry
9 Broad Pool
10 Bunkers Hill
11 Bute Park Nature Trail
12 Castle Wood Field
13 Cefn Onn Nature Trail
14 Clyne Valley Country Park
15 Coed Garn-Llwyd
16 Coed Gawdir
17 Coed-y-Bedw
18 Coed-y-Bwl
19 Common Wood
20 Cosmeston Lakes Country Park

21 Craig Cilhendre
22 Craig-y-Llyn
23 Cwm Clydach
24 Cwm Ivy Wood
25 Cwmllwyd Wood
26 Cwm Risca
27 Dare Valley Country Park
28 Dunraven Park
29 Frog Lane
30 Gelli Hir Wood
31 The Glais
32 Glamorgan Canal
33 Goitre Coed Fach
34 Graig Fawr
35 Hambury Wood
36 Ilston Quarry
37 Kenfig Pool and Dunes
38 Lavernock Point
39 Llanrhidian Hill
40 Llantwit Major Beach

41 Margam Country Park
42 Melincourt Waterfall
43 Nightingale's Bush
44 Ogmore Down
45 Oxwich
46 Pant-y-Sais
47 Peel Wood
48 Penmoelallt Forest
49 Porthkerry Country Park
50 Prior's Wood and Meadow
51 Pwll Waun Cynon
52 Redley Cliff
53 Ridgewood Park
54 Rudry Common Wood
55 South Gower Coast
56 Swansea Canal
57 Taf Fechan
58 Wenallt Nature Trail
59 Whiteford

Glamorgan

Most people think of Glamorgan as industrialised; few realise how much open country remains. Climb to the brink of a mining valley and houses, mines and factories disappear: a great expanse of mountain moorland stretches east and west, putting the ribbon development along the valley bottoms in perspective. To the north the coalfield hills ascend to 660m and beyond them the Brecon Beacons to almost 1000m. To the south they descend to 330m before dropping abruptly to the coastal plain and the Bristol Channel.

The region, now administratively divided into West, Mid and South Glamorgan, falls naturally into upland similar to the rest of Wales, and the sunnier, more fertile Vale of Glamorgan along the southern seaboard. In the west the grey cliffs of the Gower Peninsula stand four-square to the south westerlies.

On the roof of the coalfield, where dipper and ring ouzel nest, rainfall is high and the climate bleak. The southern shores receive less rain and plants and insects known in southern Europe thrive. The extremes of climate are governed largely by altitude, but it is the wide range of rock types that determines plant and animal life.

Devonian old red sandstones dip below the south Wales coalfield to surface north and south of it. Mid Glamorgan extends across the northern outcrop into the BRECON BEACONS NATIONAL PARK (Powys), where reservoirs harbour brown and rainbow trout and amphibians.

Carboniferous limestones over the old red marls, brownstones and quartz conglomerates offer the chance to see white trout, white cave spiders and other subterranean rarities. Crevice plants escaping the inexorable munching of sheep include saxifrages and meadow-rue, with endemic whitebeams in river gorges.

The alternation of hard grits and soft shales gives some splendid waterfalls. Mountain tops are of rain-soaked acid moorland, with deergrass, bilberry, cottongrass and bog asphodel. Corrie lakes lie under the north scarp of the coalfield and upper valleys. Quillwort, water lobelia and narrow bur-reed occupy the water, with crowberry, stone bramble and roseroot on the crags. Buzzard, raven, merlin and heron are typical; foxes roam the hills and there are polecat and badger.

Much of the coalfield is blanketed by 'Molinia desert' and mat-grass moor. Heathery slopes are sprinkled with cranberry and crowberry, inaccessible cliffs with club-mosses and filmy-ferns, quagmires with bog pimpernel and ivy-leaved bellflower, streams with monkeyflower and rare red algae.

Wooded tributary valleys are the home of redstart, pied flycatcher, wood warbler and woodpeckers. Sessile oakwood formerly clothed far more, but much fell to the charcoal burners who supplied the early iron foundries; mercifully coal took over as the source of power. Soil once forested is now usually bracken- or larch-clad.

To the south the mountain limestone surfaces as a ridge which is dolomitised in the east, the red, iron-stained magnesian limestone supporting a different flora from the purer limestones of the west. Much is beech-covered, with early-purple and bird's-nest orchid, broad-leaved helleborine and columbine, spindle and dogwood among the beech leaves, centaury and yellow-wort on the paths, green spleenwort and golden-saxifrage near ancient lead mines. In the west there is more rock-rose, horseshoe vetch and squinancywort and there are some fine limestone heaths.

The Triassic rocks near Cardiff and the flaky black Rhaetic strata are characterised by narrow-leaved everlasting-pea, dyer's greenweed and flax. Warm soils of the younger Jurassic limestones support woolly thistle and wild cabbage, with clustered bellflower and marjoram, tuberous thistle and pepper-saxifrage. Stinking hellebore, stinking iris and spurge-laurel defy the hungry sheep.

Bee orchid abounds locally and the insects are reminiscent of warmer climates. Herring gull, jackdaw and house martin nest on the vertical cliffs of the Vale and a remarkable platform has been carved from the soft strata by marine erosion. The northern part of the Vale lies under boulder clay; less suited to agriculture, it has some interesting heath and bogland and peaty pools, with riverside monk's-hood and orange balsam.

FLAT HOLM, 5km offshore, is of carboniferous limestone, its spray-washed slopes bringing thrift, sea campion and rock sea-lavender well up-channel. Herring, lesser black-backed and a few greater black-backed gull nest, with the inevitable impact on other wildlife, but there are still great sweeps of scurvygrass, cowslips are surviving the rain of guano, wallflowers clothe more sheltered cliffs and the rare wild leek is thriving.

Mainland Glamorgan is blessed with vast sand dunes, each with national rarities. Plants and insects encroach on the intrusions along with the advancing sand. Dunes started to build up in the Middle Ages, and at present sand is accreting at a phenomenal rate east of Swansea. Slacks are colourful with marsh-orchid and fragrant orchid, marsh helleborine and round-leaved wintergreen, dunes with viper's-bugloss and restharrow, spinneys with yellow bird's-nest and valerian. Burnet rose and dewberry cover more stable areas, creeping willow the older slacks.

KENFIG POOL adds an extra dimension with wintering waterfowl, the occasional bittern and bearded tit, harvest mouse and water shrew. CRYMLYN BOG and associated fenland are rich in plant and bird life, dragonflies and other insects, and have been classified as Grade I conservation areas.

Alluvial flats seaward of the old sea cliffs were once visited by thousands of white-fronted geese, but have suffered lamentably at the hands of the developers. Flowering-rush, arrowhead and frogbit persist, and yellow wagtail, reed bunting and water rail still nest, but the black-headed gull colony succumbed in 1977. Gulls, kestrel, crows, starling and pied wagtail are now found nesting in and on the industrial sites.

Saltmarshes range from the vast sandy expanses at the mouth of the River Neath to the muddier saltings alongside the Bristol Channel at Rumney Mouth, just upstream from Cardiff. Both are wriggling with invertebrate life which attracts a wealth of shorebirds to feed. A fascinating complex of salt, brackish and freshwater marsh exists within a series of old and new storm beaches at ABERTHAW and there are fine ungrazed marshes around the Taff–Ely Basin.

Gower is a Glamorgan in miniature, having all these habitats from coalfield to saltmarsh. It is famous for its limestone cliffs backing sandy bays and pockets of sand dunes. Southerners like yellow whitlow-grass and spiked speedwell, clary and golden samphire, hoary rock-rose and spring cinquefoil find sanctuary on south-facing rocks. Old red sandstone pops up as moorland ridges, and the sandy saltings of the Burry Inlet are favoured by Brent geese and summering eider, well south of their breeding latitutes. There are also thousands of oystercatcher to be found feeding on the cockles of Penclawdd.

Gower nurtures rare fen orchid and dune gentian, strand beetle and money spiders and an awe-inspiring number of marine creatures. Kittiwake, fulmar, guillemot and razorbill breed and puffin have recently returned to a traditional site. The future for the conservation of this part of Glamorgan at least, now enjoying considerable official protection, is optimistic.

MARY E. GILLHAM

Aberdare Canal

SO 013024; 3ha; Cynon Valley BC reserve
Disused canal and woodland
Spring, summer

Part of the canal has been cleared to provide an open pool with a good stand of bulrush. Moorhen and heron may be seen at the pool while the rest of the reserve, grown over with large willow trees, provides a good habitat for warblers and other songbirds.

Abergelli Wood

SN 655015; 1.1ha; GWT reserve
Woodland with small pool
Spring, summer

Rowan, alder, alder buckthorn and downy birch grow above plants such as bluebell, opposite-leaved golden-saxifrage, yellow pimpernel and marsh violet. Buzzard nest in the woodland and heron visit the pools. There is a badger sett to be found here.

Aberthaw Shore

ST 043659; 36.3ha; GWT reserve
Foreshore, saltmarsh and limestone cliffs
Spring, summer, autumn

The seaward edge of the reserve is bounded by a pebble storm beach where yellow horned-poppy and sea radish flower. In the lee of the storm beach is an extensive saltmarsh, with plant life dominated by sea-purslane, sea aster and rock sea-lavender, and which supports several rare invertebrate species.

Relict sand dunes at the eastern end of the marsh are decorated with sea-holly. Patches of the rare purple gromwell and maidenhair fern are present on the tall scrubby cliffs, where crevices and ledges provide nest sites for raven and shelter for a large population of adder. In addition, a good variety of seabirds can be observed along the shoreline.

Afan Argoed Country Park

SS 821951; 56ha; West Glamorgan CC
Afforested steep valley
Leaflet from countryside centre or WGCC
All year

The fir forest rises above the twisting Afon Afan, a typical valley river. The area was once mined for coal but the tips are now grassed. Pockets of natural woodland occur among the conifers – oak, birch, ash and rowan, with alder and grey willow in the wetter places. Ivy-leaved bellflower and mountain fern may occur and the old tips have developed an interesting plant life. Woodland and waterside birds are amongst the wildlife to be seen in the park.

Berry Wood

SS 436858; 6.8ha; GWT reserve
Coastal oak woodland
Spring, summer

Although chiefly an oak woodland, there is a good mixture of other trees, including crab apple and aspen. As in many coastal woods the trees are pruned by salt-laden sea breezes. Lichens, mosses and ferns flourish in this unpolluted environment. Narrow buckler-fern grows here, as does wood millet. There is a good range of birds, from the tiny goldcrest to the broad-winged wheeling buzzard.

Bishop's Wood

SS 594878; 19.2ha; Swansea City Council
Dry limestone valley
Leaflet from SCC
Spring, summer

Above Caswell Bay, the reserve includes habitats ranging from cliff top, through slopes wooded with ash, oak, beech and sycamore, to open grassland in the valley bottom. A good variety of birds and mammals breed within the reserve.

Blaenrhondda Waterfalls Walk

SN 922021; 4km; Mid Glamorgan CC-FC
Moorland walk
Leaflet from MGCC
Spring, summer

A walk in the uplands at the head of the Rhondda Valley, it contains characteristic moorland vegetation such as heather, bilberry and tormentil, and birds such as buzzard, raven and wheatear. Grey wagtail and dipper may be seen at the streams below the waterfalls.

Bolgoed Quarry

SN 603027; 0.8ha; GWT reserve
Woodland and sandstone quarry
Spring, summer

Ash, birch and oak make up the mixed deciduous woodland which stands in an old sandstone quarry. The remainder of the area is dominated by dense gorse scrub.

Broad Pool

SS 510910; 11ha; GWT reserve
Freshwater pool and bog
Spring, summer, autumn

The pool contains white and fringed water-lily, the latter rare in west Wales. The bog is rich with bog asphodel and cross-leaved heath – a level mosaic of colour which lies in a shallow basin rising to dry heath on the slopes around.

Bunkers Hill

SS 428881; 0.4ha; GWT reserve
Scrub and grassland
Spring, summer

This tiny hillside reserve is an area of bracken-covered grassland with open scrub, the haunt of linnet and stonechat.

Bute Park Nature Trail

ST 182767; 3.5km; Cardiff City Council
Parkland nature trail beside River Taff
Booklet from Leisure and Amenities Dept, CCC
Spring, summer

The variety of both native and exotic broad-leaved and coniferous trees and the range of natural and planted flowers make this an attractive trail. Other habitats include riverside, a feeder stream, and the castle moat. The native plants include woodland species such as dog's mercury and toothwort and wetland species such as water-plantain and meadowsweet. The many birds are characteristic of these habitats.

Castle Wood Field

SS 472931; 0.3ha; GWT reserve
Saltmarsh
Spring, summer, autumn

This small area of saltmarsh within the extensive north Gower marshes supports typical plants of this habitat, such as thrift and sea plantain.

Cefn Onn Nature Trail

ST 184843; 2.5km; Cardiff City Council
Trail through limestone and sandstone woodlands
Booklet from Leisure and Amenities Dept, CCC
Spring, summer

The trail climbs out of the limestone ridges north of Cardiff to sandstone areas. Ash and birch, oak and hazel, oak and birch, beechwoods – all show their characteristics along the course of the trail.

Clyne Valley Country Park

SS 610915; 294ha; Swansea City Council
Wet valley floor and wooded hillside
Leaflet from SCC
All year

The Clyne River is quite out of proportion to its valley, which was enlarged during the Ice Age when the soft coal-measures were easily eroded. The valley was exploited for its coal and also for clay, which was used at the nearby brickworks. The pathway occupies the track of the LMS route into Swansea. The wet valley floor is noted for its show of marsh-marigolds beneath the predominantly alder woodland. The oak woods of the valley sides are partly invaded by rhododendrons and in places the three-cornered leek is found – both invaders from the private estates that formerly owned much of the area.

Coed Garn-Llwyd

ST 062715; 13ha; GWT reserve
Limestone woodland
Spring, summer

Mixed deciduous woodland with tufa springs on a hillside shelters lime-loving shrubs such as spindle and wayfaring-tree; herb-Paris, goldilocks buttercup and butterfly-orchid thrive in the base-rich soils.

Coed Gawdir

SN 783007; 0.1ha; GWT reserve
Small pool
Spring, summer

Sweet-grass, around the tiny artificial pool, forms an attractive habitat for small birds such as buntings and for waterbirds such as moorhen. There is a bird hide from which the pool may be observed.

At the head of the Rhondda Valley – Blaenrhondda Falls in winter.

Coed-y-Bedw

ST 117829; 16.6ha; GWT reserve
Rich valley woodland
Spring, early summer

In early spring, when the sunlight falls almost unfiltered to the valley floor, the dark trunks of the streamside alders stand out against the yellow of marsh-marigold. The main stream drains from west to east and the woodland grades with it from drier beech in the west to wet oak and birch woodland in the east. Alder, ash and hazel are found throughout. As these trees progressively leaf over, the shade within the wood deepens and the spring show of bluebell and ramsons becomes a variation of greens, broken by shrubs which can reach upwards for light – spindle, alder buckthorn and guelder-rose.

In autumn whole trees are cloaked with the fruit clusters of traveller's-joy. In the more acid area lousewort and heath bedstraw are found.

Among the trees there is a rich profusion of lichens, mosses and ferns and the spectacular great horsetail, which may grow as tall as a man. Where spoil from the old coal workings was tipped there are two grassy clearings. Here brimstone and speckled wood may be seen, two of the 17 butterfly species recorded.

The reserve is frequented by many birds, including green and great spotted woodpecker, grey wagtail, pied flycatcher and woodcock. Above the calcium-enriched stream Britain's largest lacewing, *Osmylus fulvicephalus,* may be seen.

Coed-y-Bwl

SS 909749; 2.4ha; GWT reserve
Elm woodland
Spring, early summer

Elm, over ash and field maple, stands above a spring show of lesser celandine, wild daffodil, wood anemone and bluebell. Woodland birds include great spotted and green woodpecker, nuthatch, tawny owl and sparrowhawk.

Common Wood

SS 508926; 16.4ha; WdT reserve
Mixed woodland
Spring, summer

Much of this ancient woodland was felled in the 1960s and replanted with conifers. However, a good number of woodland plants remain and some old oak and alder trees can still be found in the northern part of the reserve. Encouragement of the natural regeneration of ash, oak, birch, willow and hazel should restore the wood to its former state.

Cosmeston Lakes Country Park

ST 180693; 84ha; Vale of Glamorgan BC–South Glamorgan CC
Two large lakes, limestone grassland, woods, scrub
Leaflet from VGBC or SGCC
Spring, summer

A large 'natural' area, within the park, includes one of the lakes. There is a good range of limestone plants, including some spectacular orchids, and, with water, wood and grassland, there is a great variety of bird and insect life.

Craig Cilhendre

SN 719022; 16.1ha; GWT reserve
Escarpment woodland
Spring, summer

Lying on a coal-measure escarpment on the east side of the Swansea Valley, the woodland is mainly oak and birch with substantial stands of beech, and a hazel and holly understorey. There is alder on the lower, wetter parts. Birds are abundant with pied flycatcher, redstart, willow warbler and tree pipit.

Craig-y-Llyn

SN 905038; 16.2ha; GWT reserve
Corrie lake and crags
Spring, summer, autumn

Llyn Fach lies in the curve of the Craig-y-Llyn crags, a double horseshoe of sandstone cliffs above steep fans of scree which spill down as far as the lake. A Forestry Commission plantation fringes the lake on its northern and eastern sides and there is a boggy wetland where water flows in at the western end.

The lake and wetland contain many interesting plants, including spring quillwort, floating bur-reed and water lobelia, which grows here at its most southerly station in Britain.

The screes and higher slopes on the south of the lake vary in steepness and wetness and have a typical moorland cover of heather and bilberry with cross-leaved heath in wet areas; their chief interest, however, lies in the presence of some high-altitude and arctic–alpine species such as roseroot and lesser meadow-rue. Three unusual ferns are found here – parsley fern, Wilson's filmy-fern and a dwarf variety of male-fern. Fir clubmoss, not really a moss at all, may also be found.

The crags, cold, wet and exposed, offer little to the more delicate bird species; raven, nesting in February and March, followed by ring ouzel in May, are the main species of the rocks. Peregrine used to nest here, but plantations and coalmining have now destroyed much of their territory and they will probably never return. Buzzard, kestrel and sparrowhawk, however, hunt the reserve and short-eared owl has been seen.

Crymlyn Bog

No access; 234ha; various bodies
Large wetland
Can be overlooked from lanes around, e.g. at SS 700963
All year

A site of national conservation importance, this is the largest area of lowland fen in Wales. With a range from *Sphagnum* mosses through bulrush, common reed and great fen-sedge swamps, the bog contains many uncommon plants and provides a haven for bird life and a rich variety of insects.

Cwm Clydach

SN 682953; 49ha; RSPB reserve
Woodland and heathland
Keep to footpath along river
Spring, summer

In this area of mixed deciduous woodland along the banks of the River Clydach pied flycatcher, redstart and wood warblers nest. Buzzards and ravens can be seen overhead, while dipper and grey wagtail frequent the river. On the higher ground, wheatear and tree pipit occur among the heather and bracken. Badgers and foxes, and purple hairstreak and silver-washed fritillary butterflies are also found on the reserve.

Cwm Ivy Wood

SS 443938; 5.5ha; GWT reserve
Mixed wood and small quarry
Spring, summer

The mixed ash wood has a shrub layer which includes holly and dogwood and the quarry is thick with traveller's-joy. Spring flowers include primrose, cowslip and early-purple orchid, and in summer dog's mercury and hart's-tongue appear. Birds are plentiful; there is a badger sett.

Cwmllwyd Wood

SS 610946; 6.4ha; West Glamorgan CC reserve
Woodland, grassland and marsh
Leaflet from WGCC
Spring, summer

Cwmllwyd has mixed oak woodland and bracken-covered grassland above marshland, each habitat showing characteristic plants. A tiny bog contains

Deep shade ensures a stretch of open water on the Glamorgan Canal.

bog asphodel, heath spotted-orchid and cross-leaved heath. Typical woodland birds are present and snipe and woodcock visit in winter.

Cwm Risca

SS 881843; 1.6ha; GWT reserve
Woodland and pond
Spring, summer

The woods are chiefly oak, with ash, elm and some very fine small-leaved limes. The pond is bordered by marsh and wet grassland, fringed with willows and wetland flowers. Snipe visit the marsh and meadow and the willow scrub shelters tits and finches. Moorhen breed around the pool, adjacent to the Nature Centre.

Dare Valley Country Park

SN 962027; 320ha; Cynon Valley BC
Reclaimed mining valley
Leaflets from warden or CVBC
Spring, summer

The country park has been landscaped in a valley once mined for coal. Three nature trails in the upper reaches of the valley show examples of plants and animals typical of the coalfield.

Dunraven Park

SS 890729; 22.7ha; Glamorgan Heritage Coast
Project–Mid Glamorgan CC
Parkland and restored gardens
Leaflets from Heritage Centre
Spring, summer

The parkland has magnificent views and historic walled gardens interpreted according to various themes, including a plant-explorers' garden. Nearby are limestone cliffs and Dunraven beach.

Flat Holm

Permit only; 28.8ha; South Glamorgan CC reserve
Small island in Bristol Channel
Permit required for landing: from Project Manager, Flat Holm Project, Harbour Road, Barry
Leaflets from SGCC and Project Manager
Spring, summer

The island slopes from west to east, exposing much of the plateau to the prevailing off-sea winds. Dense clumps of nettles and thistles indicate the gull colonies' past domination, but the numbers of both lesser black-backed gull and herring gull have now declined. Because of the general lack of cover and the gull numbers, which are still high, other breeding species are few, although shelduck, oystercatcher and some smaller birds do nest. The island is one of the few British sites for wild leek.

Frog Lane

SS 447933; 0.45ha; GWT reserve
Hedgerow, scrub and meadow
Summer

The southern two-thirds is field and scrub bounded by hedges with oak and elm which has

succumbed to Dutch elm disease. The northern edge is alluvial and is periodically flooded. There are stands of yellow iris and marsh-mallow.

Gelli Hir Wood

SS 563925; 28.7ha; GWT reserve
Mixed lowland woodland
Spring, early summer

The open heathlands of East Gower were once covered with deciduous woodland like Gelli Hir but most were cleared for grazing. Much of the reserve is wet and acid, like the modern heaths, but is thick with oak and birch, with alder and willow by the pools and stream, and hawthorn and rowan in the drier places. Other parts of the wood are less acid and drier, and trees such as ash and wych elm with beech, hazel, sweet chestnut and small-leaved lime predominate.

The smaller pools along the main ride are bright with lesser spearwort but the chief wetland interest is the main pool, perfectly circled by trees, sheltered and undisturbed. Bulrush grows at the water's edge with water-plantain, wild angelica, blinks, branched bur-reed, greater tussock-sedge and purple-loosestrife.

Mallard and teal nest here while, deeper in the wood, sparrowhawk, tawny owl and buzzard may breed. Of the many different moths and butterflies there are several which are uncommon in the area. These include comma, silver-washed fritillary and holly blue.

The Glais

SO 041105; 3.5ha; GWT reserve
Woodland, stream and limestone caves
Access by permit only
Spring, summer

The reserve follows the lower reaches of the Nant-y-glais stream and is on carboniferous limestone. The southern section is mixed deciduous woodland, the middle has a limestone cave system and the northern contains a collapsed cavern and further caves of geological interest.

Glamorgan Canal

ST 143803; 23ha; Cardiff City Council
Canal, old railway cutting, grassland, marsh and woodland
Permit only to marsh
Spring, summer

The canal and marsh contain plants such as arrowhead, yellow loosestrife, branched and unbranched bur-reed, cyperus sedge and purple-loosestrife. The alder carr and mixed woodland support many spring flowers. Birds include all three woodpeckers, kingfisher and redpoll.

Goitre Coed Fach

ST 092965; 4.3ha; WdT reserve
Deciduous woodland
Spring, summer

This attractive amenity woodland by the side of the River Taff is especially important in this built-up area of the county. It contains mainly oak and birch with scattered beech trees.

Graig Fawr

SS 795867; 52ha; WdT reserve
Mixed woodland
Spring, summer

The wood, which is adjacent to MARGAM COUNTRY PARK, consists of broadleaves and conifers. Part of the site is believed to be ancient woodland and there are various earthworks probably dating from the Iron Age.

Hambury Wood

SS 472929; 4.8ha; GWT reserve
Oak woodland
Spring, summer

A mixed, chiefly oak woodland with an understorey of coppiced hazel, Hambury Wood is a haven for a range of woodland birds including breeding buzzard. There is an active badger sett.

Ilston Quarry

SS 555905; 7.6ha; GWT reserve
Mixed woodland and pool
Spring, summer

The quarry is dominated by a steep limestone cliff, bare rock and scree slopes which are being colonised by plants. These, together with the plants of the woodland and pool, encourage many insect species and woodland insect-eating birds.

Kenfig Pool and Dunes

SS 802815; 810ha; Mid Glamorgan CC
Dune system and pool
Leaflets from MGCC or reserve centre
All year

A superb spread of plant-rich dunes and a clear reed-fringed pool contrast with the heavy industry of Port Talbot not far to the north. The primary colonisers of the dunes are typical species such as sea couch, sea rocket, sea sandwort and prickly saltwort, followed by marram, seaholly and sea spurge – then the lime-richness of the dunes encourages an enormous range of species. Over 500 flowering plants have been recorded: those of the dunes include restharrow, wild pansy, evening primrose and burnet rose with viper's-bugloss; kidney vetch and autumn lady's-tresses. In the damp slacks yellow rattle fringes roundleaved wintergreen and marsh-orchids sit among creeping willow. The pool is mainly fringed with a reedswamp of sea club-rush and common reed, with water horsetail and bulrush and with an area rich in plants such as yellow loosestrife, tubular water-dropwort and purple loosestrife. It lies among the older dunes which are now well grown with grasses, bramble and dewberry, tending to a scrub of hawthorn, birch and other trees.

Sedge and grasshopper warbler breed around the pool, where waterbirds may include mallard, tufted duck and great crested grebe, while winter brings goldeneye, pochard and teal, with Bewick's and whooper swan. Passage birds often visit the reserve and curlew, greenshank, redshank, sanderling and whimbrel may be seen. Kestrel and short-eared owl come here to hunt.

The pool and the dunes are rich in insects and other small animal life, with a good range of mammals including fox and hare.

Lavernock Point

ST 182680; 5.8ha; GWT reserve
Limestone grassland and scrub
Spring, summer, autumn

Lavernock is a coastal reserve with areas of dense hawthorn scrub on rich limestone grassland. The grassland contains adder's-tongue and several orchids, including lesser butterfly-orchid, green-winged and bee orchid. Greenfinch and linnet are typical of the small birds of the hawthorn scrub which, during migration times, may shelter less common species.

Llanrhidian Hill

SS 497922; 3.1ha; GWT reserve
Grassland, scrub and rock
Spring, summer

Two old quarry sites, together with elder, hawthorn and ash scrub and limestone grassland, provide a good habitat range rich in plant and insect life. Linnet and stonechat flick from shrub to shrub and kestrel hunt the steep slopes.

Llantwit Major Beach

SS 956675; 17.8ha; Glamorgan Heritage Coast Project–South Glamorgan CC
Coastal cliffs and rocky shore
Five leaflets from Glamorgan Heritage Coast Project
Spring, summer

Col-huw Beach, Llantwit Major, is the starting point for walks, which take in the vertical sea cliffs and wide rocky platform exposed at low tide. The varied flora incudes sea cabbage, wild carrot, rock sea-lavender and various algae on the rocky shore. Goldfinch, stonechat, yellowhammer and whitethroat may be seen on the cliffs and, on sunny days, there are many butterflies such as tortoiseshell, gate-keeper and common blue.

Margam Country Park

SS 813849; 240ha; West Glamorgan CC
Parkland and woodland
Permit only to Furzemill Heron Reserve
Leaflets from park or WGCC
All year

The park has several pools and some fine parkland trees. Several waymarked walks demonstrate the variation within the area. The ponds and streams have plants related to the acidity of the water, with water horsetail and shoreweed in the richest lake and water-plantain and marsh St John's-wort fringing the most acid. This is Furzemill Pond, established as a reserve to protect the heronry. Over 300 fallow deer graze within the parkland.

Melincourt Waterfall

SN 825017; 4.8ha; GWT reserve
Waterfall, river gorge and oak woodland
Spring, summer

This spectacular waterfall on a tributary of the Neath River was painted by Turner in 1794. The reserve includes some five hectares of upland oak–birch woodland which ascends steeply from the Melincourt Brook. The birdlife is typical of the habitat with species such as redstart, wood warbler, pied flycatcher, dipper and grey wagtail.

Nightingale's Bush

ST 082898; 1.1ha; GWT reserve
Disused canal
Spring, summer

Some 200m of the canal have been excavated, giving an area of slow-moving open water, rich in wetland plants. On one bank is a towpath, on the other a scrub of grey willow, osier, alder, sycamore and guelder-rose, harbouring a variety of woodland birds. Kingfisher visit the canal.

Ogmore Down

SS 897762; 26.5ha; GWT reserve
Limestone grassland and heath
Spring, early summer

Sandwiched between quarries, Ogmore Down is a reminder of the rich vegetation which once must have clothed the area. Where there are pockets of deeper soil on the hillside, the plants are often typical of lime-poor areas because much of the goodness of the limestone has been washed downwards; where the soil is shallow there is a rich mix of lime-loving plants because grazing

Purple gromwell, a rare plant of lime-rich woods.

pressures hold back the grasses and the soil is too thin for lime-haters such as gorse and heather.

On the hilltop is one of the fascinations of limestone heath: acid-lovers such as gorse, heather and bell heather grow alongside limestone plants in a dense and colourful confusion. The soil is rich enough for common rock-rose, but acid enough for cross-leaved heath and tormentil.

On the thin soil of the steep grassland, lady's bedstraw, eyebright, wild thyme, small scabious, salad burnet, harebell and autumn lady's-tresses flourish, together with a rare subspecies of hairy violet, a diploid population of horseshoe vetch and mountain everlasting, a northern heath and mountain species.

This generally dry mosaic of open grassland, tussocky heath and gorse scrub is an ideal nesting area for many typical heathland birds. One of the more unusual insects is glow-worm, a nationally decreasing species. The larvae are very active predators, feeding mainly on snails, which are most plentiful in chalk and limestone grassland. The decrease of these beetles is due, in part, to the destruction of such grassland.

Oxwich

SS 501865; 258ha; NCC reserve
Dunes, saltmarsh and freshwater marsh between wooded limestone headlands
Permit required except on dunes and on footpaths through woodlands
Booklets from NCC information centre in car park
Spring, summer, autumn

Two nature trails give the flavour of the reserve. The sand dune trail begins with the first land plants of the sandy beach. These, such as sea-holly and prickly saltwort, trap some of the blown sand to form foredunes. Marram continues the consolidation and then dewberry and sea bind-weed form a lattice of runners through which ragwort and common evening-primrose grow. The sand here is rich in calcium and in the damp hollows between the dunes lime-loving plants such as yellow-wort, common centaury and dune gentian grow among creeping willow and downy birch. In June both early and southern marsh-orchid and marsh helleborine may flower.

Behind the seaward dunes bracken and wood sage grow where rain has washed most of the calcium out of the top layers of the soil. Wild privet and carline thistle, two characteristic lime-loving species, are plentiful. At the back of the dunes clovers and grasses form a more meadow-like sward and damp places are filled with meadowsweet and rushes.

The main woodland is of high-forest oak and ash with an understorey of hazel and holly. In spring there are bluebell, ramsons, wood anemone, common dog-violet and lesser celandine. Dog's mercury, enchanter's-nightshade and many ferns follow later in the year. The drier slopes have bracken and scrub of blackthorn, hawthorn and gorse, perfect cover for heathland birds and for badger, fox and weasel. Adder, slow-worm and grass snake may occur. From the clifftop grassland, oystercatcher and redshank may be seen.

Mewslade Bay shows some of the splendid sea cliffs that distinguish the South Gower Coast.

The areas open only to permit holders are extensive freshwater marshes with fen, carr and open pools, and Crawley Wood, another limestone wood, with an interesting flora including the rare whitebeam *Sorbus rupicola*.

Pant-y-Sais

SS 713939; 17.8ha; Neath BC
Narrow strip of rich fen
Spring, summer, autumn

Tall stands of common reed, a belt of fenland unexpectedly surviving between the Skewen road and the Tennant Canal, crossed by a railway line, close to huge oil refineries, Pant-y-Sais is a rare and exciting treasure. Among the reeds are rosebay willowherb, greater bird's-foot-trefoil, bulrush and royal fern. In the canal, white water-lily lifts above the water. A towpath separates the fen from the canal and has its own contrasting plants, such as common toadflax and the more unusual pale toadflax. Heather and gorse make a rather unexpected show here. Creeping willow, too, grows on the towpath. Alders line the east side of the canal and there is a scattering of birch and hawthorn in the fen itself. These obviously grow in the drier parts, a supposition reinforced by areas of bracken around some of them – bracken does not like wet conditions. Yellow iris and fleabane show where conditions are wet and skullcap, hemp-agrimony and marsh cinque-foil may be seen at the canal edge.

Peel Wood

SS 607883; 1.2ha; GWT reserve
Wooded old quarry
Spring, summer

Sycamore and elm, with oak and ash, form the main tree cover over a shrub layer which includes rhododendron and snowberry. The quarry is rich in ferns, including hart's-tongue and soft shield-fern, and there is a good range of woodland birds including breeding tawny owl.

Penmoelallt Forest

SS 995093; 7ha; NCC–FC reserve
Mixed woodland
Leaflet from NCC
Spring, summer

The tree cover varies from ash, with wych elm and rowan, on the limestone screes to oak with ash, elm, rowan and silver birch where the soil is deeper. Small-leaved lime and hazel are also present and there are many spring flowers. This diversity means a good range of woodland birds, but the chief interest is the rare whitebeams, one of which is known only in this valley.

Porthkerry Country Park

ST 092672; 91ha; Vale of Glamorgan BC
Woodland, grassland, cliff and shingle
Booklet from car park
Spring, summer

Only Cliff Wood, the coastal woodland, is actually scheduled as a reserve, but the whole park is a rich mix of varied habitats which encourages a good range of mammals and common birds.

The long curve of the shingle beach which closes the mouth of the valley has typical plants such as sea beet, bulbous foxtail and yarrow. Above the beach is a spectacular limestone cliff on which the rare maidenhair fern grows.

The cliff is topped by a typical limestone woodland, Cliff Wood, which protects another rare plant, purple gromwell, a trailing, creeping plant with dark blue-purple flowers which show in early summer. The trees are chiefly oak and ash and have been managed in a coppice-with-standards system which, with the hawthorn, hazel, field maple and yew that also grow in the wood, has resulted in a very varied structure.

Beneath the tall standards the coppiced trees form an interlaced canopy over the smaller plants. This obviously poses problems for plants which depend on light, and most of them flower in spring when the shade is less dense. Some, such as wild madder on the sea edge of the wood, and traveller's-joy, can climb to reach the light.

Prior's Wood and Meadow

SS 577938; 17.4ha; GWT reserve
Wood and wet meadow
Spring, summer

A lowland wood on the eastern Gower coal measures and an important landscape feature on the neck which divides the Gower peninsula from suburban Swansea. It is mainly oak and birch, with planted beech and some sweet chestnut. Part of the wood was felled and is regenerating. Alder and willow grow in the southern wetter patches. The southern of the two unimproved meadows has a wide variety of plants including yellow iris, ragged-Robin and several species of orchid.

Pwll Waun Cynon

ST 034997; 7.2ha; GWT reserve
Pool and river meadow
Summer

The meadow, which is regularly flooded, supports yellow iris, bulrush, water horsetail, greater burnet and meadowsweet, while the pool contains fat duckweed. There is also a small alder copse. Kingfisher, heron, moorhen and yellow wagtail are seen on the reserve.

Redley Cliff

SS 589875; 3.6ha; GWT reserve
Coastal grassland and scrub
Spring, summer

The north-facing slope is covered with scrub woodland – ash, hazel, hawthorn and blackthorn – with a dense ground cover of dog's mercury and ramsons. The south-facing slope is a more open coastal heathland. From the headland, seabirds such as oystercatcher may be seen.

Ridgewood Park

SS 611906; 0.3ha; GWT reserve
Grassland, scrub and immature woodland
Summer

It is hoped that this small building plot will provide an undisturbed habitat for wildlife, particularly birds, in a highly populated urban area. Trees have already been planted by the Trust.

Rudry Common Walk

ST 183865; 3.2km; Mid Glamorgan CC
Moorland and valley walk
Spring, early summer

A climb to the peak of Mynydd Rudry near Caerphilly which includes dry heathland with damp valleyland and small areas of *Sphagnum* bog. Typical grassland birds such as skylark and meadow pipit may be seen, with woodland birds in the lower scrub and in the nearby oakwood.

South Gower Coast

See map; 30km; GWT–NCC–NT
Foreshore, cliffs, dunes and marshes
Leaflets from NCC
Spring, summer

The Gower Peninsula is rich in natural beauty and the south coast, in particular, is fascinating.

Hard, pale carboniferous limestone has been tilted, folded and faulted, planed off to form a coastal plateau and eroded into bays and coves, faced with sand or carved into pinnacles and caves. The cliffs are dramatic and beautiful, varied with sweeps of grassland, scrub and woodland, giving way to a bay of duneland and marsh where the sea has found a fold of softer rock. The mild climate and lack of pollution, with lime-rich rocks, encourage a wonderful range of wildlife.

The cliffs and shallow limestone grasslands contain coastal species such as thrift, spring squill, rock sea-lavender and rock and golden samphire, together with lime-loving common rock-rose, carline thistle and squinancywort. Horseshoe vetch, uncommon in Wales, occurs with other less common plants including bloody crane's-bill, wild cabbage, spring cinquefoil, hoary rock-rose and hutchinsia. Yellow whitlowgrass grows on this coast and nowhere else in Britain – its nearest European site is far inland in Belgium – while small restharrow and goldilocks aster are almost as restricted, occurring only in a few western coastal sites. These last two plants are of very special interest because they seem incapable of spreading. The sites where they do occur are often far-flung – BERRY HEAD (Devon) is one – but intermediate, apparently suitable areas have not been colonised; whereas most of our plants spread back across Britain at the end of the ice ages, these species seem unable to have done so. This suggests that the cliffs on which they grow may have escaped the worst of the ice and acted as reservoirs of plant life.

Contrasting with the hard rocks are the dunes and marshes of OXWICH. Soft shales, folded into the limestone, have been eroded to form a bay, then altered to a lagoon by a bay-head barrier of sand. The lagoon now forms an expanse of freshwater marsh and saltmarsh, while a low dune system has developed behind the beach. Drainage from the millstone grit flushes the freshwater marsh – open pools lie among spreads of common reed and rich mixed fen filled with plants such as bogbean and flowering-rush, both bulrush and lesser bulrush, with yellow iris, marsh lousewort, greater bird's-foot-trefoil, lesser twayblade, marsh arrowgrass and a fine variety of sedges. The fen gives way through an area rich in marsh-mallow to a saltmarsh, draining into the bay, overlooked by the dunes which cut off the old lagoon.

The dunes show a good example of progression from open sand, with marram, sand sedge, sea spurge and sea-holly, to fixed dunes with an excellent lichen flora, bracken-clad where the sands are leached, coloured with common centaury, restharrow and dewberry. The slacks, in particular, may be filled with colour – low straggles of creeping willow patterned with early and southern marsh-orchid or marsh helleborine; other plant species include fen, green-winged and pyramidal orchid, autumn lady's-tresses and autumn and dune gentian.

On either side the bay is fringed with woodland, and areas of scrub also occur, a feature of this coastline where fine examples of wind-pruning may be seen, together with splendid spreads of limestone heath. The heaths may be as spectacular as the short-turfed coastal grasslands, curving above the sheer limestone in a sweep of bell heather, western gorse and heath bedstraw, common rock-rose, wild thyme and salad burnet. Gorse and western gorse appear in the scrub, together with blackthorn, wild privet and juniper, while, in the woodlands, dogwood, hawthorn, hazel, guelder-rose, spindle, wild privet and blackthorn predominate. The woods themselves vary from alder carr by the marshland to high-forest ash and oak, occasionally with small-leaved lime and the rare whitebeam *Sorbus rupicola*. A thick ground cover of dog's mercury, enchanter's-nightshade, sanicle, woodruff and wood spurge may be plumed with hart's-tongue and broad buckler-fern or show ramsons and meadowsweet in damper places, while more open woods on thin rocky soils stand above lime-loving yellow-wort, bloody crane's-bill, common rock-rose and marjoram, with rustyback growing on outcrops.

Its south westerly position makes the Gower a staging post for migrant birds and the offshore waters shelter thousands of wintering common scoter. The marsh provides a breeding site for large colonies of reed and sedge warbler and has become a regular nesting site for bearded tit. Occasional visitors have included rarities such as little bittern and aquatic warbler. Worm's Head, a high tide island, holds the most westerly notable seabird colonies this side of the Bristol Channel, including numbers of guillemot, razorbill, fulmar, kittiwake, shag and cormorant.

Swansea Canal (Godre'rgraig to Ynysmeudw)

SN 743060; 1.2km; West Glamorgan CC reserve
Derelict canal with carr woodland
Spring, summer

The fast-flowing disused canal supports dipper, grey wagtail and kingfishers, as well as the dark winged damselfly. Great burnet, sneezewort and heath spotted orchid may be found.

Taf Fechan

SO 045097; 41ha; Merthyr BC–Merthyr Naturalists' Soc.–GWT
Steep river valley
Booklet from MBC
Spring, summer

The steep valley sides are wooded with oak, ash and sycamore, with areas of mature trees. Oak again, with Turkey oak, small-leaved lime, beech and bird cherry and an understorey of dogwood, field maple and guelder-rose, declares the lime-

stone richness of the upper reaches. The valley floor varies from wide grassy swards to wet alder swamps, while the open slopes of the wider valley are covered with great spreads of bracken.

This wide variation is due to changes in the underlying rock, from acid millstone grit to rich limestone, to changes in the dampness, from dry slope to torrential river, and to the effect of man. The limestone has been quarried leaving a grass-land thick with lime-loving species.

The greatest influence has been the river, either as ice or running water, cutting deep into the bedrock. Where the rocks are hard and wet there are rich clusters of liverworts, mosses and ferns; where the water shallows the yellow of monkey-flower recalls the earlier brilliance of marsh-marigold. At the river edges greater tussock-sedge, water avens, common and water figwort and hemlock water-dropwort grow.

The river is rich in animal life, busy with insects and their larvae, with snails and small shrimp-like gammarids. Brown trout lie up among the weeds or hang in a mid-water eddy. Dipper and kingfisher pillage the stream while pied and grey wagtail flick and bob at the water's edge, taking, at low level, insects similar to those that pied flycatcher and redstart capture in the air above. Other birds are typical of north and mid-Wales woodlands as well as raven, buzzard and sparrowhawk.

Wenallt Nature Trails

ST 153831; 1 and 1.6km; Cardiff City Council
Two trails in woodland and heath above Cardiff
Booklet from Leisure and Amenities Dept, CCC
Spring, summer

These trails show plants typical of the soils on which they grow. The open slopes are thick with bracken, gorse and broom. The woods are birch–oak, or plantations of beech or young conifers, with elder, hawthorn, rowan and holly in scrubland or as understorey to the trees, sheltering the many flowers on the woodland floor. The birds, too, are typical of the habitats through which the trails pass.

Whiteford

SS 438938; 800ha; NCC reserve
Sand dunes, saltmarsh and foreshore
Permit only off marked paths
Leaflet from information kiosk
All year

The dunes are separated from the saltmarsh by a well defined damp transition zone in which both dune and saltmarsh plants occur together with wetland plants. A bird hide overlooks the saltmarsh and the waters of Burry Inlet – the estuary of the Loughor (see PEMBREY COUNTRY PARK (Dyfed)) – which are renowned for winter waders and wildfowl. Oystercatcher frequently exceed 10,000, with almost as many dunlin and knot, and large numbers of golden plover, turnstone and redshank. Other waders include bar-tailed and black-tailed godwit and spotted redshank.

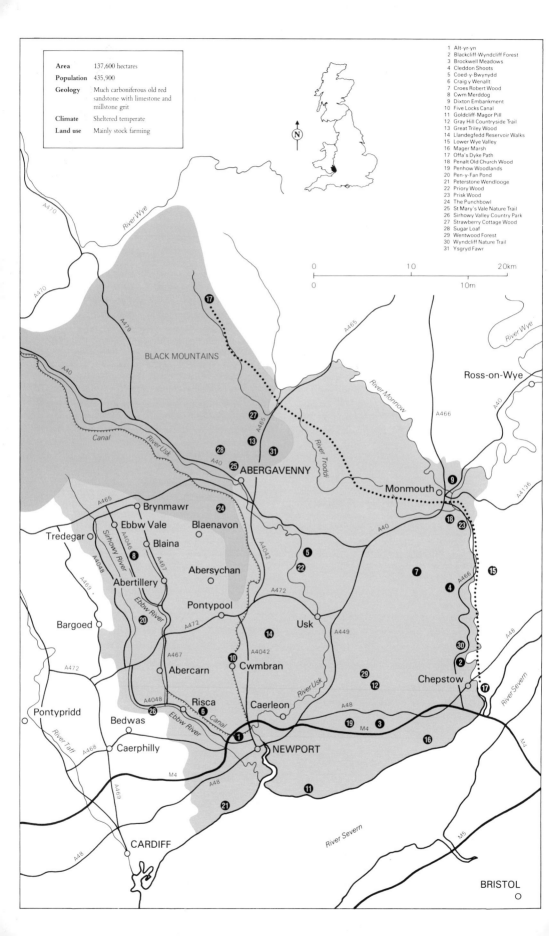

Area	137,600 hectares
Population	435,900
Geology	Much carboniferous old red sandstone with limestone and millstone grit
Climate	Sheltered temperate
Land use	Mainly stock farming

1 Alt-yr-yn
2 Blackcliff-Wyndcliff Forest
3 Brockwell Meadows
4 Cleddon Shoots
5 Coed-y-Bwynydd
6 Craig y Wenallt
7 Croes Robert Wood
8 Cwm Merddog
9 Dixton Embankment
10 Five Locks Canal
11 Goldcliff-Magor Pill
12 Gray Hill Countryside Trail
13 Great Triley Wood
14 Llandegfedd Reservoir Walks
15 Lower Wye Valley
16 Mager Marsh
17 Offa's Dyke Path
18 Penalt Old Church Wood
19 Penhow Woodlands
20 Pen-y-Fan Pond
21 Peterstone Wendlooge
22 Priory Wood
23 Prisk Wood
24 The Punchbowl
25 St Mary's Vale Nature Trail
26 Sirhowy Valley Country Park
27 Strawberry Cottage Wood
28 Sugar Loaf
29 Wentwood Forest
30 Wyndcliff Nature Trail
31 Ysgryd Fawr

N

0   10   20km

0   10m

BLACK MOUNTAINS

Ross-on-Wye

ABERGAVENNY

Monmouth

Brynmawr

Ebbw Vale   Blaenavon

Tredegar   Blaina

Abersychan

Abertillery

Pontypool

Bargoed

Abercarn   Cwmbran

Usk

Chepstow

Pontypridd

Bedwas   Risca

Caerleon

Caerphilly

NEWPORT

CARDIFF

River Wye
River Usk
River Monnow
River Troddi
River Severn
River Taff
Ebbw River
Sirhowy River
Canal

BRISTOL

Gwent

The most southerly of the Welsh border counties, Gwent is probably still better known by its ancient name of Monmouthshire. A small county, it can nevertheless boast most habitats except the classic marine ones of dune, cliff and sandy beaches.

The northern third of Gwent is contiguous with mountainous Breconshire (now part of Powys) and contains much land over 330m, including the SUGAR LOAF and Skirrid Mountains, the Blorenge near Abergavenny and the Black Mountains, all within the BRECON BEACONS NATIONAL PARK (Powys). This area is rich in mountain wildlife and offers ample scope for walking, camping and pony trekking.

Between the mountains and the sea lies the agricultural heart of the county. This is largely a landscape of small farms and very little of the traditional patchwork pattern has been disturbed. There are a number of comparatively small deciduous woodlands and many more tiny ones. Although some corn and maize is grown, it is predominantly a stock-rearing district, beef, milk and lamb being the primary products. In the west, the farmland is bounded by the industrial valleys and former coalmining areas which once gave south Wales a bad name for dirt and dereliction; valleys run down to Newport at the mouth of the Usk where the river joins the Bristol Channel. Eastern Gwent is bordered by the Wye, one of the great salmon rivers of Britain, which carves a spectacular valley for itself, cutting down through the limestone between the FOREST OF DEAN (Gloucestershire) and the adjacent Tintern Forest in Gwent towards its confluence with the Severn at Chepstow.

A narrow strip of land, known locally as the Monmouthshire Moors, runs along the coast, defended against the ferocious tides of the Severn by a sea wall said to have been erected originally by the Romans. This area has a great reputation for grazing cattle, though at one time it supplied the vast quantities of hay needed for the horses working in the local industrial areas. On the other side of the wall lie the banks of silt and sand which, when exposed at low tide, form feeding grounds for countless waders and ducks which use the estuary as a refuelling station on their long migrations north and south.

Geologically the county consists of the eastern and western ridges of carboniferous limestone, those in the west overlying the coal measures which gave rise to the great mining industry of the nineteenth and early twentieth century. Some millstone grit is also present in the north west and forms a durable cap to the aptly named Sugar Loaf Mountain. Most of the rest of Gwent lies on the old red sandstone which gives a characteristically red colour to the soil, though not as red as in neighbouring Herefordshire. In the Llanthony Valley in the Black Mountains evidence of glaciation is very evident. In the coastal belt, for about a kilometre inland from the sea wall the reclaimed silt land lies on a deep layer of sedge peat, evidence of a former fenland type of habitat now only represented by the MAGOR marshland reserve. The climate is comparatively mild at least as far north as Usk, but in the mountainous areas of the north west the rainfall is about 1500mm annually, falling to about 1000mm in the central districts near Raglan and Usk.

The two main rivers, the Usk and the Wye, both rise in central Wales and are swift, clear and excellent for salmon and trout, being almost unpolluted except at their mouths. The Monnow, which joins the Wye at Monmouth, is a little-known and delightful river running for much of its course along the Herefordshire border. There are a number of smaller rivers and streams; some of the ones in the west of the county, such as the Ebbw and Affon Llwyd, have been more or less restored to normality, after more than a century's gross industrial pollution. All the Gwent rivers are good for such species as dipper, kingfisher, grey wagtail and siskin, the last-named being common in the many alders that line the banks.

LLANDEGFEDD RESERVOIR, near Pontypool, carries large flocks of mallard, wigeon and coot in the winter, with smaller numbers of other species such as pochard, tufted duck and great crested grebe. Migrating terns are often recorded in late summer.

The mountains of the north and west support a typical plant life of moorland grasses with much bracken and patches of heather, bilberry and crowberry. The Blorenge and its neighbouring ranges still have a population of grouse, though much reduced from its heyday in the nineteenth century. Other birds to be seen are buzzard, wheatear, whinchat and ring ouzel as well as great numbers of meadow pipit and skylark. Raven, although nesting in many places in the county, are most commonly spotted in the mountains, giving voice to their ominous croak as they soar and dive in the wind.

A number of small mountain ponds support a remarkably large population of amphibians in the summer, including palmate newt in one or two places. A number of rare dragonflies and Lepidoptera have been recorded breeding in these districts too. Adder is the commonest reptile on the mountains and in the forestry rides, grass snake being mostly restricted to damper lowland habitats. Slow-worm and common lizard can also be found by those who know where to look for them.

In the east the principal habitat is that created by the Wye Valley, bounded by the great deciduous mass of the Forest of Dean and the lesser but still magnificent Tintern Forest. The whole area between Chepstow and Monmouth is a paradise for the botanist and lepidopterist and many species of rare plants, ferns, moths and butterflies can be discovered by the enthusiast. With the noble ruins of Tintern Abbey at its heart, the beauty of the Wye Valley, especially in the autumn, is internationally famous, and even in the spring and summer, with different but subtler shades lighting the woodland, the region is full of interest.

The coast of Gwent is probably of no great attraction except to the ornithologist, the walker or the wildfowler. To others the great estuary of the Severn seems bleak and grey most of the time and is rarely very warm even in the summer; but there is a good path along the top of the sea wall and one can walk for hours and meet only the occasional farmer or birdwatcher. The ever-changing colours of the rushing water, sometimes lapping the sea wall but more often far away beyond the silt banks, together with the constantly shifting flocks of gulls and waders and the reflected patterns of the clouds, create a unique atmosphere, heightened by the constant music of curlew, dunlin, redshank, oystercatcher and lapwing and the strange discordant notes of shelduck as they continually search for food.

P.N. HUMPHREYS

Allt-yr-yn

ST 295888; 15ha; Newport BC–GWT reserve
Woodland, grassland and wetland
All year

Semi-natural woodland, old pasture, a canal and ponds, and a quarry with remnants of heathland create a rich oasis for wildlife close to Newport.

Blackcliff–Wyndcliff Forest

ST 533985 and ST 525972; 81ha; FC reserve
Mixed woodland
Spring, early summer

Part of the reserve, a mix of high-forest and old coppiced woodland on steep limestone slopes, may be seen from the WYNDCLIFF NATURE TRAIL.

Brockwells Meadows

ST 471896; 4.6ha; GWT reserve
Limestone hay meadows
Permit from GWT otherwise 3 public open days per year
Spring, summer

In spring the limestone flora is at its best, with green-winged orchids being the main attraction. Midsummer is the best time to see insects on the reserve, the highlight being the nationally rare great robber fly, while in late summer there is a fine display of autumn lady's-tresses.

Burness Castle Quarry

Permit only; 2ha; GWT reserve
Disused limestone quarry, grassland and woodland
Spring, summer

This shallow disused limestone quarry is an interesting mixture of grassland and secondary woodland. Many of the species present are scarce in Gwent, including star-of-Bethlehem and viper's-bugloss. There is also a good selection of mosses.

Caldicot Bee Orchid Site

Permit only; 1.5ha; GWT reserve
Limestone grassland
Spring, summer

The sites lie above the Severn tunnel between a rapidly expanding housing estate and the main South Wales railway line. There is a typical limestone flora, including bee orchid, kidney vetch and yellow-wort. It is also a good area for butterflies and the locally distributed marbled white can be seen.

Cleddon Bog

Permit only; 15ha; GCC reserve
Lowland wet heath
Spring, summer

The finest small basin mire in Gwent, the bog is a spread of purple moor-grass sheltering typical wet heath species. An area of willow carr and an open scrub of birch and conifers add further interest.

Cleddon Shoots

SO 520040; 8ha; GWT reserve
Steep mixed woodland with streams
Spring, summer

Cleddon Brook keeps the air damp and suitable for ferns and mosses. Wild cherry, oak and beech with holly and yew, show the richness of the underlying rock but throw a dense shade with little light for late-flowering plants, although providing nest sites for birds.

Coed-y-Bwynydd

SO 365068; 10ha; NT
Mixed woodland
Spring, summer

Bracken and rosebay willowherb give way to
grassland under magnificent oak and beech trees
at the top of this wooded hill. Ash and beech
grow on the slopes where ivy-covered oaks make
ideal nest sites for small birds. Holly and yew
occur occasionally in the understorey together
with field maple, hazel and elder.

Craig y Wenallt

ST 260908; 7.2ha; WdT reserve
Deciduous woodland
Spring, summer

Some fine mature beech trees enhance this prominent woodland on the side of the Ebbw Valley.
Bluebells grow in abundance under birch and oak,
and there are also areas of scrub and young
woodland.

Croes Robert Wood

SO 480060; 14ha; GWT reserve
Coppiced deciduous woodland
Spring, summer

The dominant trees on this steep hillside woodland are ash and wych elm, and there is a wide
variety of birdlife.

Cwm Clydach

Permit only; 23.3ha; NCC reserve
Very steep valley and beech wood
Spring, summer

Beech, here at its western limit, shows a dense
shade under which few plants can thrive, but the
limestone of much of the reserve encourages a
rich ground cover where there are gaps in the
canopy, and in other open areas. Slender, delicate
grasses and the rare soft-leaved sedge grow in the
valley, together with early and common dog-
violet, wild thyme and the rarer large thyme. Oak,
wych elm, downy birch, holly, with yew and an
uncommon whitebeam, *Sorbus porrigentiformis*,
break the monopoly of the beech with which
yellow bird's-nest and bird's-nest orchid grow.
Another section of the wood is more acid in
character, with hard fern, scaly male-fern and wiry
clumps of bilberry. There is a good variety of
woodland birds and both grey wagtail and dipper
breed by the river. Common blue and small copper
are among the butterflies recorded.

Cwm Coed-y-Cerrig

Permit only; 4.5ha; BBNPC
Wet alder woodland and marsh
Spring, summer

A narrow alder swamp where early marsh-orchid
is followed by yellow loosestrife and alternate-
leaved golden-saxifrage. Plentiful insects attract a
good range of woodland birds.

Cwm Merddog

SO 185065; 20ha; GWT reserve
Ancient woodland and wet flushes
Spring, summer

The reserve is a mixture of old beech woodland,
wet flushes with alder and willow, regenerating
spoil-tips and moorland. It is a good site for ferns
and orchids, and the common land above the
reserve is one of the most attractive heather moors
in Gwent.

Dixton Embankment

SO 524147; 2ha; GWT reserve
Limestone grassland
Spring, summer

The reserve lies between the A40 and the River
Wye, and is very similar to the CALDICOT BEE
ORCHID SITE, with a good range of lime-loving
plants, including bee orchids.

Five Locks Canal

ST 287968–292978; 1km; GWT reserve
Disused canal
Spring, summer

Slow-moving waters are uncommon in Gwent and
the canal provides an opportunity to see plants
and animals otherwise scarce in the county.

Around 120 plants have been recorded from the
water and the banks, and the reserve provides a
breeding site for newts, frog and common toad.
In the canal are water plants such as rigid
hornwort, whorled water-milfoil and several species of duckweed, pondweed and water-starwort.
Attractive plants such as arrowhead, yellow water-
lily and water-plantain lift above the surface or
float on the water while the margin and banks
may be filled with colourful plants. Monkeyflower,
a bright yellow alien which has spread through
many of our waterways, complements yellow
iris, contrasting with marsh woundwort and
gipsywort. Reed canary-grass and branched bur-
reed provide cover for breeding moorhen.

The nearby alders provide a winter feeding
ground for redpoll, siskin and twite and, in
summer, their overhanging branches are often
used as perches by kingfisher. Good numbers of
dragonflies and damselflies may be seen, with a
range of water beetles, leeches and water snails
which could not survive the surge of a rapid
stream.

The reserve is managed mainly as an educational
site but also includes an attractive walk by the
old Monmouthshire–Brecon Canal.

Goldcliff–Magor Pill

ST 375820–ST 438848; 7km; GWT reserve
Estuarine foreshore
No access off rights of way
Spring, autumn

The GWT has acquired the shooting rights over
the estuary foreshore, thus protecting an area of
tidal flats important for many waders and migrant
birds which use the River Severn as a flight path.

Gray Hill Countryside Trail

ST 429936; 5km; GCC
Moorland and woodland trail
Leaflet from GCC
Spring, early summer

From Gray Hill, above Wentwood Reservoir, the trail circles through WENTWOOD FOREST. A fine range of moorland and forest habitats may be seen from this path.

Great Triley Wood

SO 310182; 6.4ha; WdT
Deciduous woodland
Spring, summer

Lying on the marsh banks of the River Gavanny, the wood contains many fine oak and ash trees, while in the wetter areas there are large alders and willows. The ground flora is rich and varied, including herb-Paris.

Henllys Bog

Permit only; 0.6ha; GWT reserve
Damp grassland
Spring, summer

The good diversity of plants can be found here which includes some which are rare or uncommon in the county.

Lady Park Wood

Permit only; 46ha; NCC reserve
Mixed woodland
Spring, early summer

An exceptionally rich mixed woodland, the reserve contains several rare tree species and, although in the past it was considerably modified by felling, it is to be left unmanaged so that natural return to the wildwood can be studied.

Llandegfedd Reservoir Walks

ST 329985–323978; 6.5–10km; GCC
Varied walks
Leaflet from GCC
All year

The walks circle in the hills, woods and steep valley around Llandegfedd Reservoir, itself of ornithological interest. Winter wildfowl include mallard, wigeon and coot, with great crested grebe, pochard and tufted duck. At migration times more unusual birds, including terns, may be seen.

Llwyn-y-Celyn Bog

Permit only; 0.4ha; GWT reserve
Lowland bog
Spring, summer

This very fine small marsh holds a great number of species, including water avens, bogbean, marsh lousewort, marsh-mallow, monk's-hood and lesser skullcap among a wealth of colourful wetland plants.

Lower Wye Valley

See map; 35km; various bodies
Spectacular river gorge
Spring, summer

Rising close to the source of the River Severn on the eastern slopes of Plynlimon, the River Wye cuts a more direct course to their confluence below Chepstow. This, one of the finest rivers in the country, has been scheduled as a Grade I site by the NCC: in its lower reaches it has cut a spectacular winding gorge which shelters one of the four most important woodland areas in Britain.

Compared with most of our major rivers, the lower reaches of the Wye have been little altered by man and the geological interest and range of wildlife is possibly unequalled in the country.

Within the gorges, below THE DOWARD GROUP (Hereford and Worcester) and from Wyesham to Chepstow, the river is now deep and slow-flowing, tidal in the lower sections where it gradually changes to estuarine conditions. It holds a gradation of freshwater to brackish and marine animals and provides the route by which the uncommon Allis shad migrates to spawn in higher waters. It also provides a site where a number of uncommon insects breed.

The Lower Wye Valley: the pinnacles of the Seven Sisters look across the Lady Park Wood.

The carboniferous limestone forms spectacular cliffs in the gorges and is largely responsible for the magnificent range of unusual plants. The sandstones, though, increase the habitat range by providing more acidic areas and the woodlands here hold over 60 species – most of our native trees and shrubs – in essentially natural groupings.

The woods have been modified by man but mainly by coppicing, a practice which does not destroy the natural communities, and, except where alien species have been planted, these steeply sloping woods are considered to be ancient woodland.

Oak–beech woods occur on the sandstones, with a characteristic acid-loving ground flora, but many of the sites contain a mix of soils – light or heavy loams depending on their origin, areas of glacial drift and dry stony limestone soils. A typical sloping woodland might contain a mix of ash, beech, wych elm, small-leaved lime and yew at the rather acid summit falling through ash, wych elm and hazel to riverside alder on the damp rich valley flood plain. Species such as wild cherry might occur throughout and the ground cover would vary with the richness. Some of the finest limestone woods contain several rare whitebeam species including Cheddar whitebeam,

Sorbus rupicola, Sorbus porrigentiformis and even the rare hybrid between common whitebeam and wild service-tree.

The ground cover of such woods is also extremely rich. Dog's mercury often forms a dense green carpet but is varied with yellow archangel, bluebell, ramsons and woodruff, with hart's-tongue and soft shield-fern, with herb-Paris and spurge-laurel. Clearings and woodland edges might show lime-loving species such as marjoram and ploughman's-spikenard while less common plants of the woodlands include yellow bird's-nest, wood crane's-bill, wood fescue, mountain melick, fingered sedge, thin-spiked wood-sedge and common wintergreen. The gorge, too, is a site for upright spurge, a small plant of clearings and open ground which occurs nowhere else in Britain.

This rich variety is underlined by the occurrence of almost half the British butterflies including common and holly blue, silver-washed fritillary and speckled wood.

Mammals are those expected of a large and varied woodland area and include yellow-necked mouse with greater horseshoe bat which roost in limestone caves by the riverside cliffs. Typical woodland birds are complemented by those of river and estuary sites, such as heron and cormorant, while the cliffs provide ideal nesting places for crag-loving birds such as jackdaw.

This is a truly spectacular area, from the deep ravine below LADY PARK WOOD to the dramatic curve of cliff at LANCAUT (Gloucestershire). Few views can be more impressive than that from the Eagle's Nest, on the WYNDCLIFF NATURE TRAIL, over 200m above a great curve of the river.

Magor Marsh

ST 424867; 24ha; GWT reserve
Relict fen
Spring, summer

The reserve contains a remnant of the once extensive Monmouthshire fens and is a mosaic of damp pasture fields, hay fields and ditches (or reens). The old fields are, in places, reverting to scrub and woodland, adding to the wide range of habitat. The whole area is extremely wet and is filled with a wonderful variety of fen and marshland wildlife.

Grazing is continued in some of the drier fields but even these are wet enough for plants such as ragged-Robin, for lesser and greater spearwort, marsh-marigold and meadowsweet. Ungrazed fields are waist-high stands of wild angelica, purple-loosestrife, great willowherb and yellow iris, laced with marsh bedstraw, scented with water mint and filled with a fine variety of sedges. Reed canary-grass and common reed grow in these damper meadows while wetter areas hold stands of reed sweet-grass.

Old willow pollards often stand by the reens and these ditches, paralleled by the rhynes of the Somerset Levels, contain some of the special plants of Magor. Arrowhead occurs, as at FIVE LOCKS CANAL but here too are flowering-rush and frogbit – all three rare in Wales. Mare's-tail, scarce in Gwent, grows in one of the pools and the poolside stands of bulrush provide excellent cover for birds.

A hide overlooks the main pool and provides opportunities for seeing some of the many birds of Magor. This is a site, near the flight path of the Severn, where many rarities have been recorded, where garganey have bred and where one of the most important Gwent colonies of reed warbler breed. Other breeding species include reed bunting, sedge and grasshopper warbler, mallard and water rail, yellow wagtail, redshank and snipe. The rich wetland encourages a good range of insects and small water-animals, including a number of nationally rare dragonflies.

Offa's Dyke Path

SO 267323–ST 553928; 70km; CC
Long-distance way
Booklet from HMSO bookshops
Spring, summer

The old defensive wall of the English against the Welsh, the path runs from Prestatyn (Clwyd) to Chepstow and passes through some of the most spectacular and richly interesting country in east Wales.

Penalt Old Church Wood

SO 525105; 4ha; GWT reserve
Valley woodland
Spring, early summer

The sloping oakwood lies on old red sandstone in the LOWER WYE VALLEY. A typical range of woodland birds including pied flycatcher, adds to the beautiful spring display of wild daffodil.

Penhow Woodlands

ST 418901; 24ha; NCC reserve
Woodland
Access to south-western part of reserve only
Spring, summer

These woods contain a large variety of tree species and support a wealth of characteristic woodland plants and insects.

Pen-y-Fan Pond

SO 197006; 13.5ha; GCC
Pond and heathland
Spring, summer

Although disturbed by rowing, model boat sailing and fishing, the park contains an interesting area of dry heath, with bracken, gorse and heather, which grades into acid bog beside the pool.

Peterstone Wentlooge

ST 278807; 4km; GWT reserve
Extensive mudflats and saltmarsh
All year

The mudflats and saltmarsh are probably the most important habitat types here, but the land behind the sea wall has been reclaimed and ditched and the influences here are more typical of farmland than of sea coast but there are a number of interesting plants including bristly oxtongue and spiny restharrow – both uncommon and usually found only near the coast in Wales.

Across the sea wall annual sea-blite edges areas of open mud on which glasswort grows. The grassland is thick with sea plantain and sea aster around the small salt pans and greater sea-spurrey grows in the rock jumble of the lower wall.

The land side of the sea wall is clumped with bramble and scrub and the dykes are often fenced with hawthorn hedges. In the dykes themselves are stands of common reed and bulrush, with branched bur-reed and water-plantain. The water is often covered with duckweed which shows the tracks of swimming moorhen or water vole.

The saltmarsh and mudflats are favourite sites for waders and wildfowl. On one day in 1977 a mixed flock of dunlin and knot was estimated at 11,000 strong. A number of duck uncommon in Gwent may occur here, including long-tailed duck, a winter visitor unusual anywhere in the west of England and Wales, with shoveler and common scoter. Other rarities in Wales, avocet, ruff, wood sandpiper and little stint, have been seen. In winter merlin, peregrine and short-eared owl may patrol the area. Redshank and yellow wagtail breed in summer, while autumn brings flocks of finches and other small birds, with swallows gathering before their long migration. Thousands of fieldfare and redwing feed on the hawthorn hedges in cold weather.

Priory Wood

SO 352057; 5ha; GWT reserve
Mixed woodland
Spring, early summer

This small wood has a tremendous variety of woodland types within it, including oak, birch, cherry and beech above the old quarry. The birdlife is particularly rich, with pied flycatchers being a recent addition to the breeding list.

Prisk Wood

SO 533087; 6ha; GWT reserve
Deciduous woodland
Spring, summer

Small streams, rocky gullies and disused quarries add diversity to this typical Wye Valley wood with wild cherry and small-leaved lime. Sparrowhawk, woodcock and woodpecker breed. Fallow deer and badgers frequent the reserve.

The Punchbowl

SO 284115; 38ha; WdT
Woodland and pond
Spring, summer

This bowl-like depression in Mount Blorenge is a most unusual feature set on the edge of the BRECON BEACONS NATIONAL PARK (Powys). Only part of the site is wooded and this consists of a fine mixture of mature beech and ash, many of which have been pollarded. A large pond adds considerably to the reserve's wildlife interest.

St Mary's Vale Nature Trail

SO 283162; 3.2km; BBNPC–NT
Steep-sided valley walk in foothills of Sugar Loaf
Booklet from BBNPC
Spring, summer

The trail rises through woodland – alder and ash beside the stream with beech, probably planted, on one side and native oakwood on the other. The oaks grade into open moorland as the valley side climbs towards the SUGAR LOAF, with stands of heather, bilberry and bracken.

Sirhowy Valley Country Park

ST 200908; 325ha; Gwent CC
Woodland, grassland and riverside
Spring, summer, autumn

The Country Park is based on a disused railway line with regenerating birch, oak and alder, and adjoining woodland and meadowland next to the River Sirhowy. Buzzards, herons and foxes frequent the area and bluebells carpet the woodland in spring. There is a visitor centre at the former Babell Chapel, Cwmfelin Fach.

Strawberry Cottage Wood

SO 314215; 6ha; GWT reserve
Steep oak woodland
Spring, summer

This hanging oak woodland with some birch clings to the side of a steep old red sandstone slope. Buzzard, wood warbler and great spotted and green woodpecker frequent the wood.

Sugar Loaf

SO 268168; 852ha; NT
Fine upland
Spring, summer

The Sugar Loaf is one of the last of the old red sandstone hills which make up the greater part of the Brecon Beacons. The summit, capped with millstone grit, is bare and open but grades down through bilberry and bracken to sheltered woodlands on the lower slopes where buzzard and kestrel breed.

Wentwood Forest

ST 436936; 1005ha; FC
Mixed woodland
Spring, early summer

Wentwood is mainly larch forest, set on a ridge of old red sandstone above the lower meanders of the River Usk. Its southern slopes have been cut into valleys by the streams which fed the Monmouthshire fens – of which nearby MAGOR is a relic – while unwooded hills close to the forest are heather–bracken moors. Trails and bridleways provide ample scope for exploring the woodland and include the GRAY HILL COUNTRYSIDE TRAIL.

Its large size and the mosaic of conifers at various stages of growth, with blocks of broad-leaved trees, wide rides and clearings, offer a range of habitat which varies from areas of acid bog, where ivy-leaved bellflower occurs, to richer sites on lime-rich cornstone conglomerate where ash stands over woodruff. Broad-leaved hellebor-ine may be found in the woodland, with adder's-tongue in remnants of old pasture, and spring may bring a magnificent display of wild daffodil.

The mature native trees provide holes and crevices for long-eared, noctule and whiskered bat and larger mammals include fallow deer, badger and fox. Both dormouse and harvest mouse have been recorded. The breeding birds are very varied and may range from shelduck on the reservoir to redstart and wood warbler in the native trees, nightjar in the clearings and occasional crossbill in the conifers. Other breeding species include raven, buzzard and sparrowhawk, tree pipit, grasshopper warbler and woodcock.

Pools provide breeding sites for all three British newts and for common toad and frog, while adder and common lizard are plentiful in the heathland. Heather attracts emperor moth, and other insects include peach blossom, Chinese character and wood tiger moths, with many butterflies in the forest rides as well as eyed ladybird, a species associated with conifers.

Wyndcliff Nature Trail

ST 525973; 1km; FC
Woodland walk
Leaflet from Welsh Tourist Board, Tintern or GWT
Spring, early summer

The trail, in the BLACKCLIFF–WYNDCLIFF FOREST, includes the viewpoint of the Eagle's Nest with its spectacular outlook across the LOWER WYE VALLEY.

Ysgyryd Fawr

SO 330180; 83ha; NT
Steep knoll, grassland and woods
Spring, summer, autumn

Ysgyryd Fawr, rendered into English as Skirrid Fawr, is a sudden shoulder of hill, rising from the farmland around, looking westward to the better-known SUGAR LOAF and inland, across the Vale of Usk, to the MALVERN HILLS (Hereford and Worcester). An outlier of the old red sandstone Black Mountains, the hill is flanked by woodlands to the west and south and has areas of open scrub around its lower slopes. There are high stands of bracken with gorse and foxglove and the scrub is chiefly hawthorn with a mixture of ash, birch, crab apple, elder and oak. The bracken opens where flushes and wet areas drain through the scrub and sheep-grazing keeps the turf short.

Above the scrub the hill rises steeply to reach the summit at 486m. Here there are extensive spreads of bilberry and rough grassland which run on the western side to the vertical crags of a rocky scarp. Below the crags long slopes of tumbled scree are broken by grassy plateaus and massive rock outcrops with harebell, wild thyme and bilberry. Mosses and lichens cover the long-fallen rocks and among the screes herb-Robert and hart's-tongue can be found.

The woodlands grade from open scrub to more mature woods with attractive ash woodland in the damper, richer areas. Here there is a profusion of ferns with raspberry and in spring wood-sorrel and common dog-violet. The hill is long-backed, running from south to north, and scrub and woodland climb high up the sheltered southern slopes. This is a superb site for hill woodland birds such as redstart and the open scrub is a perfect hunting ground for both kestrel and sparrowhawk. Buzzard circle above the area.

Sheep grazing here is not over-hard and there is a good balance between close-grazed areas, the sweeter grasses around the streams and wet places, and the rough grassland on the slopes and summit. The habitat varies from open scrub, suitable for linnet and stonechat, rabbit and fox, to thicker woodland where bank vole and wood mouse may be prey to stoat, weasel or tawny owl.

Sugar Loaf and Ysgyryd Fawr, backed by the Black Mountains.

Gwynedd

Nature has bestowed a magnificent mantle on Gwynedd – from its mountainous shoulders down to the vast and superbly varied coastline. The region's bold and breathtaking contrasts are mirrored by an abundance of nature reserves and conservation sites. Anglesey, Caernarvonshire and Merioneth have been administratively recombined to form Gwynedd, once the county of Welsh princes and now the stronghold of Welsh culture.

Half the county lies in the SNOWDONIA NATIONAL PARK, a land of hill farms that enjoys the true alpine scenery of Snowdonia and its neighbours. The coastal plateaus of Anglesey and the Lleyn Peninsula display a mosaic of ever more productive grassland mixed farms. Most of the few towns are strung along the coast. Upland climate, poorly developed soils and marshes have prevented man from greatly changing the vegetation of many parts of the county; in this lies much of its outstanding interest for nature conservation.

Gwynedd's diverse habitats owe much to its complex rock formations and the scouring of ice and water. This complexity, unusual even in Britain, ranges from some of the oldest to some of the youngest rocks; many of them are acid, with mineral-deficient soils. Other, more basic, soils are found on limestone, sand dunes and some of the volcanic rocks. Snowdonia's rugged land shows all the signs of the forces which squeezed and folded its rocks. Gwynant and Padarn are just two of the valley lakes bequeathed by ice age glaciers.

In contrast to Snowdonia the island of Anglesey is a succession of broad, flat-topped ridges and straight valleys, more or less parallel with the Menai Strait, itself deepened by moving and melted ice. Further south, on the Meirionnydd coast, are the broad triangular forelands, originally of shingle, of MORFA HARLECH and MORFA DYFFRYN.

Strong, warm, moist winds from the Irish Sea play their part in shaping the vegetation. Windy, sunny Anglesey is less often in cloud and rain than the mainland mountains where a varied landscape produces a range of local climates. The treeless natural vegetation on the thin soil of Snowdonia's harsh mountain slopes was mainly heather moor and grass fell. Deciduous forest covered the coastal lowlands and most valleys

below the tree line, with marshes and fens on the extensive areas of poor drainage.

An interesting arctic–alpine flora survives on the higher mountains, on YR WYDDFA (Snowdon) and CADER IDRIS, for example. Here fescue dominates, reindeer-moss is found, and the cliffs are the habitat for some plants found also on the coast – sea-plantain, thrift and creeping willow. Man's main impact on the mountain vegetation has been through sheep, which favour grass rather than heath on the rough grazings; the Rhinogydd, inland of the Meirionnydd Ardudwy coast, are an exception. Elsewhere on the cold, wet, southern uplands purple moor-grass and mat-grass abound. East of Blaenau Ffestiniog are hill peats, cotton-grass moors and flush bogs.

In Snowdonia, as elsewhere in Britain's uplands, there has been an ebb and flow of the upper limit of grassland management. Above the lowland winter grazing is a band of *ffriddoedd*. Rushes, heather and bracken have invaded parts of the less intensively managed hill farms. Overhead, kite, buzzard and kestrel hunt their prey.

Modified remnants of the once natural western oak woodlands can be found on many steep valley sides. Though mainly of sessile oak, a range of hybrids with pedunculate oak is common. Several woods are nature reserves notable for their abundant mosses and liverworts, and management of these woods for conservation, beauty and timber is gaining attention. Under-planted conifers have altered many of the woods in recent years.

Coniferous afforestation, not only of deciduous woodland, has rapidly been changing wildlife habitats. Most of Gwynedd's lowland woodland has long been replaced by a patchwork of grass and arable fields interlaced with other vegetation less easily used for farming. The decline in rabbit numbers has reduced the supply of small flowering herbs, food plants for butterfly larvae.

Anglesey's valleys abound in small lakes, sluggish rivers and marshes, but it is the non-acidic fens, rich in nutrients and with high, fluctuating water levels, which are most prized, with their characteristic background of saw-sedge and black bog-rush. Columbine is an impressive early summer sight on CORS ERDDREINIOG, while orchids and pale dog-violet have been encouraged on

CORS GOCH. One of the island's most attractive plants is the delicate blue marsh gentian, still found on some of the damp unimproved acid soils; another is spotted rock-rose, whose petals drop within hours of opening.

Over half the county's long boundary is coast, mostly very beautiful and much of outstanding conservation interest. From the Little Orme round to the southern DYFI (Dyfed), cliff-fronted headlands of infinitely subtle variety separate sand and shingle beaches, estuaries and saltings. The Lleyn cliffs, including BARDSEY Island, are some of the least disturbed and, along with those around Anglesey, support populations of breeding seabirds. Puffin Island, beyond Beaumaris, supports more of the tougher guillemots, with their 'anti-roll'-shaped eggs. This island also possesses one of the largest herring gull colonies in Britain. The oil-spitting fulmar too has been competing successfully for cliff-nesting sites. Holyhead Mountain's SOUTH STACK CLIFFS are the finest place in Gwynedd for watching seabirds.

On the low-lying southern sector of the island's coast is the large NEWBOROUGH WARREN–YNYS LLANDDWYN reserve, the finest of its kind in Wales; it includes the Cefni Estuary, loved by Charles Tunnicliffe, the wildlife artist. The county's intertidal and marine habitats are almost as diverse as the British coast; the coast of Anglesey is an especially valued scientific resource. Along the dune-edged arc of Tremadog Bay, planning and conservation interests are working to protect the coast from excessive tourist pressures. This is the kind of co-operation that is essential to safeguard our wildlife and its natural environment for future generations.

D.M. EAGAR

Abercorris

SH 749085; 1.1ha; NWWT reserve
Mixed woodland
Spring, early summer

Ash, birch, oak and sycamore form a steep riverside woodland where nesting birds include pied flycatcher, wood warbler and grey wagtail.

Bala Lake Foreshore

SH 918339; 1ha; NWWT reserve
Lake shore woodland
Spring, summer

Ash, sycamore, birch, hazel and holly make up this narrow strip of mature, unevenly aged woodland between the railway line and the shore of Lake Bala. A rich variety of woodland plants occurs, including primrose, wood anemone, pignut and wild strawberry. Nearer the water's edge wet woodland of alder and willow supports marsh-marigold, opposite-leaved golden-saxifrage and bugle. The many dead and dying trees are ideal for bryophytes and fungi.

Bardsey

Permit only; 175ha; Bardsey Island Trust
Inshore island
Permit from observatory bookings secretary, tel. Newton Abbot 68580
Spring, summer, autumn

The island is a landmark for migrant birds monitored by the observatory. Rabbits keep the coastal grassland short and the varied rocks encourage plants such as spring squill, sharp rush, Wilson's filmy-fern and lesser meadow-rue. There is a large population of Manx shearwater, with smaller numbers of kittiwake, guillemot, razorbill and shag. Grey seal are often plentiful.

Bryn Pydew

SH 818798; 5ha; NWWT reserve
Limestone pavement, quarries and grassland
Spring, summer

The reserve is rich in such lime-loving plants as common rock-rose, bloody crane's-bill, lily-of-the-valley and dark-red helleborine, together with juniper, common whitebeam and yew. Insects include dingy skipper and brown Argus butterflies with reddish light arches, heath rustic and cistus forester moths. Glow-worm may also be seen.

Bwlch Gwynt Observation Hide

SH 774601; FC
Waterside bird hide
Spring, summer

The hide overlooks a small reservoir, fringed with alder, birch and grey willow. Mallard, teal, moorhen and little grebe breed and a variety of other birds may be seen; buzzard, raven and sparrowhawk are not uncommon.

Cader Idris

SH 730114; 392ha; NT–NCC reserve
Mountain range, crags, lake and woodland
Permit only to enclosed woodland
Leaflet from NCC
Early summer

The path to Cader Idris rises steeply along the edge of the Afon Cau and through a mixed woodland of oak with alder, ash, hawthorn and rowan. The valley widens and then opens into the huge bowl which holds the lake of Llyn Cau and is a superb example of an upland cwm. Climbing the valley towards the lake the impression is that of a traditional sheep walk: grazed mat-grass, heather and bilberry, but with richer grasses such as sheep's-fescue and common bent where the soil is better. Where poor drainage causes boggy areas, round-leaved sundew grows on the spongy masses of *Sphagnum* moss. Common butterwort may also be found here.

The crags are a mixture of hard, acid rocks and calcareous ashes and lavas. Their steepness protects the vegetation from sheep grazing and the north-facing aspect provides a suitable environment for plants of the last ice age whose usual habitat is the high Alps and Arctic. A good example of these, flowering from June to July, is moss campion. Other attractive plants include globeflower, Welsh poppy, spring sandwort and purple and mossy saxifrage.

Of particular interest are a number of ferns: the rare alpine woodsia and both green and forked spleenwort. Green spleenwort is well known as a highly sensitive lime indicator and will only be found in the areas of calcareous rocks; forked spleenwort, on the other hand, grows only on the acid rocks. Their presence together underlines the highly varied nature of the reserve.

In February or March, raven nest in these crags, which in May become nest sites for a summer visitor, the ring ouzel. At about the same time wheatear nest among the lower rocks and meadow pipit in the open sheep walk.

The reserve rises to a maximum of 893m and, where the soil is deep enough, moles have been recorded 43m from the top.

Caeau Tan y Bwlch

SH 432489; 5ha; NWWT reserve
Unimproved grassland and mire
Summer

There is a very large colony of greater butterfly orchids on the meadows, along with heath and common spotted orchids, fairy flax, lady's-mantle, knapweed and yellow rattle. The soligenous mire is dominated by rushes with purple moor-grass tussocks. Bilberry and cranberry are common and sundew can easily be found. Grasshopper warblers breed and buzzard, raven, curlew and snipe are frequent visitors. Butterflies recorded include green-veined white, small heath, ringlet, peacock and small tortoiseshell.

Cemlyn

SH 336932; 16ha; NT–NWWT reserve
Brackish pools and shingle bank; small enclosure
Permit only to enclosure at Ty'n Llan
Spring, winter

The shingle bar is a storm beach: once pebbles have been thrown above the normal tideline plants begin to move in. Nearest the waterline are strong, fleshy plants, sea kale, sea beet and orache, which can stand being battered by pebbles and drenched at spring tides. When out of reach of all but the heaviest gales the plants become more slender and include spring squill and, in some years, autumn lady's-tresses.

Behind the bank is the water of the pool, brackish and muddy, fringed by saltmarsh plants. These are not usually subjected to the battering that plants on the seaward side may suffer, but they are just as likely to be covered by a high tide, so have evolved similar protection. Glasswort grows at the water's edge, as fleshy as a smooth cactus; sea aster and thrift, both with fleshy leaves, can also stand occasional flooding.

In spring several hundred pairs of tern breed at Cemlyn. Three of Britain's native species, arctic, common and sometimes Sandwich tern, breed,

together with a few pairs of black-headed gull. Several other species nest on or near the reserve: oystercatcher on the shingle and shelduck in old rabbit burrows around the pool. Other breeding species include mallard, red-breasted merganser and redshank. In winter wigeon, mallard, shoveler and teal may be seen, together with diving duck such as goldeneye, and little grebe. Dunlin, turnstone, lapwing and golden and grey plover come into the reserve for shelter and food.

Tasselweed grows in the Ty'n Llan pool: it is a local plant generally limited to slightly brackish ditches near the sea. The enclosure beside the pool has an area of dense blackthorn and gorse scrub and at the western end an area of rushes.

Clogwyn Cyrau Observation Hide

SH 789574; FC
Woodland bird hide
Spring, summer

The hide is on a terrace overlooking the Llugwy Valley. The woodland includes broad-leaved and coniferous trees; typical woodland birds such as chaffinch, green and great spotted woodpecker, treecreeper, wren and several tit species may be seen from this hide.

Coed Aber Artro

SH 597267; 28ha; WdT
Deciduous woodland
Spring, summer

This reserve and the adjacent COED LLETYWALTER form part of a complex of woodlands in one of the most important conservation areas of the SNOWDONIA NATIONAL PARK. There are many superb old sessile oaks in the wood that support a rich variety of lichens and mosses; and birch, wych elm and planted beech are also found. In the wetter areas ash and alder grow and there is a rich ground flora.

Coed Aber Eden

SH 725253; 2.8ha; WdT reserve
Deciduous woodland
Spring, summer

A small oak, birch and ash wood with hazel coppice in SNOWDONIA NATIONAL PARK.

Coed Allt

SH 620357; 3.2ha; WdT
Deciduous woodland
Very steep – access not recommended
Spring, summer

A young oak woodland which has been developed naturally on a steep slope after the area was fenced to exclude grazing sheep. Ravens nest in the older trees near the rocky crags.

Coed Avens

SH 476923; 0.7ha; WdT
Young broadleaf woodland
Spring, summer

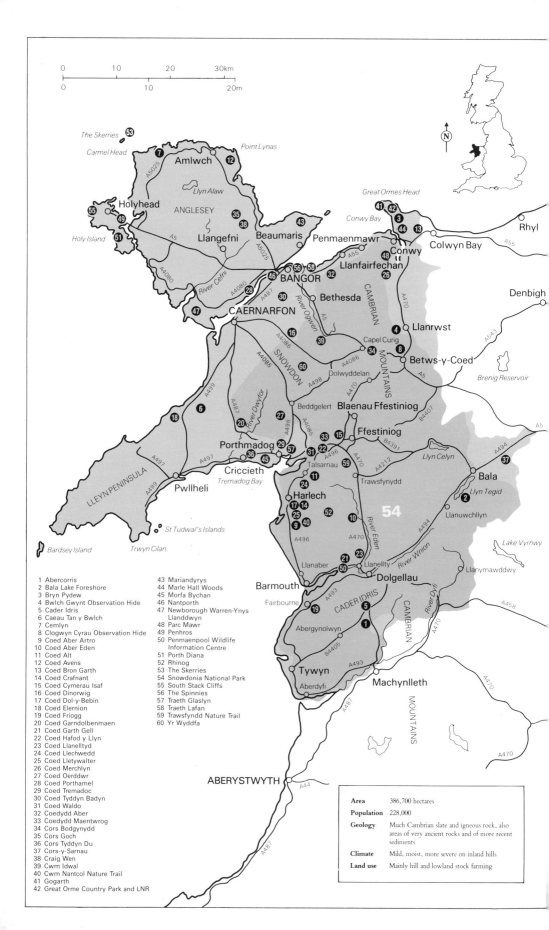

Scale:
0   10   20   30km
0   10   20m

The Skerries 53
Carmel Head
Point Lynas
7 Amlwch 12
Llyn Alaw
Holyhead 55 49 51
ANGLESEY
Holy Island
35
38
Llangefni
A5
Beaumaris 43
Penmaenmawr
Great Ormes Head
Conwy Bay 41 42 3
44 13
Rhyl
Colwyn Bay A55
Denbigh
46 BANGOR 56 58
Llanfairfechan 48 Conwy
26
CAMBRIAN
A470
28
River Cefni
47
30
CAERNARFON
Bethesda 32
16
39
River Ogwen
A5
Capel Curig 4 Llanrwst
34 8 Betws-y-Coed
Brenig Reservoir
A543
A5
60
Dolwyddelan
MOUNTAINS
18 6
River Dwyfor
SNOWDON
20 27 Beddgelert
Blaenau Ffestiniog
B4407
Porthmadog 29 57
36 45
33 15 Ffestiniog
B4391
Criccieth
31 22
59
Llyn Celyn
A4212
A494 37
Talsarnau
Trawsfynydd
Bala
Pwllheli
Tremadog Bay
24 11
LLEYN PENINSULA
A499
Harlech
Llyn Tegid
Llanuwchllyn
St Tudwal's Islands
17 14
25 52
9 40 10
54
River Eden
A494
Lake Vyrnwy
Bardsey Island
Trwyn Cilan
A496
A470
Llanymawddwy
A458
21 23
Llanaber 50 Llanellty
Dolgellau
River Wnion
Barmouth
Fairbourne
19 CADER IDRIS
5
CAMBRIAN
River Dyfi
A470
Abergynolwyn 1
MOUNTAINS
B4405
Tywyn
A493
Machynlleth
Aberdyfi
A487
A470
ABERYSTWYTH
A44

1 Abercorris
2 Bala Lake Foreshore
3 Bryn Pydew
4 Bwlch Gwynt Observation Hide
5 Cader Idris
6 Caeau Tan y Bwlch
7 Cemlyn
8 Clogwyn Cyrau Observation Hide
9 Coed Aber Artro
10 Coed Aber Eden
11 Coed Alt
12 Coed Avens
13 Coed Bron Garth
14 Coed Crafnant
15 Coed Cymerau Isaf
16 Coed Dinorwig
17 Coed Dol-y-Bebin
18 Coed Elernion
19 Coed Friogg
20 Coed Garndolbenmaen
21 Coed Garth Gell
22 Coed Hafod y Llyn
23 Coed Llanelltyd
24 Coed Llechwedd
25 Coed Lletywalter
26 Coed Merchlyn
27 Coed Oerddwr
28 Coed Porthamel
29 Coed Tremadoc
30 Coed Tyddyn Badyn
31 Coed Waldo
32 Coedydd Aber
33 Coedydd Maentwrog
34 Cors Bodgynydd
35 Cors Goch
36 Cors Tyddyn Du
37 Cors-y-Sarnau
38 Craig Wen
39 Cwm Idwal
40 Cwm Nantcol Nature Trail
41 Gogarth
42 Great Orme Country Park and LNR

43 Mariandyrys
44 Marle Hall Woods
45 Morfa Bychan
46 Nantporth
47 Newborough Warren-Ynys
   Llanddwyn
48 Parc Mawr
49 Penrhos
50 Penmaenpool Wildlife
   Information Centre
51 Porth Diana
52 Rhinog
53 The Skerries
54 Snowdonia National Park
55 South Stack Cliffs
56 The Spinnies
57 Traeth Glaslyn
58 Traeth Lafan
59 Trawsfynydd Nature Trail
60 Yr Wyddfa

Area	386,700 hectares
Population	228,000
Geology	Much Cambrian slate and igneous rock, also areas of very ancient rocks and of more recent sediments
Climate	Mild, moist, more severe on inland hills
Land use	Mainly hill and lowland stock farming

Polecat, a rare relative of stoat and weasel.

A field overlooking the sea was planted up with mixed broadleaved trees. The site faces north-west so is protected from the prevailing south-west winds on Anglesey. A public footpath runs through the reserve, which as it matures will become an important broadleaved wood on the windswept island where even individual trees are uncommon.

Coed Bron Garth

SH 821793; 5.5ha; WdT
Mixed woodland
Spring, summer

The wood supports a wide range of tree and shrub species, including small-leaved lime, hornbeam, yew and spindle – all species uncommon in the country except on this small area of limestone rocks around Llandudno and Colwyn Bay. Underplanted with some conifers before it became a reserve, these are now being removed to prevent the loss of the interesting ground flora of lime-loving plants.

Coed Camlyn

Permit only; 63.5ha; NCC reserve
Oak woodland
Spring, summer, autumn

One of the Vale of Ffestiniog oakwoods, Coed Camlyn is damp and acid with bilberry and purple moor-grass in the wetter areas and bracken where it is dry enough. The dampness encourages a good range of mosses.

Coed Crafnant

SH 618289; 20ha; NWWT reserve
Sessile oakwood
All year

For much of the year this woodland, which adjoins COED DOL-Y-BEBIN, is drenched by gales sweeping off the Atlantic and, being untouched by all but the evening and high summer sun, it has developed a special character of its own. The dimness and humidity offer 130 species of mosses and liverworts freedom from competition from other more robust plants and the woodland is therefore considered of international importance for its bryophytes. Species with extremely restricted national distribution occur here, such as the liverworts *Jamesoniella autumnalis* or *Cephaloziella pearsonii*. Other rare species incude the moss *Dicranum scottianum*, the liverworts *Porella pinnata* and *Lepidozia pinnata*, and the lichen *Sphaerophorus melanocarpus*.

Coed Cymerau

Permit only; 26ha; NCC reserve
Oak woodland
Spring, summer, autumn

Coed Cymerau is more sheltered and damper than nearby Coed Camlyn. Birch is more common among the oaks and bilberry less common on the forest floor. In addition there are several small wet mires and a grassland area. There is a wide range of ferns, mosses, liverworts and lichens.

Coed Cymerau Isaf

SH 691425; 32ha; WdT
Deciduous woodland, unimproved meadows and marsh
Spring, summer

The mixture of woodland, herb-rich grassland and marsh surrounds an old farmhouse dating back to the seventeenth century. The woodland of oak and birch with hazel in the more fertile areas has been heavily grazed in the past and this has impoverished the ground flora. The contrast between this reserve and the adjoining COED CYMERAU which is ungrazed, emphasises this effect. Several of the meadows are rich in flowers and the marshes are also interesting botanically, with both species of cottongrass. From the upper parts of the woods there are fine views of Ffestiniog Valley.

Coed Dinorwig

SH 586603; 50ha; GCC reserve
Old oak woodland
Leaflet from Padarn Country Park information centre
Spring, early summer

Part of the Padarn Country Park, on the steep slopes above Llyn Padarn, the reserve is unusual among similar Welsh hill oakwoods in having been ungrazed for many years. The wood was fenced, presumably to keep sheep from the Dinorwig quarries and this has protected what must have been the typical ground cover of many other woods from grazing.

Under the often rather small oaks, heather, bilberry and bramble form a rich tangle while, in damper areas, the ground is thick with spreads of great wood-rush. Hazel and holly form a thin understorey, best in the deeper soils where bands of slate have eroded unevenly to give a ridge-and-channel effect which runs across the slope. The sheltered dampness encourages a good range of ferns and mosses and the oaks, often thick with ivy, carry attractive sprays of polypody. Lady-fern, hard and parsley fern occur on the woodland floor and wet rocky outcrops provide a habitat for Wilson's filmy-fern; drier rocks and jumbles of block scree provide a suitable site for maidenhair spleenwort. In places where the oakwood has been cleared, the Vivian quarry for instance, birch is invading – a first step towards new woodland cover.

Insects such as mottled umber moth will sometimes completely strip the leaves from many of the oaks, an attack balanced by a second spring of fresh leaves in July – but an attack which is most important for breeding birds: it implies enormous numbers of accessible caterpillars. Pied flycatcher specialise in oakwoods such as this, with a full canopy, sparse understorey and a richness of insects for food. Buzzard, kestrel and sparrowhawk are among the other birds and mammals include fox, stoat and weasel. The reserve is sometimes hunted by the far more uncommon polecat.

Coed Dolgarrog

Permit only; 69ha; NCC reserve
Mixed deciduous woodland
Spring, summer

Coed Dolgarrog's trees include oak, wych elm, ash, small-leaved lime and crab apple. On the woodland floor there is a good varied cover where dog's mercury and enchanter's-nightshade grow with sanicle, ramsons, wild strawberry and common dog-violet. The bird and mammal life is similarly rich and the wood has a large badger population.

Coed Dol-y-Bebin

SH 614280; 29ha; NWWT reserve
Woodland and rough hillside
Spring, summer

Oak woodland, with ash, birch, holly and rowan, stands on the steep rocky hillside, thick with bracken in the clearings. Two streams give wet areas which are rich in ferns. Buzzard hunt the hillside and stands of heather on the drier slopes support occasional red grouse.

Coed Elernion

SH 378462; 20ha; WdT
Deciduous woodland
Spring, summer

Oak is the dominant canopy species in this important area of broadleaved woodland. Many other species of trees are also found.

Coed Friog

SH 621129; 3.6ha; WdT reserve
Woodland and moorland
Spring, summer

This rocky, open oak woodland with area of bracken on a west-facing hillside is an important landscape feature above the town of Fairbourne.

Coed Ganllwyd

Permit only; 24ha; NCC reserve
Oak woodland
Spring, summer, autumn

Coed Ganllwyd is chiefly oak woodland but contains other tree species; the considerable variation in the soil gives a good range of ground cover. A waterfall makes part of the wood extremely damp, encouraging a rich variety of unusual ferns, mosses and liverworts.

Coed Garndolbenmaen

SH 498444; 1.1ha; WdT
Marsh and scrub
Spring and summer

The small area of marshy land and scrub has been allowed to grow wild for some years and is beginning to be colonised by trees and bushes.

Coed Garth Gell

SH 687191; 46ha; RSPB reserve
Deciduous woodland
Spring, summer

This sessile oak and birch wood lies on a hillside overlooking the Mawddach Estuary in the SNOWDONIA NATIONAL PARK. It supports a typical bird community, including pied flycatchers, redstarts, wood warblers and great spotted woodpeckers. Buzzards and ravens also nest here. The woodland is bounded by a dramatic river gorge where grey wagtails and dippers are found. The reserve is in part of the old Dolgellau goldfield and there are the remains of a number of worked out nineteenth-century mines.

Coed Gorswen

Permit only; 13.5ha; NCC reserve
Mixed deciduous woodland
Spring, summer

Coed Gorswen, like COED DOLGARROG nearby, is much richer than most other woods in Gwynedd A similar wide range of trees and smaller plants, includes moonwort and broad-leaved helleborine.

Coed Hafod y Llyn

SH 649415; 17ha; WdT reserve
Mixed woodland
Spring, summer

Much of the boundary of this wood follows the Ffestiniog railway; on its other side is COEDYDD MAENTWROG, a National Nature Reserve. Although the Woodland Trust's site has been largely planted with conifers, some areas of sessile oak remain. Together the two reserves create a very varied area for wildlife within SNOWDONIA NATIONAL PARK.

Coed Llanelltyd

SH 723205; 3.6ha; WdT
Deciduous woodland
Spring, summer

Oak, ash, cherry, sycamore and beech are found in this narrow strip of mature woodland in the SNOWDONIA NATIONAL PARK.

Coed Llechwedd

SH 592318; 24.4ha; WdT
Steep sloping woodland
Spring, early summer

The wood is mainly oak with a variety of other species including wild cherry. Since the wood has been fenced the ground flora has become more varied and interesting.

Coed Lletywalter

SH 602275; 37.6ha; WdT
Woodland and lake
Spring, summer

The area includes a large lake with boggy wetlands and a stream through the woodland. Rocky outcrops add to the habitat range making the whole complex of great interest.

Coed Merchlyn

SH 764734; 2.7ha; WdT
Deciduous woodland
Spring, summer

This valley floor woodland supports an interesting wet ground flora and the mature timber provides a good habitat for birds and insects.

Coed Oerddwr

SH 592450; 55ha; WdT
Mixed woodland, grassland and moorland
Spring, summer

The wood is an important feature in the landscape of the Aber Glaslyn valley. It consists mostly of mature oak underplanted with conifers, but areas of unimproved grazing and semi-natural moorland give an interesting diversity of habitats.

Coed Porthamel

SH 508678; 2.4ha; NWWT reserve
Mixed woodland
Key for gate from warden at Porthamel Old Farm House or from Trust office
Spring

The reserve includes Coed Brain, a 0.5ha wood of sycamore. Green hellebore and golden-leaved saxifrage grow near the stream and ramsons cover much of the ground. The main part of the reserve is mixed deciduous woodland with good patches of brambles and nettles which attract many butterflies and provide food for birds later in the year. The most notable species of the 43 which have been recorded are merlin, stock dove, long-tailed tit and wood warbler. Records of *Catoptria falsellus* and *Teichobia filicivora* were both the first for these moths on Anglesey.

Coed Tremadoc

SH 569405; 20ha; NCC reserve
Deciduous woodland and cliffs
Strictly no access
Spring, summer

The woodland lies on the steep slope of the hill overlooking the village of Tremadoc. Much of the hillside is made up of scree of huge tumbled blocks of slate – here only a few scattered sessile oaks occur. But where there is soil – in pockets on the hill and at the base of the slope – a mixed woodland of sessile oak, ash and sycamore is found. The smaller plants are of the acid-loving type – wavy hairgrass, bilberry and wood sage with the cliff ledges holding a richer selection, including orpine, marjoram and stonecrop.

Coed Tyddyn Badyn

SH 565668; 3ha; WdT
Mixed woodland
Spring, summer

Although largely replanted with conifers, the wood still contains a mix of alder, birch and willow and is to be allowed to return to a broad-leaved woodland.

Coed Waldo

SH 628400; 2.3ha; WdT
Woodland and scrub
Spring, summer

The wood is a fine example of sessile oak woodland, and there are also areas of rowan and gorse in the more open parts of the reserve.

Coedydd Aber

SH 662720; 147ha; NCC reserve
Mixed valley woodland
Permit only off rights of way from NCC, Bangor
Nature trail leaflet from NCC
Spring, summer

To walk to the spectacular Aber Falls at the head of the valley is to walk through an immense variety of woodland and valley habitat. The dry acid oak woodland on the higher slopes is typical of many Welsh oakwoods, but the lower slopes are richer and damper and there are also wet areas of alder woodland and a fine example of cliff woodland in the spray of the Falls themselves. On the lower slopes of the valley the woods are varied, with oak, ash, wych elm, birch and hazel, with primrose, bluebell, wood anemone and wood-sorrel in spring. Here, in wet boggy areas, are alder and grey willow with creeping buttercup and opposite-leaved golden-saxifrage. On the steep ravine slopes soft shield-fern is common

The flanks of the Vale of Ffestiniog are clothed with splendid mixed oakwoods.

and, where sheep cannot graze, tutsan grows on rock ledges and wood fescue, a rare grass, may also occur.

Towards the head of the valley the woodland becomes more open, wide glades and marshy areas give more openings in the leaf canopy, and the woodland eventually grades into hawthorn and crab apple scrub, open and standing in close-grazed grassland. A litter of boulders and low hummocks sparsely grown with hawthorn signals the head of the valley and the Aber Falls. On either side of the washed slabs the cliffs are terraced and broken, soaked with spray and rich with stunted oak, birch, rowan, gorse and heather and thickly clumped with great wood-rush. The reserve also has a good lichen epiphyte flora, with a number of important rarities, and some very local Atlantic bryophytes on these cliffs situated near the Aber Falls.

There are particularly good breeding populations of pied flycatcher, redstart and wood warbler. Willow warbler and chiffchaff may be heard in the woods and the stream attracts both dipper and grey wagtail. Wheatear and ring ouzel nest in the rocky areas around the head of the valley where merlin and buzzard hunt.

Coedydd Maentwrog

SH 652414–600410; 68.5ha; NCC–NT reserve
Oak woodland in three blocks
Leaflet from NCC
Spring, early summer

Coed Llyn Mair, high above the Vale of Ffestiniog, is the smallest of the three woodland blocks and the only one to which there is unrestricted access. The NCC has laid out a nature trail to show the various facets of woodland life.

The trees are mostly oak with a scattering of birch, alder, rowan and sycamore, but the reserve also has small meadow-like clearings, a marshy wetland at the top of the wood, a good deal of woodland edge and a small area of rocky heathland. This heathland shows the sort of habitat over which the woods have grown, a thick springing stand of heather and bell heather, with bilberry, tormentil, heath bedstraw, harebell and goldenrod.

Under the trees the smaller plants change, the ferns, mosses and lichens come into their own and hard fern and polypody are common. There are also flowering plants, such as common cow-wheat, adapted to grow in shade. Primrose, lesser celandine and common dog-violet grow in the clearings.

Above and outside the present woodland is an open area of bracken with young hawthorn beginning to mark the change to scrub which precedes the change to woodland. The bracken is tangled with bramble and raspberry. Above this is a small area of wetland with grey willow standing above tussocks of purple moor-grass and meadowsweet, a warm scented corner loud with insects, very different from the shaded quiet of the woods and the stream which drops down through them into Llyn Mair below.

Although Llyn Mair is outside the reserve it adds another range of habitat to the area, with marshland becoming lakeside bog. The lake itself is fringed with willow, small birch and thick beds of rushes. This open water attracts mallard, coot, moorhen, heron and insect-taking birds such as swallow, contrasting with the reserve's typical woodland birds, pied flycatcher, wood warbler, nuthatch, treecreeper, green and great spotted woodpecker, jay and buzzard.

Coed-y-Rhygen

Permit only; 27.5ha; NCC reserve
Oak woodland
Spring, summer

The underlying rocks cause alternating belts of dry woodland and wet boggy slopes. The moss *Leucobryum glaucum* forms green-grey cushions on the forest floor while purple moor-grass and bog myrtle grow in the wet mires. In more open areas are heather and cross-leaved heath. Buzzard, pied flycatcher and great spotted woodpecker are among the birds that frequent the woodland and the reserve has wetland birds of which mallard and common sandpiper breed on the lake. Polecat has been recorded.

Cors Bodeilio

6ha; NCC reserve
Fen
Strictly no access
Spring, summer

The reserve lies in a shallow valley surrounded by limestone hills, which give the peat an interesting variety of lime-loving plants. Of particular note are the orchids, with fragrant, fly, frog, lesser butterfly, and a selection of marsh-orchids and marsh helleborines.

Cors Bodgynydd

SH 766596; 4ha; NWWT reserve
Small area of bog and heath
Spring, autumn

Bog myrtle, cross-leaved heath and purple moor-grass cover much of this reserve, important for the rare marsh clubmoss. The rich dampness encourages insects and green hairstreak butterfly and oak eggar, emperor and beautiful snout moths have been recorded, together with two national rarities: Ashworth's rustic and Weaver's wave moths.

Cors Erddreiniog

Permit only; 66ha; NCC reserve
Fen, birch woodland and heath
Spring, summer

Wetland and limestone combine to provide an exceptional range of habitat and species. There is a wide variety of fenland plants, including black bog-rush and great fen-sedge, together with orchid species such as northern and narrow-leaved marsh-orchid, fen orchid, and marsh helleborine.

Cors Goch

SH 497813; 58ha; NWWT reserve
Rich fen, limestone grassland and acid heath
Spring, summer

Rushes, sedges and great stands of common reed, scented with bog myrtle and water mint, combine with marsh fern and royal fern in one of the finest fen communities in Britain. The richness is due to drainage from the limestone higher ground. On the thickly grassed bank above the fen common rock-rose and fairy flax show among mats of salad burnet and quaking-grass. Here one of the

Dune grassland and scrub at Newborough Warren, backed by Snowdonia's mountains.

reserve's many orchid species grows – never more than locally common, and rare in north Wales, green-winged orchid occurs in the limestone grassland. Lower down, where the grassland merges into fen, fragrant orchid and lesser butter-fly-orchid grow. Rich areas of damp marshland occur around the fen and these are glorious with grass-of-Parnassus and early and northern marsh-orchid, common spotted-orchid and marsh helle-borine, another orchid uncommon in north Wales.

The area of acid heath where a belt of sandstone shows above the fen is bright with gorse, heather and bell heather and, in April and May, it is starred with spring squill. In the more acid marshy places common butterwort grows, with lesser water-plantain, uncommon throughout the country and rare in north Wales. Another rarity is greater bladderwort which grows with lesser bladderwort in the more acid fenland pools. Lesser bulrush grows together with bulrush and common reed in the largest of the pools.

Over 800 species of insect have been identified, including some 300 moth and butterfly species. Birds include grasshopper warbler, reed bunting, curlew, lapwing, redshank, snipe and nightjar.

Cors Tyddyn Du

SH 481403; 5.5ha; NWWT reserve
Wet heath, scrub and two artificial lakes
Spring, summer

The drier parts of the heath are dominated by purple moor-grass with brown bent and sharp-flowered rush, dotted with devil's-bit scabious. Cranberry, marsh cinquefoil and marsh St John's-wort grow in the wetter parts and willow scrub fringes the stream. Branched bur-reed and plants such as the three-petalled water-plantain have colonised the stream and lakes. Reed bunting, grasshopper and willow warbler and whitethroat breed; corncrake and water rail have been recorded.

Cors-y-Sarnau

SH 972390; 13ha; NWWT reserve
Marsh and alder carr
Spring, summer

The marsh formed where an old valley lake gradually silted up. Varied acid wetland plants include bog asphodel, cranberry, cross-leaved heath and round-leaved sundew while purple moor-grass grows on parts of the swamp with marsh cinquefoil, bogbean and ragged-Robin. The wet alder woodland has greater tussock-sedge, meadowsweet and marsh-marigold.

Craig Wen

SH 493803; 6ha; NWWT reserve
Damp acid heath
Spring, summer

Acid-loving plants such as bog pimpernel and bog asphodel, mountain everlasting and pale dog-violet contrast with lime-rich areas where black bog-rush may be found.

Cwm Glas Crafnant

Permit only; 15.5ha; NCC reserve
Partly wooded rocky hillside
Spring, summer

The slopes are mainly of a rich volcanic ash and the ledges carry a range of arctic–alpine plants which are unusual at such low altitude. The woodland is chiefly ash with hawthorn and hazel.

Cwm Idwal

SH 640590; 398ha; NCC reserve
High upland cwm, corrie lake and crags
Leaflet from NCC
Late spring, summer

Cwm Idwal, containing the hanging gardens of Twll Du, the Devil's Kitchen, lies at the head of the Nant Ffrancon, cupping Llyn Idwal, a small glacial lake, in the long curve of its tremendous crags. Like much of Wales it is heavily sheep-grazed but, like only a very few upland areas now, it shows how the hills must have been a glory of colour before sheep became so widespread.

Where the mat-grass cover of much of the reserve is fenced against sheep, purple moor-grass, heather and bell heather show; where the damp sward of common bent and sheep's fescue below the lime-rich cliffs is fenced, tufted hair-grass, Yorkshire-fog, bog asphodel, common cottongrass, heather, cross-leaved heath, milkwort and yarrow grow.

The cliffs above, where sheep cannot reach, are a treasure-house of flowers and ferns. Some are rarities, arctic–alpine plants which have survived here since plants first recolonised the cliffs after the last ice age; others are commoner plants enjoying the damp richness of the cliff ledges. April shows primrose, moschatel, early-purple orchid and purple saxifrage – the first of the arctic–alpines. By July the ledges are filled with flowers: alpine meadow-rue, moss campion, mossy and starry saxifrage and globeflower, with red campion, foxglove, thrift, goldenrod, sea campion, great wood-rush, brittle bladder-fern, oak fern, parsley fern and green spleenwort. The acid crags, too, have their characteristic flora. The lake has plants peculiar to its high altitude – awlwort, floating bur-reed, water lobelia, pillwort, quillwort, shoreweed, alternate water-milfoil and autumnal water-starwort.

There are trout and minnows in Llyn Idwal and it is fished by cormorant and heron. In winter goldeneye, pochard and whooper swan may be seen. In high crags there are raven and ring ouzel.

Cwm Nantcol Nature Trail

SH 605270; 1km; GCC–SNPC
Short trail in Nantcol Valley
Leaflet from car park or SNPC
Spring, summer

The trail passes through oak and birch woodland, by the rushing Nantcol stream, to the open sheep walk above. The small peat bog has common cottongrass and bogbean. The land formation and litter of great boulders shows the effects of the ice ages on the landscape.

Gogarth

SH 757833; 2ha; NWWT reserve
Limestone grassland and scree
Spring, summer

Although heather and bell heather occur, this is an outcrop of carboniferous limestone with many limestone plants. Juniper shrubs and dense scrub shelter heathland birds and seabirds may be seen along the coast. The insects include the dwarf forms of grayling and silver-studded blue butterflies and the rare horehound plume moth, otherwise found only in southern England. Glow-worm may occasionally be seen.

Great Orme Country Park, LNR and Nature Trails

SH 767834; 291ha; Aberconwy BC
Coastal headland with grassland and heath
Booklet from visitor centre on site (nature trail booklet
from tourist information centre, Llandudno)
Spring, summer, autumn

This fine carboniferous limestone headland has now become a country park and LNR. The interesting calicole flora includes wild cabbage, spring squill, bloody crane's-bill and common and hoary rockrose. Some 85 bird species may commonly be seen around the Orme. Apart from the usual breeding seabirds, spring and autumn migrants such as golden plover, ring ouzels and whinchat often stop over on the reserve, and gannets, skuas and Manx shearwaters pass offshore. In winter snow buntings and black redstarts are seen, and divers often shelter in the bays.

The trails at SH 780832 take in grassland with characteristic limestone flowers, and fine sea cliffs holding breeding colonies of birds such as fulmar, and guillemot with chough and raven.

Mariandyrys

SH 604809; 6ha; NWWT reserve
Limestone grassland
Spring, summer

The patchwork of vegetation on this reserve includes species-rich grassland with autumn gentian, rock-rose, ploughman's-spikenard, burnet saxifrage and spring squill; a sloping area dominated by Western gorse and bell heather, with grassy patches containing carline thistle, columbine and fragrant orchid; and a quarry, the floor of which supports pale flax and a small colony of bee orchids. Ten species of butterflies, including grayling, common blue, brown argus and large skipper have been recorded, and adders occur on the reserve.

Marle Hall Woods

SH 798791; 12ha; WdT
Mixed woodland, limestone pavement and cliffs,
species-rich grassland

Do not attempt to reach the top of the wood by going up the cliff face
Spring, summer

The reserve has a wide range of different habitats, including limestone pavement, cliffs, important grassland rich in limestone plants, and several different woodland types with a number of unusual plants.

Morfa Bychan

SH 548367; 11ha; NWWT reserve
Coastal dune system
Spring, summer

Morfa Bychan shows the range of duneland habitat from open seaward dune edge through stable dunes, overgrown with plants, to dune grassland and freshwater marsh. Partridge nest on the reserve and the bishop's mitre shield-bug, unusual in north Wales, has been found.

Morfa Dyffryn

Permit only; 202ha; NCC reserve
Coastal dune system
Spring, summer

These dunes have typical sand plants such as sand couch and prickly saltwort, and the sand stabiliser, marram. The stabilised dunes are rich with lichens, mosses and plants such as lady's bedstraw and thyme-leaved sandwort. In the damp slacks between the dunes sharp rush and glaucous sedge grow with sprawls of creeping willow. Seaside centaury and green-flowered helleborine are among the reserve's rarer plants.

Morfa Harlech

Permit only; 491ha; NCC reserve
Dune system and saltmarsh
Spring, summer

The saltmarsh, which is now being invaded by common cord-grass, grades into sandy grassland and then into a rich and complex system of dunes and damp dune slacks where plants such as moonwort, Portland spurge and sharp rush may be found. A freshwater marsh holds a black-headed gull colony in summer and a winter population of wildfowl, including shoveler, teal and whooper swan. Reed bunting, curlew, lapwing, oystercatcher, ringed plover, redshank and shelduck breed on the reserve.

Nantporth

SH 567718; 7ha; NWWT reserve
Small limestone quarry, woodland and foreshore
Spring, summer

In the quarry the limestone plants include common rock-rose, burnet rose, yellow-wort and salad burnet. The woodland has common twayblade, columbine, early dog-violet and woodruff. The area between high and low water demonstrates muddy shore ecology, with animals ranging from the tiny shrimp-like *Corophium* to the giant king rag bristleworm.

Spotted rock-rose grows only on Anglesey.

Newborough Warren–Ynys Llanddwyn

SH 406636; 633.5ha; NCC reserve
Dunes, saltmarsh, pool and rocky headland
Permit only off rights of way
Leaflet from NCC
All year

Newborough Warren is one of the finest dune systems in the country. The sand includes a high proportion of powdered shells which makes it rich in calcium and contributes much to the wealth of plants found here. Some 560 plant species have been identified in the open duneland and in Newborough Forest. Characteristic plants of the first, seaward, dunes are marram, sea spurge, sand cat's-tail and wild pansy, the food plant for the caterpillars of dark green fritillary. The more stable dunes have lady's bedstraw, common bird's-foot-trefoil, cuckooflower, meadow saxifrage and wild thyme. In the dune slacks creeping willow grows and the wide range of orchids includes dune helleborine.

The dunes are rich in insects but bird species are limited by lack of cover, and the characteristic birds are curlew, lapwing, oystercatcher, meadow pipit and skylark.

A large area of the duneland has been planted with trees and although most of them are conifers,

generally Corsican pine, there are some broad-leaved trees and many characteristic duneland plants, as well as more typical and some more unusual woodland ones. Although it is outside the reserve the NCC has scheduled Newborough Forest a Site of Special Scientific Interest.

Beyond the Forestry Commission plantations is the Cefni Estuary and an area of saltmarsh. This contains one of the country's largest continuous stands of sea rush. Other typical plants are sea aster, sea arrowgrass, annual sea-blite and thrift. In winter flocks of around 2000 duck, including 200 pintail, come to the estuary and several hundred Canada and greylag geese feed on the saltmarsh. Further up the estuary is Malltraeth Pool, another haven for waders and wildfowl. Most commonly seen are curlew, lapwing, redshank, cormorant and shelduck, but goldeneye, pintail, greenshank, bar-tailed and black-tailed godwit and Bewick's, mute and whooper swan have been recorded.

A narrow ridge of Pre-Cambrian rock, which runs through the middle of Newborough Forest, ends in the tidal islands and rocky islets of Ynys Llanddwyn. Cormorant and shag nest on the islets, little more than ledged spikes sticking up out of the sea. The island is larger and, due to the acid rocks topped by glacial clays and lime-rich habitat unfolds, with waders feeding at the water's edge or probing the marshy slacks.

Parc Mawr

SH 760740; 34ha; WdT
Mixed woodland
Spring, summer

Situated on a hillside overlooking the beautiful Conway Valley on the edge of the SNOWDONIA NATIONAL PARK, part of the broadleaved woodland has been felled and replanted with conifers, but sympathetic management will eventually restore the whole reserve to broadleaves once again.

Penhros

SH 276804; 140ha; Penhros Nature Reserve–Anglesey
Aluminium Ltd reserve
Coast, woodlands, scrub and marsh
Permit only to Specialist Sector: from Hon. Director,
Penhros Nature Reserve, Holyhead
Booklet from site
All year

The main part of the reserve consists of woodland, coastal grassland and rocky foreshore on the north east corner of Holyhead Island.

The mixed woods contain many typical woodland birds while the foreshore may have breeding red-breasted merganser, shelduck, oystercatcher, ringed plover and redshank. Greenshank, spotted redshank, Slavonian grebe, black-tailed godwit and whimbrel may visit and the artificial pools attract many other wild birds. The Specialist Sector, open only to bona fide ornithologists, consists of scrub and marsh and overlooks an important tern colony.

Penmaenpool Wildlife Information Centre

SH 695185; RSPB NWWT SNPC

Bird observatory
Opening times: 11.30 a.m.–5.30 p.m.
June–September

From the observatory species such as cormorant, red-breasted merganser, curlew, lapwing, oyster-catcher and heron may be seen along the tidal riverway. From here an old railway line follows the estuary and overlooks a range of habitats: grazed saltmarsh with ditches and pools, fresh-water marshes, oak woodland and patches of acid scrub.

Porth Diana

SH 255781; 2ha; NWWT reserve

Coastal heathland
Spring, summer

In this tiny reserve spring squill, bird's-foot and English stonecrop show beneath gorse, heather and cross-leaved heath. The real treasure, however, is spotted rock-rose, which only grows in certain parts of north Wales.

Rhinog

SH 657290; 598ha; NCC reserve

Acid upland and crags
Leaflet from NCC
Late spring, summer, autumn

This highly inaccessible area (the map reference marks the peak of the reserve since the nearest road access is several kilometres away from any part of it) has a wonderful sweep of heather moor with bilberry, cowberry and crowberry. Areas of blanket bog have *Sphagnum* mosses and purple moor-grass, with bog myrtle edging the wetter places. The crags provide nest sites for raven, ring ouzel and wren, while red grouse, meadow pipit and wheatear breed on the lower slopes.

The Skerries

SH 270950; 17ha; RSPB reserve
Offshore islands
No access

A small group of rocky islets 2 miles off the north-west coast of Anglesey. The islands were once a major tern colony but were deserted by the terns during the 1960s. However, arctic terns returned in 1979 and have now built up to 150 pairs. There is also a large colony of herring and lesser black-backed gulls, as well as puffins and oystercatchers breeding. The reserve is an important site for autumn migrants.

Snowdonia National Park

See map; 218,455ha; SNPC
Mountains, moorland, valleys and coast
Leaflets from National Park centres
Spring, summer

Snowdon – YR WYDDFA, the highest mountain in Wales and England – is the remains of a worndown dip in the rocks. Upheavals in the earth's crust about three million years ago, and subsequent erosion of the softer rocks have left the hard, compressed rocks of Snowdon standing as a peak among lesser remnants.

The ice-sculpted plateau forms the core of the National Park which, excluding the Lleyn Peninsula and much of the coastal strip, covers most of the land between the River Conwy, Bala

Choughs nest on cliffs such as these at South Stack, or in upland crags, quarries and old mines.

Lake and River Dyfi. It includes the ranges of Snowdon and the Carneddau, Arennig, Aran, CADER IDRIS and RHINOG, in an area second only in size to the LAKE DISTRICT NATIONAL PARK (Cumbria). Among the mountains, valleys wind between long rocky slopes of sheep-grazed grass moorland or steeply tilted woodlands, between huge splays of shattered scree or dark cliffs of stone while, everywhere, the silver threads of streams or the cold ripples of upland lakes add their beauty to the scene. Below the uplands, rich agricultural valleys drain to the dunes and marshes of the coast.

When the ice withdrew, plants began to recolonise: first, those which could live in arctic conditions and then, as the climate warmed, those which preferred more temperate ones. Birch and pine woodland, similar to the relict Caledonian forests of Scotland, spread throughout the hills and then, with a further warming, sessile oak took over. Of course, the spread of plants varied: the folding and eroding, the volcanic intrusions and changes led to a widely varying range of rocks being exposed and each rock weathered to give a different soil. In a similar way the shape of the land affected exposure and wetness.

Some sites, high in the mountains, north-facing and cold in summer, retained their arctic plants – these are some of the specialities of Snowdonia which attract botanists to the region. With a change in climate, other areas became spreads of bog, trapping remains of the earlier woods in their peat. Yet other sites, the sheltered valleys, preserved their splendid oakwoods and provided cover for many mammals and woodland birds.

The heather moorland and all but the steepest valley woods have largely gone from the mountains; birds and mammals have been hunted for many generations and the rarer, less resilient ones are gone or only survive in hidden places. A few inland-breeding chough and peregrine remain and rare and beautiful plants still show on the higher rocky ledges. The arctic–alpines, the ice age relict plants, include Snowdon lily, at its only site in Britain – a plant that grows here on lime-rich ledges but which, elsewhere in the world, normally grows in mountain ranges close to perpetual snows. The splendid range of species includes mountain avens, alpine bistort, moss campion and alpine cinquefoil, mountain crowberry, alpine meadow-rue, arctic and alpine mouse-ear, alpine saw-wort, alpine saxifrage, mountain sorrel, holly fern and alpine woodsia. Together with these are more commonly lowland species and water avens, meadowsweet, early-purple orchid, primrose and great wood-rush may be found on the upland crags.

Below, the mat-grass moors have little variation but, where heather survives on the peat mires, plants such as lesser twayblade may occur. The woods, lower still, have a wide range from acid oakwoods to sheltered valley woodlands where clays have washed down to give suitable soils for a much wider range of trees. Modern coniferous woodlands add slight variety.

The lakes are as varied as the woods, ranging from shallow upland pools to deep-scoured narrow waters in the valleys. Many are of glacial origin, formed when mountain rubble dropped from the melt-face of the glacier to form a moraine which dammed the waters above it. These lakes have native populations of minnow and small brown trout and a few contain char. Char, like the arctic-alpines, is thought to be a glacial relict species; related to trout, it is a coldwater fish limited to its deep narrow lakes and unable to survive elsewhere. Bala Lake holds gwyniad, another relict fish, which is found nowhere else in Wales.

To travel through the National Park, from the mountain tops to the sea, would encompass a marvellous range of country and a rich variety of wildlife. The mammals, of course, are seldom seen but a great diversity of birds might be observed. In the high hills buzzard and raven, wheatear and ring ouzel, meadow pipit and skylark may be seen. On the moors red grouse breed in the heather, there are curlew, lapwing, redshank, snipe, and perhaps golden plover or dunlin in the bogs, while merlin, sparrowhawk, short-eared owl, hen harrier and kite may occur. The kite nests in valley oakwoods outside the National Park but in the woods of Snowdonia a typical range of Welsh woodland birds may be seen. Here are pied flycatcher, wood warbler and redstart, with all three native woodpeckers and with buzzard, sparrowhawk and tawny owl. Where a rapid stream runs, dipper and grey wagtail come to breed and, where the valley broadens to give agricultural land, kingfisher nest in the clay banks and a whole variety of lowland birds occur. Follow the river down to the sea and there may be a wide drowned estuary, sheltered tidal waters fringed with saltmarsh, where wildfowl and waders feed. Onwards to the coastal dunes another rich habitat unfolds, with waders feeding at the water's edge or probing the marshy slacks.

South Stack Cliffs

SH 205823; 316ha; RSPB reserve
Coastal cliffs and heathland
Leaflet from RSPB
Spring, summer

In spring and early summer the northern part of the reserve is probably the most exciting, for at least nine seabird species breed there. The 120m cliffs hold a breeding population which includes around 2500 guillemot, 20 puffin and 700 razorbill pairs. Stock dove and rock pipit are among the cliff-nesting birds which are not specifically coastal, as are four members of the crow family: carrion crow, raven, jackdaw and chough.

Plants of the sea cliffs characteristic of western coasts are golden samphire, rock sea-spurrey, spring squill and English stonecrop. Sea campion, common scurvygrass, kidney vetch and restharrow also cluster the hard white twisted rock. Gogarth Bay, between South and North Stack, is a regular hauling-out place for grey seal.

The other important habitats are heathland, the hill moorland of Holyhead Mountain and the coastal heath of Penrhos Feilw Common. Holyhead

Mountain has typical acid plants such as bilberry and wavy hair-grass, with heather, bell heather, gorse and tormentil. Penrhos Feilw is more unusual, since good coastal heathland is not common in Britain. Dense masses of intermingled gorse and heather turn the heath into a deep-pile carpet of gold and green and purple, for exposure and salt-laden winds prune the heath so that it rolls smooth and even until, as it approaches the sea, the exposure becomes too great and it fades into coastal grassland. There are wet areas within the heathland, where bog pimpernel and cross-leaved heath appear. Two rarities grow here, field fleawort and spotted rock-rose.

There are small breeding populations of waders on the heathland in spring and dotterel are passage migrants in May and September. Adder and common lizard are plentiful here. Among the butterflies are marsh fritillary and silver-studded blue – the latter at its most northerly site in western Britain.

The Spinnies

SH 612721; 3ha; NWWT reserve
Coastal lagoon with scrub
Leaflet from NWWT
Winter

Despite its small size, the reserve is an excellent area for bird watching. Over 170 species have been seen on or from the Spinnies. Kingfisher, water rail and greenshank are all regular visitors and the area is a favourite hunting ground for sparrowhawk, peregrine and merlin. The many exotic species of trees include Norway maple, white poplar and western red cedar, and a variety of ferns grow in shady spots along the paths.

Traeth Glaslyn

SH 592385; 36ha; NWWT reserve
Mudflats, marsh, grassland and woodland
All year

A low-lying area at the mouth of the Afon Glaslyn, behind the cob at Porthmadog, regularly floods with brackish water. Much of the site is marshland, with marsh-orchid, ragged-Robin and whorled caraway. In the winter months wildfowl and waders such as teal, pintail, wigeon, shoveller, goldeneye, redshank and snipe can be viewed from the cob. On higher ground the alder woodland provides feeding for finches and redpoll.

Traeth Lafan

SH 614724; 2000ha; GCC reserve
Inter-tidal flats
Autumn, winter

Over 1000 waders of 10 different species, together with large numbers of duck, add to the importance of the sands and mudflats where red-breasted merganser and great crested grebe gather to moult.

Trawsfynydd Nature Trail

SH 695383; 3km; CEGB
Nature trail along edge of Trawsfynydd Reservoir

Booklet from CEGB
Spring, summer

Herring gull, greater and lesser black-backed and black-headed gull and a few common tern nest on the islands, and common sandpiper on the stony shores, of this man-made lake. The planted woodlands hold spotted flycatcher, green woodpecker, buzzard and sparrowhawk, while natural woods below the Maentwrog Dam are rich in mosses, liverworts and ferns, with birds such as pied flycatcher, redstart, dipper and barn owl.

Yr Wyddfa

SH 630530; 1677ha; NCC reserve
High upland crags, cwms and corrie lakes
Leaflets from NCC
Spring, summer

The Miner's Track nature trail rises from Pen-y-Pas to Llyn Llydaw and gives a very good idea of the sort of influences – altitude, exposure, underlying rock and the effects of man – which have brought about the present face of Snowdon, Yr Wyddfa. Much of the way is through wide slopes of rocky grassland where grazing sheep reduce the plant cover to little more than a lawn of mat-grass. Higher up, though, where rich volcanic lavas break through and the soil is better, the grasses are more varied, softer, and more small herbs appear. But again sheep keep most of the more exciting plants from growing and only a few, heath bedstraw, tormentil and wild thyme, for instance, survive the continual grazing.

Higher again, the acid rocks reappear and there are small areas of bog, bright green with *Sphagnum* mosses and vivid with bog asphodel, while common cottongrass dances in the wind. Common butterwort and round-leaved sundew lay sticky traps for small insects, a special adaptation to secure extra nutrition in this difficult habitat. Many years ago trees grew where the bogs are now, and their remains can still be found preserved in the peat, but changing climate and the hand of man have banished them from almost all the hills and grazing sheep make sure that none will grow now, although a few rowans, brilliant with reddish-orange berries in autumn, survive on rock ledges too steep for sheep to reach.

Llyn Llydaw, at the end of the nature trail, looks beautiful on a still summer day but the ripple of rising trout no longer stirs its surface: copper pollution from the mills where ore was crushed early this century has poisoned its waters.

Apart from predators, particularly peregrine, and the birds of the long-gone oakwoods, birds have not been greatly affected by man's interference here; indeed the high crags are still a haven for chough, once common on the western sea coasts and now very rare indeed. The important factor affecting mountain birds is the bleakness, and the characteristic birds are fairly few. With the chough on the crags are carrion crow, raven, ring ouzel and wren. Wheatear on the screes and meadow pipit on the grassland are the characteristic birds of the lower slopes.

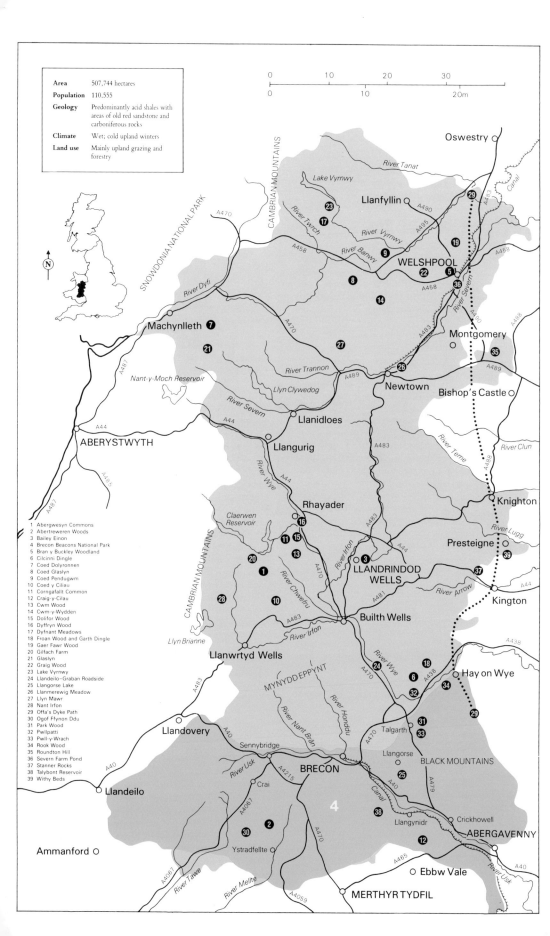

Powys

Powys, the upland heart of Wales, comprises former Montgomery, Radnor and Brecknock. Its western border follows the crest of the Cambrian Mountains, the spine of Wales, touching the sea only at the DYFI Estuary (DYFED). On the east the border with England follows ancient OFFA'S DYKE, now a long-distance footpath. The southern boundary follows the edge of the carboniferous limestone and millstone grit escarpment where it meets the coal measures of the south Wales valleys. This border is shared by the southern limit of the BRECON BEACONS NATIONAL PARK, which lies mainly in Powys and is the largest area of old red sandstone upland in Wales. These sandstones do not reach further than Builth Wells, for the rest of the county is largely of acidic shales of Silurian age.

The highest points in Powys, reaching just over 800m, are the Berwyns in the north and the Brecon Beacons in the south. Powys is essentially a county of rounded hills. On reaching the Severn, Wye and Usk valleys, the streams which issue from these hills create superb farmland and beautiful countryside. The Wye is of sufficient environmental interest to be scheduled a Grade I site by the NCC, one of the few rivers in Britain to receive this premier grading.

Few of the major reservoirs are noted for wildfowl, but an exception is TALYBONT RESERVOIR. Its attractiveness to birds is partly due to the mineral-rich waters which act as a stimulus to the whole food chain. Some 6km north is the largest natural nutrient-rich lake in Wales, LLANGORSE LAKE, now heavily over-exploited for recreation, but still worth visiting if only for the opportunity of glimpsing a migrating osprey.

Powys is the most sparsely populated county in England and Wales, and with less than 20 per cent of it below 180m sheep greatly outnumber people. In the north these quiet uplands are the territory of hen harrier, further south scavenging grounds for red kite. The relatively few craggy areas echo to the piercing cry of peregrine. In the heather above the crags the merlin rears its brood on a diet of meadow pipits.

Most of the uplands are blanketed with peat, some actively growing and supporting *Sphagnum* mosses, some eroding to leave remnants of the original surface as hags in a sea of treacherous peaty ooze. Here dunlin nests, along with scattered golden plover and redshank. Some of the plants of the uplands are distinguished more for being on the southern edge of their range than for their rarity.

In southern Powys the limestone shows itself in a maze of caverns, part of which, at OGOF FFYNON DDU, is Britain's first underground National Nature Reserve. Elsewhere limestone only outcrops at Dolyhir, midway along the eastern border, and at LLANYMYNECH HILL (Shropshire), which supports a wide range of lime-loving species, at its northern end.

Away from rocks and hills there is still much to interest the naturalist. Walk along the Montgomery Canal near Welshpool, or the Monmouthshire and Brecon Canal, both rich in plants. Look for otter along any river in this, one of its last strongholds in England and Wales. Look out for yellow rattle, saw-wort, meadow thistle, dyer's greenweed and wood bitter-vetch, which together indicate a field with an undisturbed history.

Well over 10 per cent of Powys is covered by softwood forests but some of the original sessile oakwoods still cling to hillsides. In spring these woods, some of which are the home of red kite, come alive with small migrant birds. Pied flycatcher is very common in oakwoods.

The county possesses certain plant rarities and specialities. The Wye Valley and some of the limestone crags in the south support rare species of whitebeam including three endemic to the county. At scattered volcanic outcrops spiked speedwell, sticky catchfly, perennial knawel and rock cinquefoil are found. On a few rocky ledges late winter is brightened by a small yellow crocus-like flower *Gagea bohemica*; although native, it was only discovered a few years ago, the first distinct native flowering plant found in England and Wales for decades.

Powys has relatively few formal nature reserves, although if transposed into other regions much of the county would merit such status. So come and enjoy the freedom of its hills, the summer melody of its oak woodlands and the Wordsworthian splendour of the 'sylvan Wye' without, in general, recourse to a pocketful of permits.

F.M. SLATER

Abergwesyn Commons

SN 900590; 6,600ha; NT
Grassland and mire
Spring, summer

The commons are used for rough grazing by sheep
and a few ponies. The largely blanket mire is
dominated by heather with hare's-tail cottongrass
and deergrass, or by purple moor-grass. There is
also some acid grassland and areas of heathland
with bilberry, crowberry and cowberry.

Aberithon Turbary

Permit only; 5.8ha; RWT reserve
Old peat cutting
Spring, summer

Common reed, bulrush and willow carr stand
above a wetland flora which includes lesser
bladderwort, meadow thistle and floating club-
rush and provides a varied habitat for many birds
and insects. The reserve is important for the lichen
Cetraria sepincola, probably a glacial relict species.

Abertreweren Wood

SN 922263; 7.3ha; WdT
Woodland
Spring, summer

The wood was clear-felled several years ago, but
after extensive replanting is beginning to recover.

Bailey Einon

SO 083614; 4.5ha; RWT reserve
Deciduous woodland
Keep to nature trail and public footpath
Trail leaflet from RWT
Spring, summer

Overlooking the River Ithon, the woodland is on
boulder clay. There are distinct stands of wet alder
and sallow in the south, oak and ash with hazel
coppice in the centre and oak with field maple on
the steeper northern section. In the early summer
months a good number of pied flycatchers breed.

Brecon Beacons National Park

See map; 134,421ha; BBNPC
Huge tracts of uplands and valley
Literature from BBNPC and several information centres
All year

From the high ridge above CRAIG-Y-LLYN (Glamorgan), the view across the Brecon Beacons is
breathtaking. The huge escarpments stand out
in tiered ranks, cupping the shadowed valleys,
showing a splendid range of dark reds, deep
purples, greens and yellows. The reds are due to
the old red sandstone which makes up most of
the park, but there are also areas of limestone,
at CRAIG-Y-CILAU, for instance, where the Agen
Allwedd caves run for 25km, at OGOF FFYNON DDU,
another cave system, and at Castell Cerrig where
both limestone and acid old red sandstone show
in COED-Y-CASTELL (Dyfed).

Sheep grazing has converted the great moors of
heather and bilberry into long slopes of bents and
fescues, great plains of mat-grass and wet places
where hare's-tail cottongrass can be found among
tussocks of purple moor-grass. Only the tiered
ledges of the cliff faces show what the Beacons
must have been like in earlier years. Here, where
sheep cannot graze, globeflower grows, purple
and mossy saxifrage curtain the damp rocks in
early summer, and dense clumps of great wood-
rush show dark green on the lower ledges.

The valleys, Cwm Sere below Pen-y-Fan, for
example, open smoothly down to the lowlands
from steep heads ending in the high terraced
scarps of the peaks. Rain on the high land drains
down through these valleys in streams that have
cut into the valley bed. They start as bubbling
streamlets, rising from small rushy bogs or falling
clear down the hillside, but soon the streamlets
join and the waters race and tumble, cutting steps
where the rock is harder, often forming a series
of small waterfalls. Rowans stand over the falls
and the shelter and dampness there encourage a
rich growth of ferns, mosses and lichens and a
colourful show of flowering plants.

The park as a whole naturally contains a
greater range of habitat than merely the Beacons
themselves; there are the limestone areas already
mentioned, there are woodlands such as those in
NANT SERE WOOD, and there are wetlands such as
CWM COED-Y-CERRIG (Gwent) and DAUDRAETH
ILLFUD all making this an area that is rich in flora
and fauna.

Bron y Buckley Woodland

SJ 220080; 4.9ha; WdT
Deciduous woodland
Spring, summer

Ash, sycamore, elm and oak are all to be found
scattered throughout this deciduous wood, and
there is an area of beech in the centre and eastern
section.

Burfabog

Permit only; 9.5ha; RWT reserve
Rough marsh, grassland and stream
Permit from RWT
Spring, summer

The vegetation ranges from wet marsh of marsh-
marigold, meadowsweet and lesser spearwort
through to fen communities of lesser pond-
sedge. In neutral flushes both alternate-leaved and
opposite-leaved golden saxifrage are found. Birds
include spotted and pied flycatcher, whitethroat
and redstart.

Cefn Cenarth

Permit only; 9.7ha; RWT reserve
Hillside woodland
Spring, early summer

Mainly a steep oak woodland, the reserve also
includes rowan and planted larch and rises to
some 420m. Tree pipit, redstart, pied flycatcher
and wood warbler breed.

Cilcinni Dingle

SO 175415; 17ha; WdT reserve
Deciduous woodland
Spring, summer

The fine mature trees in this ancient woodland on a steep valley side provide an excellent habitat for many plants and animals. Access to the wood is via an old pedlars' road.

Coed Dolyronnen

SN 835998; 4ha; WdT
Deciduous woodland
Spring, summer

The deciduous woodland of Coed Dolyronnen contains good specimens of oak and ash, as well as rowan, birch and cherry as the main tree species. The understorey beneath this cover is dominated by hazel and hawthorn.

Coed Glaslyn

SJ 042070; 10.9ha; WdT
Deciduous woodland
Spring, summer

In Coed Glaslyn the most common species to be found in the woodland are oak, beech, birch and willow. An interesting mixture of natural regeneration and old trees planted between 150 and 200 years ago provide an ideal habitat for a variety of wildlife.

Coed Pendugwm

SJ 103124; 3ha; MWT reserve
Mixed woodland
Leaflet from MWT office
Spring, summer

A good example of mature woodland is given by Coed Pendugwm. The trees are mainly oak and include beech, elm and ash above a typical woodland ground cover. There is a good range of insects which reflects the wood's maturity. Both red and grey squirrel are present and the bird life includes the classic Welsh trio of wood warbler, pied flycatcher and redstart, with dipper on the boundary streams.

Coed y Ciliau

SN 947543; 10ha; WdT reserve
Deciduous woodland
Spring, summer

This ancient wood lying on a steep hillside is predominantly oak coppice with occasional ash and alder. There is a rich variety of flowers, mosses and lichens, and good populations of woodland birds.

Corngafallt Common

SN 940641; 260ha; RSPB reserve
Upland heath
Access along public footpaths
Summer

The common is part of the Wye/Elan reserve which includes the nearby DYFFRYN WOOD. Red grouse, stonechat and whinchat are the moorland birds that are regularly seen, and there is always the possiblity of spotting red kite or peregrine which hunt the area.

Cors y Llyn

Permit only; 17ha; NCC reserve
Mire
Permit from warden, Penllyn, Cathedine, Bwlch, Nr Brecon, Powys
Spring, summer, autumn

The small mire lies in an irregular glacial hollow. It is an interesting area made up of dry hummocks of heather, purple moor-grass, deergrass and crowberry, which are surrounded by a floating raft of *Sphagnum* mosses. Other species supported by the reserve include white beak-sedge, cranberry and bog asphodel.

Craig Irfon

Permit only; 8.3ha; BWT reserve
Upland valley side
Spring, summer

In contrast with the rounded slopes of the BRECON BEACONS, the valley at Craig Irfon has been cut from harder rock and twists, craggy and narrow, through looming cliffs of rugged shales. Like so much of Wales the uplands here are grazed by sheep, so the sloping valley sides below the crags have lost their heather–bilberry cover and generally are blanketed with fescues, bents and mat-grass although the lower slopes have areas of scrub, hawthorn and rowan, lifting above thick stands of bracken.

The crags, where the sheep cannot graze, have a richer range of plants and stunted oak trees manage to survive. Fine clumps of heather, with bell heather and bilberry, decorate the crags. Other acid moorland plants include heath bedstraw, tormentil and sheep's sorrel. The rocks also support a range of more widespread plants including wood sage, navelwort and ivy. Ferns, among them polypody, hard fern, lady-fern and the generally northern oak fern, grow on the ledges and in the crevices which also provide nesting sites for cliff-breeding birds.

An area of bog above the crags drains downwards through the long grass slopes, the course of the seepage marked by tussocks of purple moorgrass and *Sphagnum* moss. Below small mires hold *Sphagnum* with a good variety of rushes, sedges and acid wet-bog plants including cross-leaved heath, marsh lousewort, and bog asphodel.

The bird life is somewhat restricted by the open ruggedness of the valley but the stream is exploited by dipper; stonechat and whinchat occupy the scrubby areas; wheatear breeds on the open slopes below the rocks. The crags themselves provide nest sites for wren, ring ouzel and raven.

Craig-y-Cilau

SO 188159; 63ha; NCC reserve
Limestone crags, acid heath and bog
Permit only off right of way
Leaflet from NCC
Spring, early summer

The great white sweep of the limestone cliffs hides some well-known cave systems including the Agen Allwedd, which extends for some 25km. Limestone is the champagne rock of Britain and often the most forbidding cliffs effervesce with bright, unusual and fascinating plants.

Five rare whitebeams grow here together with beech, yew, wych elm, oak and silver birch, with hawthorn scrub on the slopes below. Harebell grows in the cliff crevices with brittle bladder-fern while mountain melick, angular Solomon's-seal and several uncommon subspecies of hawkweed grow on the cliff ledges. Limestone polypody and mossy saxifrage grow on the screes with commoner plants such as herb-Robert.

The lower slopes are a jumble of moss-shrouded limestone blocks and steep slopes thickly grown with hawthorn scrub. At the base of the scarp, a small raised mire has formed in a glacial depression, with two streams at its edge, fringed with round-leaved sundew.

The caves shelter hibernating lesser horseshoe bat while fox and badger may occur on the slopes. Some 40 species of birds breed, including upland wheatear, ring ouzel and raven, with woodland species such as willow warbler and redstart.

Part of the gritstone plateau above the limestone crags lies within the reserve. This is acid moorland and heather is rather patchy, but there are good stands of bilberry and crowberry grading into common cottongrass mires and areas of mat-grass and heath rush.

Cwm Wood

SN 952633; 8ha; RSPB reserve
Deciduous woodland
Spring, summer

This wood in the upper Wye Valley has typical breeding birds such as pied flycatchers, redstarts, wood warblers and tree pipits. The wood also has a good variety of mosses and liverworts.

Cwm-y-Wydden

SJ 136025; 4ha; MWT reserve
Small steep woodland
Leaflet from MWT office
Spring, summer

The wood is a mixture of generally acid areas and pockets of richer soils where rain washes minerals down. In the latter dog's mercury, herb-Paris and soft shield-fern grow beneath a canopy of wych elm, ash and willow. The acid parts have oak above a mossy ground cover with wavy hair-grass. Mosses and liverworts are particularly good along the stream and many lichens grow on the trees. Butterflies include speckled wood and purple hairstreak; there is a good range of birds.

The Irfon Valley holds three reserves, Craig Irfon, Nant Irfon, and Abergwesyn Commons.

Daudraeth Illfud

Permit only; 5ha; BWT reserve
Wetland and bog
This site may be dangerous
Spring, summer

The heart of the bog is an area of mire and swamp, which grades into a damp grassland filled with pools and then a grazing common with clumps of gorse and bracken. The whole area is grazed, so the drier parts consist of short-cropped turf where little can survive except the grasses, although the gorse and bracken provide good cover for heathland birds such as whinchat.

The pools contain more interesting plants with sweet-grass species standing above smaller water plants such as common water-crowfoot and shore-weed while the bog-swamp central area is more diverse, not least because it is more difficult to graze, although invading downy birch shows that the progression to drier scrub and then to woodland is already under way. The range of wetland species includes flea and bottle sedge with star sedge and great fen-sedge in the more marsh-like areas while pockets of open water hold the unusual lesser marshwort.

The reserve's superb range of feeding and nesting sites for many bird species is made even more attractive by the inaccessible nature of the wet heart of the area. Duck include mallard and teal. Black-headed gull nest and the wader population includes curlew and lapwing, together with snipe. Other birds include heron, buzzard and raven.

Dolifor Wood

SN 960655; 11.6ha; WdT
Mixed woodland
Spring, summer

A recently planted woodland in the Elan Valley, an area of dramatic landscape where the young trees are beginning to make impact, though the wood blends in well with the surrounding scenery.

Dyffryn Wood

SN 976667; 26.3ha; RSPB reserve
Woodland
Spring, summer

A good example of sessile oak wood on a hillside where pied flycatcher, wood warbler and redstart nest. Ravens and buzzards also breed, and grey wagtails and dippers occur along the streams.

Dyfnant Meadows

SH 998156; 9ha; MWT reserve
Grassland
Leaflet from MWT
Summer

The boggy flushes of this wet acid grassland are particularly rich with ragged-Robin, and marsh- and spotted-orchids, as well as a good variety of rushes and sedges. The grassland is full of tormentil and heath bedstraw, while more heathy areas contain bog asphodel and cross-leaved heath.

The mixed woodland of Pwll-y-Wrach falls to a swift clear stream.

Fron Wood and Garth Dingle

SO 191421; 7.7ha; WdT reserve
Deciduous woodland
Spring, summer

These two adjacent woods have a great variety of trees, including sessile and pedunculate oak, wych elm, yew, rowan and wild cherry. There is a rich ground flora and a varied bird population.

Gaer Fawr Wood

SJ 223128; 30ha; WdT
Mixed woodland, grassland
Spring, summer

The reserve is set on a steep, saddlebacked hill overlooking the Severn Valley close to the Welsh border. This natural look-out was once a hill fort and the banks and ditches of this important archaeological site can still be seen clearly. The wood itself has a wide variety of trees and shrubs, including naturally regenerated birch, old coppice, oak and many other species. Small groups of conifers can be seen near the summit.

Gilfach Farm

SN 905617; 53ha; RWT reserve
Grassland, woodland and moorland
All year

The farm contains a wide variety of wildlife typical of mid-Wales. On the moorland wheatear, whinchat and stonechat are found, while by the river there are dippers, grey wagtail and common sandpiper. There are woods of dry oak and wet ash and alder where pied flycatcher, redstart, woodwarbler and buzzard breed. The plant life is particularly rich in oceanic mosses and lichen, particularly in the river gorge. More unusual higher plants include globeflower, wood bitter-vetch, mountain pansies, butterwort and sundews.

Glaslyn

SN 824937; 216ha; MWT reserve
Heather moorland
Leaflet from MWT office
Spring, summer

There is a fine spread of heather, with bell heather, cross-leaved heath, bilberry, crowberry and areas of *Sphagnum* bog. The moorland and a steep rocky gorge provide a hunting ground for red kite, merlin and peregrine, and breeding sites for golden plover, red grouse and ring ouzel.

Graig Wood

SJ 175085; 3.2ha; WdT
Deciduous woodland
Spring, summer

This lovely hillside wood consists largely of sessile oak standards over coppice with a few beech and ash trees on the boundaries.

Lake Vyrnwy

SH 985215; 7090ha; RSPB
Flooded valley, grassland, moor and woodland
Leaflets and trail guide from visitor centre
All year

At the south western end of the Berwyn Mountains a deep steep-sided valley has been flooded to form the reservoir of Vyrnwy. Around and above the reservoir are some 2000ha of conifers, pockets of broad-leaved trees and great spreads of moorland. Grass moor and old-meadow pastures increase the habitat range, together with crags and upland streams, scrubland and valley bogs. The reservoir is largely screened by a belt of trees but the road offers several vantage points and a public hide provides views across the northern shallows to the towering crags beyond.

Its depth and the steepness of its banks are not ideal for waterbirds but mallard, teal and occasional great crested grebe nest here while goosander breeds at one of its very few Welsh sites. The stony edges of the lake provide nest sites for common sandpiper and grey wagtail which, with dipper and kingfisher, also breed on the feeder streams. In winter the reservoir may be bleak, at 250m above sea level, but mallard and teal may be joined by goldeneye, pochard and tufted duck, wigeon and whooper swan. The lake itself has become a pre-breeding roost for up to 6000 black-headed gulls, which congregate before flying on to their nest sites. In autumn, too, a good passage occurs and, although they may not pause unless the year is a good one for rowan and hawthorn berries, large numbers of fieldfare and redwing may be seen.

Over 120 species have been recorded; few are resident because of the hardness of the winters – the moorland rises to 600m – but the valley provides an important flightpath for migrants and spring brings an influx of breeding birds to Vyrnwy. Crossbill, in the plantations, and raven, in the taller conifers or the crags, are the earliest to nest – usually sitting while snow is on the ground. Siskin and redpoll also breed in the conifers; black and red grouse, ring ouzel and wheatear nest in the moorland, together with curlew, lapwing, golden plover and snipe; the mixed woods and scrub provide habitats for pied and spotted flycatcher, redstart, wood warbler, tree pipit and whinchat. Breeding numbers may not always be large but the diversity is impressive, underlined by nesting predators: buzzard, kestrel, sparrowhawk and tawny owl.

Over 24 species of butterflies include a fine range of fritillaries and hairstreaks with the now uncommon large heath on the moors. Among the mammals, pride of place must go to the polecat, present but rarely seen, with a good population of badger and thriving colonies of red squirrel.

Over 200 flowering plants and 13 ferns have been recorded, together with a wide range of fungi, lichens, liverworts and mosses. The lakeside and roadside verges contribute such plants as betony, Welsh poppy and goldenrod, the grasslands harebell, sheep's-bit and heath bedstraw; the rocky crags have English stonecrop and navelwort while the woods contain species such as wood anemone, enchanter's-nightshade and climbing corydalis. The unimproved pastures hold an attractive range of hay-meadow plants including yellow rattle and field scabious with petty whin, pignut and heath spotted-orchid. Scattered here and there are uncommon ferns such as beech, oak and parsley fern and, as is so often the case in moorland areas, a wealth of beautiful plants occurs in and around the bogs: among the typical species the occasional bog asphodel and bog pimpernel. Ivy-leaved bellflower, globeflower, marsh lousewort and starry saxifrage are infrequent here but lesser twayblade, very rare in Wales, is fairly well represented.

The reserve was established mainly for the interest of its bird life and a measure of its potential was seen in August 1981. In a two-hour watching period, one hen harrier, one merlin, two buzzards and two sparrowhawks, four peregrines and five kestrels were observed: few birdwatchers could ask for a more exciting experience.

Llandeilo–Graban Roadside

SO 090438–112419; 3km; RWT reserve
Old railway line
Spring, summer

Overlooking the River Wye, the reserve includes a range from meadowland to marsh and woodland plants. Slow-worm and common lizard occur on the slopes, with a good variety of butterflies and other insects, while the river and the wayside woods are rich in bird life.

Llangorse Lake

SO 133262; 22ha; Privately owned
Large shallow lake
All year

This shallow lake attracts a wide variety of wetland migrant and breeding birds. The lake is fringed with many plant species including common reed and bulrush; there are several species of pondweed and fringed, white and yellow water-lily occur. Roach, perch, pike and eel are in the lake, which would be an outstanding refuge for wildlife were it subjected to fewer public pressures.

Llanmerewig Meadow

SO 129929; 1ha; MWT reserve
Hay meadow
Leaflet from MWT office
Spring, summer

The plants of this unimproved hay meadow include cowslip, yarrow, lady's-mantle and the rare autumn-flowering meadow saffron. Along a small stream valerian, brooklime and meadow-sweet grow. Redstart, sparrowhawk, chiffchaff and tawny owl are among the birds to be seen.

Llyn Mawr

SO 008972; 12ha; MWT reserve
Lake and marsh area
Leaflet from MTNC office
All year

The margins of the lake are rich in plants typical of lower-level waters, such as marsh cinquefoil, marsh lousewort and early and northern marsh-orchid, as well as more characteristic species such as round-leaved sundew, butterwort and bog asphodel. The reserve is noted for its black-headed gull, mallard and teal, with tufted duck, great crested grebe, snipe and curlew. Stonechat and whinchat nest in the scrubland. Pochard, wigeon, goldeneye, goosander and whooper swan may visit the lake in winter.

Mynydd Ffoesidoes

Permit only; 26.8ha; RWT reserve
Upland moor
Spring, summer

This fine heather moorland, with bilberry, cowberry and crowberry, provides a breeding site for red grouse and a hunting ground for buzzard and merlin. Damper areas are marked by plants such as purple moor-grass, hare's-tail and common cottongrass with pockets of *Sphagnum* moss.

Nant Irfon

SN 829532; 136ha; NCC reserve
Upland grassland and valley woods
Spring, summer

The grazed grassland contains the typical associ-ation of fescue, bent and mat-grass found in these hills, with extensive areas of purple moorgrass. High altitude hanging oak woodlands have gener-ally uncoppiced oak, rowan, hazel and ash. There is a good range of woodland and upland birds including redstart, pied flycatcher and whinchat.

Nant Sere Wood

Permit only; 17.5ha; BWT reserve
Valley woodland
Spring, summer

Sheltered in the bottom of a spectacular BRECON BEACONS valley, the wood is a fascinating mosaic of wet and damp woodland with a varied range of habitat: grassland, scrub and woodland, sloping steeply down to a torrential stream.

Open grazing gives way to the woodland through old walled fields, thick with bracken where they are driest but otherwise grassed, with typical plants of the sheep walk such as heath bedstraw and tormentil. An open scrub of haw-thorn spreads across these fields. The fairly dry grassland then grades into a wet meadow, full of rushes and sedges, showing a good range of marsh plants. Old walls within the fields show a contrasting, drier variation, supporting ash trees and clumps of heather. Alder and downy birch colonise the wet meadow area.

The woodland proper contains much alder; other trees include oak, holly and field maple. There is an ash coppice-with-standard.

On drier slopes within the wood foxglove, common dog-violet, wood-sorrel and herb-Robert grow, with bluebell and the occasional rowan tree, while the damper areas have yellow pimpernel, wood horsetail and lesser spearwort. Most of the wood is damp and boggy, encouraging a strong and varied growth of ferns and mosses with a good range of liverworts and a rich autumn crop of fungi.

The birds are those characteristic of gladed lowland woods in Wales.

Offa's Dyke Path

SJ 267206–SO 267323; 115km; CC
Long-distance way
Booklet from HMSO bookshops
Spring, summer

Generally following the line of the Welsh border, the footpath passes through spectacular country-side as rich in wildlife as it is beautiful.

Ogof Ffynon Ddu

SN 867155; 413ha; NCC reserve
Cave system, limestone pavement, grassland and heather moorland
Access to caves permit only
Leaflet from NCC
Spring, summer

Above the extensive cave system, one of the largest and deepest in Britain, the reserve demon-strates the difference between rich limestone and acid millstone grit. Mountain everlasting, mossy saxifrage, mountain melick and lily-of-the-valley contrast with heather and bilberry. Ring ouzel and wheatear breed, and merlin and kestrel hunt.

Park Wood

SO 167338; 57ha; WdT
Mixed woodland
Spring, summer

The reserve is sited on a prominent hillside above Talgarth and on the north east edge of the BRECON BEACONS NATIONAL PARK. A former broadleaf woodland, which follows the hillside above the upper Wye Valley for about 3km, is an important feature of the landscape. About half has been converted to a mixture of conifers and hardwood, but the rest remains in a semi-natural state.

Pentwyn Reservoir

Permit only; 76ha; BWT reserve
Small reservoir
Autumn, winter, spring

Occasional migrant waders such as redshank and common sandpiper feed in the shallows and on exposed muds when the reservoir is low; duck include mallard, teal and wigeon. Scrub and woodland around the reservoir ensure a range of other birds and winter brings a good variety of wildfowl.

Pwllpatti

SO 165390; 2ha; Powys CC–RWT reserve
Old river bed
Permit only but good viewing from nearby layby
Winter

In winter Pwllpatti is completely flooded and supports a wide variety of wildfowl including all three species of swans.

Pwll-y-Wrach

SO 163327; 8.3ha; BWT reserve
Steep valley woodland
Visitors must keep to pathways
Spring, summer

The structure of Pwll-y-Wrach is good: tall oak trees stand above an understorey varied with ash, birch, hawthorn, hazel, holly, field maple and spindle. This richness is due to richer bands within the predominant old red sandstone. Along the river bed a shelf of hard cornstone forms a sculpted waterfall, where the rocks are thick with liverworts, mosses and ferns and ash takes over from oak as the main tree species.

The ground cover in this riverside ashwood has been virtually destroyed by grazing, but within the main body of the wood there is much variety, with an abundance of spring-flowering plants such as bluebell, wood-sorrel, woodruff, dog's mercury, enchanter's-nightshade, wild strawberry and common dog-violet. The edges of the paths in summer contain plants which cannot grow beneath the trees, such as devil's-bit scabious, betony and St John's-wort species. The range of habitat includes the river itself and the river edge, and a boundary bank with heathland plants such as heather, gorse and broom growing together with lime-loving dogwood – perhaps the bank was mounded on a wall of cornstone.

Dipper and grey and pied wagtail may be seen while other birds include a range of woodland species such as treecreeper and nuthatch. Mammals include the rare dormouse.

Rhos Goch

Permit only; 45ha; NCC reserve
Mire and damp woodland
Permit from warden, Penllyn, Cathedine, Bwlch, Nr Brecon, Powys
Spring, summer, autumn

The raised mire is notable for the well-developed hummock and hollow network on its surface. The only other example of this habitat in Britain is found at WEM MOSS in Shropshire. The hollows have mainly been colonised by *Sphagnum* mosses, water horsetail, bogbean and common cottongrass with bog asphodel fringing the pools. On the drier ridges, heather, purple moor-grass, bilberry and hare's-tail cottongrass grow.

Rook Wood

SO 218408; 10.4ha; WdT
Deciduous woodland
Spring, summer

On rising land just to the south of Hay-on-Wye in the BRECON BEACONS NATIONAL PARK. Much of the wood was planted with beech about 30 years ago but there is still a good spread of mature oak, ash and cherry.

Roundton Hill

SO 294949; 35ha; MWT reserve
Unimproved heath grassland
Leaflet from MWT office
Spring, summer

Roundton Hill is an important site for its unusual plant communities developed on thin volcanic-derived soils. Species include rock stonecrop, wild thyme and carline thistle, and over 100 species of lichen have been recorded. The area supports an interesting range of birds such as wheatear, redstart and woodpeckers.

Severn Farm Pond

SJ 228068; 1.3ha; MWT reserve
Pond
Leaflet from MWT office
All year

This small pond close to the centre of Welshpool is fringed with gipsywort, bur-reed, water mint, water-pepper and yellow iris. Moorhen, coot, snipe and reed bunting can be seen.

Sidelands

Permit only; 2ha; RWT reserve
Woodland
Spring

The reserve is the only woodland site in Radnorshire for adder's-tongue. This delicate little plant grows alongside other typical species such as bluebell, yellow pimpernel and broad buckler-fern. The woodland itself has a mix of oak, birch, hawthorn and the occasional rowan and crab apple which attracts a good range of birds.

Stanner Rocks

SO 262583; 5ha; NCC reserve
Deciduous woodland with rocky outcrops and grassland
Access to quarry floor only
Leaflet from Dyfed–Powys Office
Spring, summer

Sessile oak, with occasional ash and wych elm, and a hazel and elder shrub layer form the woodlands. The cliffs, facing south-east and some 230–300m in height, are subject to summer drought, thus maintaining open communities of plants of base-rich and base-poor soils. There are some interesting mosses and lichens.

Talybont Reservoir

SO 098190; 146ha; WWA–BBNPC reserve
Flooded valley reservoir
No access to the reservoir area
Autumn, winter, spring

This long, narrow body of water set in a steep, forested valley is ideal for diving birds. The shores are variable, sometimes gently sloping, sometimes with shallow muddy cliffs, so the range of 'edge' habitat is considerable.

Mallard, teal and wigeon are the commonest of the dabbling ducks seen here and may be joined at the water's edge by occasional waders such as curlew, redshank, common and green sandpiper and greenshank. The waders long legs hold them above the icy waters while their long beaks probe down deep into the mud. A range of different styles of beak ensures that each species takes a different type of food, reducing competition to a minimum.

Three of the largest birds seen at the reservoir are the swans, resident mute swan and the two winter visitors, Bewick's and whooper swan, which fly in from Russia and northern Europe.

Withy Beds

SO 310649; 1.2ha; RWT–Radnorshire DC
Wet woodland and river
Spring, summer

An area of carr woodland on an island formed by an old mill leet and the River Lugg. White willow is the dominant tree but there is also some small-leaved lime. In spring there is a spectacular display of marsh-marigolds and ransoms in flower. Other plants include opposite-leaved golden-saxifrage, burnet saxifrage and lady-fern.

Abbreviations Used in the Guide

Note: county councils are given in the following form, e.g. CCT for Cheshire Conservation Trust; the county is always the same as the section title unless otherwise stated, and these abbreviations do not appear in the list below. All county names beginning with the letter N are spelt out to avoid confusion with the NCC (Nature Conservancy Council); CC alone stands for the Countryside Commission. For convenience the managing body named in line 1 of each entry is sometimes given an obvious abbreviation in line 3, when indicating for instance the availability of a leaflet (e.g. KAMT for Kenneth Allsop Memorial Trust). Such abbreviations are not listed below.

BBNPC	Brecon Beacons National Park Committee
BC	After a place name: Borough Council
BR	British Rail
BTCV	British Trust for Conservation Volunteers
BWB	British Waterways Board
BWT	Brecknock Wildlife Trust
CC	Countryside Commission/after a place name: County Council
CCT	Cheshire Conservation Trust
CEGB	Central Electricity Generating Board
CPRE	Council for the Preservation of Rural England
DC	After a place name: District Council
DWT	Dyfed Wildlife Trust
FC	Forestry Commission
FSC	Field Studies Council
GWT	Glamorgan Wildlife Trust/Gwent Wildlife Trust (according to context)
HNT	Herefordshire Nature Trust
HMSO	Her Majesty's Stationery Office
LNR	Local Nature Reserve
MBC	After a place name: Metropolitan Borough Council
MOD	Ministry of Defence
MWT	Montgomeryshire Wildlife Trust
NCC	Nature Conservancy Council
NNR	National Nature Reserve
NT	National Trust
NWWT	North Wales Wildlife Trust
PC	After a place name: Parish Council
PCNPA	Pembrokeshire Coast National Park Authority
RC	After a place name: Regional Council
RSNC	Royal Society for Nature Conservation
RSPB	Royal Society for the Protection of Birds
RSPCA	Royal Society for the Prevention of Cruelty to Animals
RWT	Radnorshire Wildlife Trust
SNPC	Snowdonia National Park Committee
SSSI	Site of Special Scientific Interest
SWT	Shropshire Wildlife Trust/Staffordshire Wildlife Trust (according to context)
UWT	Urban Wildlife Trust
WARNACT	Warwickshire Nature Conservation Trust
WdT	Woodland Trust
WNCT	Worcestershire Nature Conservation Trust
WWT	Wildfowl and Wetland Trust
WWA	Welsh Water plc

Addresses

The following is a list of the major wildlife organisations in Wales and the West Midlands, together with those owners and managing bodies from whom information and/or permits may be obtained, but whose addresses are not already given in the text. All requests should be accompanied by a stamped addressed envelope, and readers should understand that permits may be refused at the managing bodies' discretion.

The local Wildlife Trusts of Wales and the West Midlands

Birmingham
See Urban Wildlife Trust

Brecknock Wildlife Trust
Lion House, 7 Lion Street
Brecon
Powys
LD3 7AY

Dyfed Wildlife Trust
7 Market Street
Haverfordwest
Dyfed SA61 1NF

Glamorgan Wildlife Trust
Nature Centre
Fountain Road
Tondu
Mid Glamorgan
CF32 0EH

Gwent Wildlife Trust
16 White Swan Court
Church Street
Monmouth
Gwent NP5 3BR

Herefordshire Nature Trust
Community House
25 Castle Street
Hereford
HR1 2NW

Montgomeryshire Wildlife Trust
8 Severn Square
Newtown
Powys
SY16 2AG

North Wales Wildlife Trust
376 High Street
Bangor
Gwynedd
LL57 1YE

Radnorshire Wildlife Trust
1 Gwalia Annexe
Ithon Road
Llandrindod Wells
Powys
LD1 6AS

Shropshire Wildlife Trust
St George's Primary School
Frankwell
Shrewsbury
Shropshire SY3 8JP

Staffordshire Wildlife Trust
Coutts House
Sandon
Staffordshire
ST18 0DN

Urban Wildlife Trust
Unit 213, Jubilee Trade Centre
130 Pershore Street
Birmingham
B5 6ND

Warwickshire Wildlife Trust (WARNACT)
Montague Road
Warwick
CV34 5LW

Worcestershire Wildlife Trust
Lower Smite Farm
Smite Hill
Hindlip
Worcestershire
WR3 8SZ

Other Organisations

Birmingham City Council
The Council House
Birmingham B1 1BB

Brecon Beacons National Park Committee
Information Centre
Monk Street
Abergavenny
Gwent
NP7 5NA

British Trust for Conservation Volunteers
36 St Mary's Street
Wallingford
Oxford
OX10 0EU

British Waterways Board
Melbury House
Melbury Terrace
London NW1 6JX

Central Electricity Generating Board
The Surveyor
Sudbury House
15 Newgate Street
London EC1A 7AU

Countryside Commission
John Dower House
Crescent Place
Cheltenham
Gloucestershire
GL50 3RA

Cynon Valley Borough Council
Rock Grounds
High Street
Aberdare
CF44 7AE

Dudley Metropolitan Borough Council
Ednum Road
Dudley
DY1 1HL

Forestry Commission

Headquarters for England, Wales and Scotland
231 Corstorphine Road
Edinburgh
EH12 7AT

Wales
Victoria House
Victoria Terrace
Aberystwyth
Dyfed
SY23 2DQ

Gwent County Council
County Hall
Cwmbran
Gwent
NP4 2XH

Hereford and Worcester County Council
County Hall
Spetchley Road
Worcester
WR5 2NP

Her Majesty's Stationery Office

Government bookshops
258 Broad Street
Birmingham
B1 2HE

Knowle Society
24 Apsley Grove
Dorridge
West Midlands

Llanelli Borough Council
Elwyn House
Llanelli
Dyfed
SA15 3AP

Methyr Tydfil Borough Council
Town Hall
Merthyr Tydfil
CF47 8AN

Mid Glamorgan County Council
County Hall
Cathays Park
Cardiff
CF1 3NE

Ministry of Defence
Lands Dept
Tolworth Tower
Ewell Road
Surbiton
Surrey
KT6 7DR

National Trust
42 Queen Anne's Gate
London
SW1H 9AS

There are also 15 regional offices in England and Wales: their addresses are obtainable from the address above

Nature Conservancy Council

Headquarters
Northminster House
Peterborough PE1 1VA

West Midlands
Attingham Park
Shrewsbury
Shropshire
SY4 4TW

Wales

North
Plas Penrhos
Ffordd Penrhos
Bangor
Gwynedd
LL57 2LQ

Dyfed-Powys
Plas Goggerddan
Aberystwyth
Dyfed
SY23 3EB

South
43 The Parade
Roath
Cardiff
CF2 3UH

Pembrokeshire Coast National Park Authority
Dyfed County Council
County Offices
Haversfordwest
Dyfed
SA61 1QZ

Royal Society for Nature Conservation
The Green
Witham Park
Lincoln
LN5 7JR

Royal Society for the Protection of Birds
The Lodge
Sandy
Bedfordshire
SG19 2DL

Royal Society for the Prevention of Cruelty to Animals
Causeway
Horsham
West Sussex
RH12 1HG

Sandwell Metropolitan Borough Council
Town Hall
West Bromwich
West Midlands
B70 8DX

Shropshire County Council
The Shirehall
Abbey Foregate
Shrewsbury
SY2 6ND

Shropshire Ornithological Society
Arnsheen
Betley Lane
Bayston Hill
Shrewsbury

Snowdonia National Park Committee
Snowdonia National Park
Penrhyndeudraeth
Gwynedd
LL48 6LS

South Glamorgan County Council
Newport Road
Cardiff
CF2 1XA

South Staffordshire Waterworks Co.
50 Sheepcote St
Birmingham
B16 8AR

Staffordshire County Council
County Buildings
Stafford
ST16 2LH

Swansea City Council
The Guildhall
Swansea
SA1 4PA

Tamworth Borough Council
Municipal Offices
Marmion House
Lichfield Street
Tamworth
B79 7BZ

Trust for Urban Ecology
South Bank House
Black Prince Road
London SE1

Vale of Glamorgan Borough Council
Civic Offices
Barry
CF6 6RU

Walsall Metropolitan Borough Council
Civic Centre
Darwell Street
Walsall
WS1 1TZ

Wansbeck District Council
Council Offices
Newbiggin-by-the-Sea
NE64 6PL

Warwickshire County Council
Shire Hall
Warwick
CV34 4RR

Warwickshire County Museum
Market Hall
Market Place
Warwick
CV34 4SA

Water Authority reservoirs
See British Waterways Board

Welsh Water Authority
Cambrian Way
Brecon
Powys
LD3 7HP

West Glamorgan County Council
Guildhall
Swansea
SA1 3SN

West Midland Bird Club
1 Lansdowne Road
Studley
Warwickshire
B80 7JG

Wildfowl and Wetland Trust
Slimbridge
Gloucester
GL2 7BT

Woodland Trust
Autumn Park
Dysart Road
Grantham
Lincolnshire
NG31 6LL

Index